C000293060

"Because the Bible remains foundational to ... to be reminded regularly how it should be pu ... and historically well-informed book explair ... digesting Scripture that draw their wisdom ... provides welcome encouragement not only to learn from but to love the written Word of God."

Mark Noll, author of *In the Beginning Was the Word*

"Glenn Paauw has written a serious and compelling book on the Bible. The tone of his writing is puckish enough to keep us turning pages for more. After identifying our lazy readiness to reduce the Bible to convenient 'scripturettes,' Paauw guides us to a way to the adult work of serious engagement with the Bible. When the Bible is taken with such seriousness, it will indeed serve to refresh and revive the missional energy of the church. His argument is propelled by the deep conviction that gospel alternatives are on offer for the bold, alert and passionate who engage the biblical text beyond our narcoticized habits of reading."

Walter Brueggemann, Columbia Theological Seminary

SAVING THE BIBLE
FROM OURSELVES

Learning to Read & Live the Bible Well

GLENN R. PAAUW

IVP Books

An imprint of InterVarsity Press
Downers Grove, Illinois

InterVarsity Press
P.O. Box 1400,
Downers Grove, IL 60515-1426
ivpress.com
email@ivpress.com

InterVarsity Press® is the book-publishing division of InterVarsity Christian Fellowship/USA®, a movement of students and faculty active on campus at hundreds of universities, colleges and schools of nursing in the United States of America, and a member movement of the International Fellowship of Evangelical Students. For information about local and regional activities, visit intervarsity.org.

All Scripture quotations, unless otherwise indicated, are taken from THE HOLY BIBLE, NEW INTERNATIONAL VERSION®, NIV® Copyright © 1973, 1978, 1984, 2011 by Biblica, Inc.™ Used by permission. All rights reserved worldwide.

While any stories in this book are true, some names and identifying information may have been changed to protect the privacy of individuals.

Photos in figures 1.1, 1.2, 1.3, 1.4 and 2.1 are by Steve Crow.

Cover design: Cindy Kiple
Interior design: Beth McGill
Images: book pages: malerapaso/iStockphoto
  torn paper edge: hudiemm/iStockphoto

ISBN 978-0-8308-5124-9 (print)
ISBN 978-0-8308-9969-2 (digital)

Printed in the United States of America ♾

 As a member of the Green Press Initiative, InterVarsity Press is committed to protecting the environment and to the responsible use of natural resources. To learn more, visit greenpressinitiative.org.

Library of Congress Cataloging-in-Publication Data
Names: Paauw, Glenn R., 1958- author.
Title: Saving the Bible from ourselves : learning to read and live the Bible
  well / Glenn R. Paauw.
Description: Downers Grove : InterVarsity Press, 2016. | Includes
  bibliographical references.
Identifiers: LCCN 2015050887 (print) | LCCN 2016002222 (ebook) | ISBN
  9780830851249 (pbk. : alk. paper) | ISBN 9780830899692 (eBook)
Subjects: LCSH: Bible—Hermeneutics. | Bible--Criticism, interpretation, etc.
  | Bible--Reading.
Classification: LCC BS476 .P25 2016 (print) | LCC BS476 (ebook) | DDC
  220.6—dc23
LC record available at http://lccn.loc.gov/2015050887

P	23	22	21	20	19	18	17	16	15	14	13	12	11	10	9	8	7	6	5	4	3	2	1
Y	35	34	33	32	31	30	29	28	27	26	25	24	23	22	21	20	19	18	17	16			

Maybe, in the end, this is the best argument for higher purpose: that the history of life on earth is too good a story not to have been written.

ROBERT WRIGHT

for M:

Beauty is truth, truth beauty

JOHN KEATS

CONTENTS

PREFACE

In the early 1990s George Barna spoke at a gathering of ministry leaders sponsored by International Bible Society. I had been at the Bible Society for a few years and had personally invested in their then 180-year-old mission of making the Bible widely available. But that night the ministry model I had bought into was challenged: easy access to well-translated Bibles isn't enough, he said. Bibles are everywhere in this country but the research shows an alarming disconnection problem. People find the Bible to be a difficult book, don't understand it, and are in fact abandoning it in droves.

His presentation made a deep impact on me. Right then and there I made a commitment: *I don't know how long I'll work here, but for as long as I do I will not be content to just sell or distribute Bibles. I am going to work on understanding and overcoming this disconnection problem. I don't want George Barna Jr. coming back here in thirty years to tell us the same story.*

In the late 1990s I was spending a leisurely morning in Moby Dickens bookshop in Taos, New Mexico, when it first really registered with me how differently the Bible is formatted compared to all the other books in that shop. They, I noticed, are so very readable. The Bible, I noticed again, is so very not.

A few years later, in the early 2000s, I was in a Sunday morning worship service at International Anglican Church in the sublime Shove Chapel on the campus of Colorado College. My Bible had a bookmark from Moby Dickens stuck in it. At one particular moment during the sermon the seven big ideas of this book came together in my mind. I pulled out that bookmark and wrote them all down on the back. That was the moment I decided I should try to write about them, and that bookmark remained my guide through the entire journey.

- Introduction -

EMBARKING

This book is a journey to the center of the Bible. Some people—those prone toward counting things—will tell you that the center of the Bible is Psalm 117, since there are 594 chapters before it and the same number following it. But counting is about precision, and verses, which measure smaller units, are more precise. Alas! There is no center verse of the Bible, since the overall count is an even number: 31,174 (in most English Bibles). But this may be a case in which counting is not the thing to do. I propose instead a voyage to the heart of the Bible, an exploration of the paths we might take to get there and a quest to unearth essential, but largely forgotten Bible practices.

The purpose of this book is to contribute to the construction of a new paradigm for engaging the Bible in the Christian community. It is an intervention for a Bible in crisis. Seven new "Bibles" will be introduced to the reader as steps on the path to recovering one deeply engaged Bible. The chapters are set up in groups. Each grouping reviews a key deficiency in how we currently see or interact with the Bible followed by a recommendation for a new presentation or practice.

My core argument is that for most of us, most of the time, small readings prevail over big readings. "Small" and "big" refer to more than the length of the passages we take in. I define *small readings* as those diminished samplings of Scripture in which individuals take in fragmentary bits outside of the Bible's literary, historical and dramatic contexts. Also implicated here is a correspondingly meager soteriology—that narrow, individualistic and escapist view of salvation so common among Christians. My hope is that these deficiencies will come to be corrected by *big readings*. These are the more

magnified experiences that result when communities engage natural segments of text, or whole books, taking full account of the Bible's various
contexts. This will foster the apprehension of the story's goal in a majestic
regeneration that is as wide as God's good creation.

Closely related to these small and big readings are various other aspects
of our current Bible culture, including related issues such as our typical
visual presentation of the Bible, the inseparable connection of the Bible to
our complicated life on earth, the way we make sense of (or don't bother
with) the library of Scripture as a whole, and the role of aesthetics in what
we do with the Bible.

Overall, I examine some of the ways the Bible has "fallen" in contemporary Christianity, followed by my own proposals for the Bible's restoration.
I believe the journey to the Bible's redemption—just like our own—lies in
incarnational recovery. Just as we require a holistic salvation that includes
our bodies, so the Bible needs a restoration that includes its physical form.
And the point of this redemption—also similar to our own—is a retrieval of
original purpose and intended mission. The Word of God was sent into the
world to be an agent of God's transformative power. When we harm the
Bible, we hinder that errand.

WHY DOES THE BIBLE NEED TO BE SAVED?

The American presidency has its own fascinating history and has gone
through significant mutations as the times have changed along with those
who've held the position. August of 1974, however, was a unique moment
in that history. Gerald Ford assumed the office on the ninth day of the
month following the resignation of Richard Nixon over the Watergate
scandal. In his first address to the nation as president, Ford spoke of his
commitment to restoring trust in the nation's highest office. This need arose
as a result of the long and painful national crisis. Ford articulated the national mood by noting, "This is an hour of history that troubles our minds
and hurts our hearts."

Those of us with a commitment to and love for the Bible might be excused
for thinking similar words could be applied to the situation of the Scriptures
in this hour. I've worked in Bible teaching, publishing and ministry outreach
for nearly three decades now. I'm more familiar than I want to be with the

widespread use and abuse of this text. My heart does hurt and my mind is indeed troubled. There may not be some idyllic golden age of the Bible in the past, but that should not diminish our sense of the seriousness of its troubles today.

Troubles? I thought the Bible was still a very popular book. What troubles?

You may have heard that the Bible is the bestselling book of all time. And that's true, but that's not the half of it: the Bible is the bestselling book *every single year*. By any measure, this is remarkable. God didn't have a blockbuster once upon a time. He has THE blockbuster year after year after year. And if the Bible didn't need saving, this accomplishment would mean more than it actually does. It might mean that the content of the Bible would be extremely well known—after all, there are all those copies out there. Given the sheer distribution numbers, we should have Bible trivia experts on every corner. *Who's Melchizedek? I know! I know!* We certainly buy enough Bibles for this to be the case. But the researchers have been telling us for some time that the knowledge base isn't there. Regardless of the number of times we've rolled the Bible presses, the words on the page are not common currency.

Now, it's true that Bible literacy is not really the goal—the Bible's mission is more properly focused on deeper matters. Still, a deficient awareness of Bible basics like facts and storylines is revealing of a more profound loss. If I can't tell you who Moses, Paul, Abraham, Jesus and David are, and in what order they appear in the Bible's drama, I can't possibly know much about what's really going on there.

But there's more at stake here than a widespread cloning of the Bible Answer Man. Given Christian convictions about the Bible, we would expect (hope? pray?) that its unique content would be transforming people on a very significant scale. We would anticipate a deep cultural awareness of the themes, stories and truths of the Bible. We should be finding substantial engagement, both positive and negative, with key biblical claims. We should see, in other words, the Bible taken seriously as a culture-shaping force. But do we?

Well, increasingly no. There may be a kind of shadow that survives, the ghost of Bibles past, when sacred stories, phrases and echoes were interwoven in our literature, art and music, and when its memorable expressions were common parlance. But most of these allusions and references are now lost on people. The whole Bible thing has become blurry for folks today. We might be swimming in millions of Bibles, but we are not a Scripture-soaked society.

But what about the Bible-believing community? Isn't there a group of people still immersed in the Bible and very familiar with its contents? Isn't the Bible doing well there?

There is such a group, it's true, and they are typically quite serious about the Bible. They do study their Bibles and read their devotionals. They go to churches where the Bible is expounded every week. They do better on their Bible literacy questionnaires. (Exactly how many people this describes is open to discussion.) But there may be more to this seeming success story than first meets the eye. It's worth scratching the surface a bit.

There are two stories here, one official and one underground. To get the gist of the official story, consider the things we in the Christian community regularly tell ourselves about the Scriptures. Superlatives abound: The Bible is dynamic, special, inspired and inspiring—the crucial spiritual tool God himself has given us; the Bible is God's instruction manual for life; the Lord of the universe has written a personal love letter to us; it is our passport to heaven; it contains the words of life; it contains the announcements of God—an utterly unique discourse of the divine. We also highlight key biblical self-descriptions: The Bible is God-breathed and the Spirit's own spiritual sword; it is living and active; it is a light for our path; when God sends his word out, it doesn't return to him without accomplishing what he wants. A recent survey of the role of the Bible in American life reports that close to eight out of ten Americans describe the Bible as either inspired by God or as the literal word of God.[1] We are not lacking for a positive view of the Bible.

We talk about the Bible and its importance for the Christian life all the time. In fact, we can't stop talking about it. Everyone knows that a serious believer is supposed to spend a lot of time "in the Word"—soaking it up, praying about it, applying it on a daily basis. Typically, the exhortation to be diligent in our Bible study is followed by the clear promise of big spiritual payoff. The expectation is that believers will spend significant time getting to know their Bibles. But we are also assured that even if we spend only a few minutes in the morning, we're sure to find the spiritual gem to get us through. The Bible will brighten our day, encourage us and strengthen us, if only we will faithfully open it—even if just for a few moments. Those "Scriptures"—which more typically refer to presorted sentences and snippets—are said to be powerful.

And yet.

We know there is more to this story than the official line. The Christian community doesn't talk about it nearly as much, but there is an underside to the life of the Bible in our midst. This is the story of frustration, boredom and lack of connection. This is the story of failed expectations. Many of us try out the advice promoted in the official line and find that it doesn't work. We commit to a daily "quiet time," but after a while we give up. We read our little spiritual morsel and discover it doesn't nourish us all that much, and certainly not enough to carry us through the day. Actually, we kind of forget it pretty quickly. The unofficial line regarding the Bible is the story of weird, indecipherable passages. The "and yet" comes down to this: there is more guilt about secret noncompliance with Bible-reading standards in the self-proclaimed Bible-believing community than there is gratitude for promises realized. For far too many folks there is a hoped-for-but-as-yet-undiscovered spiritual meal in the Bible. After too long a wait they begin to doubt there is any real food there at all.

And now for the bad news. It's not just the obvious failures that are failures. Even when we think we have success, the reality is often not very good. Fragmentary, superficial and out-of-context readings and misapplications abound. One of the core reasons for our Bible engagement breakdown is that so many would-be Bible readers have been sold the mistaken notion that the Bible is a look-it-up-and-find-the-answer handy guide to life. They've been encouraged to treat the Scriptures as if they were a collection of doctrinal, devotional and moralistic statements that can be accessed and chosen at will. This topical-search mode of Bible use directly undermines authentic Bible engagement. The advent of electronic Bibles with their speedy find-a-verse feature is only making it worse.

One glaring failure of such an approach is that it ignores huge swaths of the biblical text that don't comfortably fit the model. Many books have no candidates for the My-Favorite-Scripturette award and are studiously avoided by the verse-pickers and therefore effectively decanonized. The grave danger here is that people think they are getting to know the Bible when actually they are being led to a small sampling of Bible passages—and often misreadings of them. Because this approach is so widely practiced and officially endorsed in Christian communities, even well-intentioned readers are inoculated against real Bible encounters, which differ significantly from the plucking procedure. This superficial use of the Scriptures is actually destructive because those who practice it operate under the illusion that they are engaging the Bible when they are not. They're rarely even aware of what they're missing.

The Bible needs to be saved because of what it has not become. It has not become a collection of books we know, the narrative we stew in, the words that form us. The Bible needs to be saved because it has been falsely promised to us and falsely delivered. It has been packaged aplenty, but unpacked not so much. The truth is the Bible is not easy. The Bible is a challenge—a sizeable library with a wide variety of ancient writings collected over a long period of time. There is no good reason to mislead folks about this fact. And yet, those who take the biggest shortcuts with the Bible are frequently those who have the greatest things to say about it. Unwilling to face the daunting truth, or finding it harder to sell, they push the Easy Button. But, as the saying goes, reality is a stubborn thing. It doesn't go away just because we pretend.

Religious scholar Timothy Beal provocatively contends that the current proliferation of Bibles has all the signs of a "distress crop." The analogy is of a dying fruit tree that puts all its energy into one last burst of abundance, supplying a superharvest of produce, providing the best possible chance that more seeds will be sown and future trees grown. But soon after this sweet explosion, the tree dies. While the Bible industry appears to be thriving, says Beal, this is a superficiality that masks a deeper malaise. Even as people are failing to connect with the Bible, they keep buying more. The promise of a better outcome delivered through more additives or customized notes is ever before us. Our motto, according to Beal: "If at first we don't succeed, buy, buy again."[2]

The Bible needs saving, not because of any defect in itself, but because we've buried it, boxed it in, wallpapered over it, neutered it, distorted it, isolated it, individualized it, minimized it, misread it, lied about it, debased it and oversold it. We have over-complicated its form while over-simplifying its content. We've become cavalier and even cheesy with our Bibles. We'll do almost anything with them. What we have not done, truth be told, is trusted it to be itself. It may not be far off the mark to say that the Bible is completely different from what we've been led to believe it is.

Do we want the Bible to flourish, to have the meaningful life and effective mission that God intended for it? If so, then something must be done, because it is not achieving this mission. The evidence repeatedly shows that for all its sales the Bible remains a foreign book for the vast majority of us. And this is not only a problem in the United States: global mission agencies are now acknowledging an epidemic of biblical illiteracy worldwide.[3] Widespread positive assessment of the Bible combined with widespread ignorance of it amounts to the maintenance of a hollow cultural icon of the past and nothing more.

How Can We Save the Bible from Ourselves?

The direction of the answer seems clear enough: if we are the ones who have enslaved the Bible, then it's the chains we've imposed that have to come off. We need to undo the damage we've done. The Bible is still there, after all. Even with all its injuries, like the indefatigable Black Knight of Monty Python fame, soldiering on despite limbs cut off—*Mere flesh wounds! I've had worse!*—the Bible presses forward. Its words can still pulsate with power, despite centuries of being covered over, chopped up, fenced in, overcontrolled and carefully selected. As always, God does his work despite us as much as because of us. But this is no excuse for knowingly persisting in error. We can do better, and we must.

And here's the way: we need more Bibles. *No you didn't! You didn't just say we need more Bibles!*

More Bibles? At least in the cultural context of late capitalism in Western culture, isn't the problem that there are already too many Bibles? We have Bibles of every sort, Bibles infected with the niche-marketing virus and artificially, awkwardly—dare we say it, dishonestly—slanted toward every conceivable target audience. Don't we have more Bibles and more kinds of Bibles than we know what to do with? (The one that pretends to be a teen girls' magazine—or is it the other way around, a teen girls' magazine pretending to be a Bible?—the Bible that's green because the word *wilderness* shows up a few times, the Bible with the favorite verses of people just like me highlighted in soft blue, or *The Playful Puppies Bible*. All of these are real Bibles, by the way.) More Bibles? Bible publishers are already successfully selling more Bibles to people who are ignoring the ones they have.[4]

More Bibles? Yes. Specifically, seven more Bibles.

But I don't mean more Bibles in *that* sense. These Bibles won't be found at your favorite retail dispenser of spiritual goods. These seven new Bibles are not "products," especially since the commodification of what are supposed to be our sacred writings has been a big contributor to our problems with the Bible. Instead, I'm referring to something like seven new understandings of the Bible. These seven perspectives will come together to form a new paradigm for the Bible. I'm offering a way of seeing the Bible comprehensively that will lead to discovering (or rediscovering) Bible practices that fit what the Bible really is.

So I'd like to introduce seven Bibles on the road to one new Bible. Of course, this Bible is not really unprecedented. "New" here merely means new to us. I'm looking for a Bible that is mostly unknown in our consumer-centric, late-modern world. It is new to us because we've lost our way with the Bible. So I'm proposing seven new Bibles to recover one Bible that we can take seriously in practice, not just in theory. One Bible we can do justice to. One Bible we can pursue by means of big readings, not small ones. One Bible seen and treated as a holy book. (Have we forgotten what the word *sacred* means?) One Bible that, to use C. S. Lewis's phrase, *we accept on its own terms rather than merely use on ours.*

What if we quit ignoring that dark underside of the Bible's story in our time and instead face it head on? Why are so many people struggling with their Bible reading? What can we do about it? What if we start saying things about the Bible that actually line up with what we find when we open it? What if we set aside our slick superlatives for a moment and take a good, hard look at the Bible itself? (Not that we can't have good things to say about the Bible; we can, but we need to arrive at them honestly.) And what if we developed Bible practices more fitting to what we discovered after that good, hard look?

It comes down to being attentive to two key questions: What is the Bible? and What are we supposed to do with it?

There and Back Again: The Plan of This Book

My answer to these two questions constitutes this book. Each of the seven new Bibles I propose is clearly worth a book-length treatment in its own right. My project here can be no more than an introductory outline of a would-be path to recovery. I am hoping to chart the course of the journey, not detail every step and nuance of the way. Some of this larger task of recovery will involve the decisions of Bible makers and publishers. Other parts will fall mostly to those who teach and preach the Bible in our church communities—leaders both lay and ordained are invited into what I hope is a holistic and healthy perspective on the Bible. But ultimately it will come down to what whole communities of Jesus followers do with the Bible. My prayer is that we all will become more reflective and intentional about our answers to the two core questions, and that this reflection and intentionality will result in renewed Bible practices. Because our hearts should be hurt by the current state of the Bible.

I will attempt to make the case for all this in an orderly way. One common literary structure found throughout the Bible is the chiasm, a way of arranging material in a reverse symmetrical pattern. The chiasm pattern (at its most basic: A-B-B-A) brings a pleasing, easy-to-remember structure to more complex parts of the Bible, both large and small. This book is built in a chiasm:

> The Elegant Bible (chapters 1–2)
>> The Feasting Bible (chapters 3–4)
>>> The Historical Bible (chapters 5–6)
>>>> The Storiented Bible (chapters 7–9)
>>> The Earthly Bible (chapters 10–11)
>> The Synagogue Bible (chapters 12–13)
> The Iconic Bible (chapters 14–15)

The first six chapters explore what the Bible is and how it came to be and recommend ways we can engage it that match what it really is. The final six chapters correspond to the first six in a reverse pattern, extending the opening themes in further directions. Once we regain an elegantly simple presentation of the Bible's natural complexity and literary variety (chapters 1–2), we can once again marry our sacred book of truth to beauty (chapters

14–15). If the Bible is a collection of meaty books best eaten in natural, whole forms (chapters 3–4), it is also true that meals are best experienced in community (chapters 12–13). If the Bible came to us in and through the rough and tumble of history (chapters 5–6), the meaning and direction of history is likewise the direct concern of the Bible's story (chapters 10–11). All of this leads to or flows from the climax of the chiasm: the restoration of the Bible as the story above all stories, a drama that we are invited to play a role in (chapters 7–9).

The chiastic journey of this book, then, is the proposed recovery of the Bible—a Bible that is presented as literature, eaten in natural forms, grounded in history, inviting in its narrative, restorative in its theme, engaged in community, and honored in its aesthetic presentation. My plea is that we deconstruct the crusty apparatus we've layered over our Bibles and, borrowing the language of my friend and colleague Christopher Smith, rediscover the beauty that lies beneath.[5]

If the Bible isn't what we've thought, we have to face the implications. If this is not a user's manual I'm holding in my hands or a collection of individual statements numbered for handy reference, I'm going to have to rethink my strategy for what to do with the Bible. After looking at what the Bible's current format seems to be telling us the Bible is, I will attempt to clear the deck by briefly looking at what the Bible actually is: a collection of ancient writings. This will lead to a discussion about why *this* Bible needs a slower, smarter, deeper engagement. I'll be talking about immersion in the deep blue sea of the Bible rather than skimming across the versified surface. I'll be making the case for eating good meals rather than speed snacking on what Philip Yancey calls Scripture McNuggets. My first plea will thus be for biblical holism, for exploring the Bible's smaller, richly-textured tellings in light of the complete compositions of which they are a part. And I'll argue for reading first, study second.

My case will then move on to the claim that when we pay good, close attention to this collection of writings, there is no other conclusion we can come to except that God's story (theology) is so embedded in and intertwined with our story (history) that the only good Bible reading and understanding is "grounded." That is, the Bible is tied to, bound up together with, arises from, addresses and redeems *this* place, *these* people, *our* lives. If we try to divorce the Bible and its spiritual teachings from the blood and guts and failures and hopes of God's people in history, we will sorely miss its point. One thing we've most certainly learned from the last one hundred years of historical study of the Bible is that the Bible is not a systematics—a timeless, organized scheme of otherworldly salvation. The surprising drama is rooted in this earth, and its promises will only be realized on this earth. Yes, the Bible is divine discourse, but God chose to speak in the Bible only in and through fully human voices. A dehistoricized Bible, pontificating to us from some point safely above the fray, is an unreal Bible, as unhelpful to us as a docetic Christ, who only seems to be human but really isn't. If we are determined to take flight to some higher, more noble realm above, we should be honest and go get our story from somewhere other than the Bible. The early church faced this option and dismissed world-denying, fly-away salvation as a heresy—gnosticism. But it's a very persistent, hydra-headed error and every generation faces the need to denounce it again.

Throughout the discussion I take seriously the fact that the Bibles we have are cultural artifacts. What we do with our Bibles—physically, tangibly, experientially—both reveals and shapes what we think the Bible is. God's world is a connected world and we have ignored for far too long the relationship between the forms of the Bible and its content. We do a lot of things with the Bible without thinking very much about *what* we're doing. But the Bible is not an ethereal book of spiritual ideas. The Bible itself is part of our world: it is a thing, an object, an artifact we make and form. When it is well-made—crafted, we might say—it will do more than say or teach things; it will embody them. To think we can sever this connection without consequence is to fail to think as good creational monotheists. The one, true God made the world to be a place in which form and content are meant to work together.

Since we are in the midst of a transition from traditional print to electronic forms of text, this principle is more important than ever. When sacred words move to the realm of floating electronic bits, the temptation to ignore their form is made stronger. But historic, orthodox Christian teaching stands on the connection of salvation with creation. The principle behind this is that when God saves, he is saving what he has already made. Just as we are not saved if there is no resurrection (though one might not know this from listening to typical funeral orations), the saving of the Bible will involve some physical restoration work as well. Beauty and the Bible will have to be addressed.

What does a journey to the center of the Bible look like? Any decent adventure into the Bible will take full account of both its form and its content. It will begin with knowledge of the messages of whole books and a clear perception of the uniqueness of their contributions. It will be followed by growing insight into how these books come together to form a single narrative—of God, Israel and the world—that comes into its own in the utterly remarkable story of Jesus of Nazareth and the new community he launched. We'll know we've hit the heart of it all—that is, that the Bible is achieving its purpose—when we realize that this ancient tribal tale has somehow become *our* center. When many more of us are engaged in communities that breathe this story and find their purpose in living this drama, then perhaps troubled minds and hurting hearts can be put at ease. The Bible too can be saved.

Ending with Love

Why did God give us the kind of Bible he did? Why did God give us a Bible at all? Why do we so often try to turn the Bible into something it manifestly is not? What is the *telos* (the great goal) of the Bible? Is the Bible itself part of God's mission to the world? If so, how exactly?

I invite you to ponder these big background questions (along with the two key ones I mentioned earlier: What is the Bible? What are we supposed to do with it?) as we begin our journey to the center of the Bible. Good answers can best be found by intentionally adopting the practice of sympathetic reading. I believe what C. S. Lewis said, that one's first responsibility regarding any piece of literature is to follow where it would lead. We are obligated to *receive* the submitted writing on the author's terms before we take over with our own attempts to *use* it on ours.[6] In the case of the Bible we are sorely tempted to get things backwards, to begin with our demands for immediate and obvious relevance on terms that we dictate. Indeed, much Bible publishing is built on this dishonoring practice. Call it submission, call it a willing suspension of disbelief, call it respecting an author—it comes down to stifling myself and to not letting my own questions, concerns and inner voices overrule what it is I'm first of all supposed to *receive*. Reading openly, deeply and slowly, and thus receiving the text as it was first meant—

this is the key discipline for all good reading. So it is with the Bible. The beginning of good Bible engagement is a bit of reflection on what it means to be a virtuous reader in general.

God was willing to take a great risk with the Bible: he left it in our hands. And we've done all kinds of things to it through the ages. We make it in certain ways and we read it in certain ways. Apparently this is what God planned all along. He expected and expects us to bring something of our-selves to it. The Bible is not magic. Nor is it kept away from us, safe and untouchable. To think we can simply be passive with the Bible, withholding our own active thought, reflection and shared community engagement, is to not accept the responsibility of being human.

We do best by the Bible when what we bring to it is our love. In the face of postmodernism's hermeneutic of suspicion, I, along with others, rec-ommend an epistemology of love in order to truly come to know the Bible. As N. T. Wright emphasizes, this is not the usual modernist proposal in which the knower stands dominantly over the known:

> Knowledge has to do with the interrelation of humans and the created world. This brings it within the sphere of the biblical belief that humans are made in the image of the creator, and that in consequence they are entrusted with the task of exercising wise responsibility within the created order. They are neither detached observers of, nor predators upon, creation. From this point of view, knowledge can be a form of *redeeming* stewardship; it can be, in one sense, a form of love.[7]

Wright goes on to identify the result of this kind of stewardship of knowledge:

> To know is to be in a relation with the known, which means that the 'knower' must be open to the possibility of the 'known' being other than had been expected or even desired, and must be prepared to respond accordingly, not merely to observe from a distance.[8]

Wright's critical realism can help to protect us from ourselves. Which reader of the Bible is not prone to remaking the text in their own image? How many of us profess a love for the Bible that is really no more than an affection for our own predetermined ideas? May we all be open to discov-ering in our sacred book things we had not seen, had not known, had not expected. May we, in other words, love the Scriptures as something bigger than and other than ourselves. We need a love that is truly and fully open to something coming to us from outside the imaginings of our own minds and hearts, something than can illumine our world and our stories. This is the kind of love we must bring to the Bible.

I embark on this journey knowing that it is a dangerous thing to mess with people's Bibles. Folks of all kinds and representing various perspectives tend to be pretty attached to what they believe about it, tend to be pretty certain about their certainties. I'm no different. But as Wendell Berry has reminded us, "The reason we need to have our *false* certainties shaken is so that we may see the possibility of better orders than we have."[9]

Protestants in particular will always say they love the Bible, in part because we understand our own history as a story of *biblical* reformation and recovery. But we are also the ones especially prone to instrumentalist and manipulative approaches to the Bible. Too often our well-intentioned biblical devotion comes down to merely using the Bible with our agenda already in place. So let us test this love we so constantly proclaim. A genuine love for the Bible won't mind a bit of reflection on the state of the Bible, on what the Bible once was, on what it has become and on what it could be again. As opposed to bibliolatry, this love will not be a worship of the thing itself, but a love *through* it to meet the one who stands behind it, who woos us into his story and ultimately to himself. But if we hear *him* calling to us through the mighty drama of the Bible, we will of course want to do right by his script.

one

OUR COMPLICATED BIBLE

Perfection is achieved, not when there is nothing more to add, but when there is nothing left to take away.

ANTOINE DE SAINT EXUPÉRY

W hat is the Bible?

There are the usual answers: The Bible is the Word of God. The Bible is God's inspired truth. The Bible is divine revelation. Or, the Bible is an ancient, mythological and unscientific book. Others jump to more descriptive answers—adjectives more than answers, really. The Bible is perfect, wonderful, insightful, helpful, encouraging and so on. Alternatively, for some it is incomprehensible, irrelevant, bloody, damaging or worse. But we haven't really answered the question: What is the Bible? When I open the book or turn on the screen, what is it precisely that I'm encountering?

Many people claim the Bible as the foundation of their life. Churches around the world and through the ages have pledged their commitment and faithfulness to it. It is therefore somewhat astonishing that we rarely stop to answer this question: What is it, exactly? I suspect that we pick up signals *based on how we see the Bible being used* and deduce from them what the Bible actually is. But our practices send confusing and conflicted messages. Most people simply haven't worked out clearly and consistently what they think the Bible is. And I would venture that most churches don't expressly address this question either; more likely they just go about their business, using the Bible in various ways. Again, I say, this is quite remarkable given the vital importance we claim for the Bible. You'd think we'd make sure those within our spiritual communities know what the Bible is in the interest of helping them interact with it appropriately.

I do know a man who addressed this question head-on in an adult Sunday School class. The class was an introduction to the Bible and at the end the following question was included in the review test:

Which of the following is the Bible most like: (A) Bartlett's Familiar Quotations, (B) The Reader's Digest Guide to Home Repairs, or (C) The Collected Papers of the American Antislavery Society?

What was this teacher looking for? He summarized it this way: "The correct answer is C, although we most often use the Bible like A and expect it to be like B." Part of his intention in the class was to help the students realize that "the Bible is a series of occasional pieces of various genres that traces the development of a transformational movement."[1] To this we will return—when we reach the climax of our journey to the center of the Bible, we will need a good, summarizing description like this one.

But our task in this chapter is more limited. We need a first-level answer to the question. Let's begin by simply trying to see the Bible clearly. After all, we identify many things based on how they present themselves to us. So, what does the Bible look like it is? How is it presented?

A SHORT HISTORY OF THE COMPLEXIFICATION OF THE BIBLE

We've never been able to leave the Bible alone. Ancient manuscript collections of the Bible reveal a fairly universal compulsion to tamper with the sacred text. From very early on, Christian scribes did more than record bare words. They began to interact with the sacred writings, minimally at first. Things begin to happen in, around and under the Bible's own words.

While the wider cultural aesthetic preference was for *scriptio continua* (no spaces between words and no punctuation), early Scripture manuscripts began introducing new features. Many of these seem to be related to providing "helps" for the public reading of the Bible. We should remember that most people did not see these manuscripts, but rather heard them being read. Writing material was scarce and expensive and not many people could read and write. So the first additions to the Bible's pages were there for those who read them to others. Breathing marks, paragraph or other sense unit markings, visual cues used to mark the beginnings of new words, and page numbering all appear.

There were also special abbreviated ways of presenting the divine names. Monogram-like combinations of Greek letters superimposed on each other debuted as with the *tau-rho* and later *chi-rho* pairs that functioned as shorthand ways of referring to Christ. Other symbols were creatively scripted in among the words. Visually pure Bible texts are pretty hard to come by.[2]

What began as very circumspect intervention, however, grew into something more. We moved from textual glosses, marks, symbols and chapter divisions to full-blown commentary and ornate artwork. All of this shows up not only in the margins but also in the spaces between lines and wrapped around the holy words. The temptation to comment directly on the biblical page has been indulged by copyists from the start. It's inevitable—and a healthy sign anyway—that a text as significant as the Bible's provokes strong responses and interactions. However, dangers lurk here.

First, it's essential that the boundaries of what is sacred and what is not remain clear. For receivers of the text, the aura of authority can easily start to float over our own commentary. Second, even when the boundaries are clear, the additions can become bloated and overwhelm the Bible text in appearance and thus perceived importance. Third, commentary in particular can become a kind of overbearing boss, fencing in the text and restricting the interpretive possibilities. It becomes very easy to squeeze the Bible into a mold, reversing roles with a text that is seeking to reshape us around its story.

Marking divisions in the text is perhaps the key intervention made through the Bible's history. These divisions could include paragraphs, marked sections for readings or the topical gospel canons produced by the fourth-century church historian Eusebius. (Paragraph markings in the First Testament, inserted to aid in the weekly synagogue readings, predate even the writing of the New Testament.[3]) Various chapter systems of the New Testament were made, including one that broke Matthew into sixty-eight sections, Mark into forty-eight, Luke into eighty-three and so on. Chapters were organizing principles, developed to structure liturgical readings or to help speed the finding of passages and topics within the Bible. Their guiding principle tended to be breaking up the text into sections of roughly equal length rather than attentively revealing the natural literary sections of the Bible.

We tend to think of our ever-present modern Bible companions—chapter and verse numbers—as belonging inexorably together. But they actually have separate histories. The chapter system we know today was developed around the year 1200 by the English church leader Stephen Langton. But this system wasn't immediately standardized. For example, the famous printed Bibles of Johannes Gutenberg, beginning in the 1450s, didn't include it. Eventually, however, Langton's chapter divisions would be married to verse markings, and the new arrangement would become a dynasty. That's a bit of a story, and we'll get to it shortly.

The story of Bible verses brings us to the real birth of the modern Bible. We can see this momentous emergence by focusing on the few short years from 1525 to 1557. Once the new cultural form took shape, it spread remarkably quickly and soon became the assumed, standard presentation of the Bible. The reasons for this are historically intriguing, revealing of what a lot of folks apparently *wanted* the Bible to be.

This particular chapter of the story we are concerned with has a pleasant enough beginning. William Tyndale's first New Testament in 1525 was a readable, coherent presentation: a single-column setting fairly attuned to literary form. For example, in Luke's Gospel lists and songs are presented in unique forms, appropriate to embedded subgenres. There are no intrusions to the text save for chapter headings. Overall it is an accessible work that invites big readings.

But the changes began quickly. In the 1530s extrabiblical material was increasingly poking into the sacred text itself (not just the margins) and two-column settings became the norm. The decisive turn for the modernist Bible, however, was the introduction of numbered verse divisions. By the sixteenth century the chapter numbers that we know today had been in place for three hundred years. But Reformation-era Bible dueling required a greater level of fine-tuning. The first attempt at inserting numbered verse markings was made by an Italian scholar, Santi Pagnini, who in 1528 versified a Latin New Testament. But as with those earlier alternate chapter divisions, Pagnini's numbering system didn't take hold.

THE GOSPEL OF ST LUKE

1¹⁻¹⁹

Forasmuch as many have taken in hand to compile a treatise of those things, which are surely known among us, even as they declared them unto us, which from the beginning saw them theirselves, and were ministers at the doing: I determined also, as soon as I had searched out diligently all things from the beginning, that then I would write unto thee, good Theophilus: that thou mightest know the certainty of those things, whereof thou art informed.

CHAPTER ONE

There was in the days of Herod king of Jewry, a certain priest named **A** Zacharias, of the course of Abia. And his wife was of the daughters of Aaron: And her name was Elizabeth. Both were perfect before God, and walked in all the laws and ordinances of the Lord, that no man could find fault with them. And they had no child, because that Elizabeth was barren and both were well stricken in age.

And it came to pass, as he executed the priest's office before God, as his course came (according to the custom of the priest's office) his lot was to burn incense. And went into the temple of the Lord and the whole multitude of the people were without in prayer while the incense was a-burning. And there appeared unto him an angel of the lord standing on the right side of the altar of incense. And when Zacharias saw him, he was abashed, and fear came on him.

And the angel said unto him: fear not Zachary, for thy prayer is heard: And **B** thy wife Elizabeth shall bear thee a son, and thou shalt call his name John, and thou shalt have joy and gladness, and many shall rejoice at his birth. For he shall be great in the sight of the lord, and shall neither drink wine nor strong drink. And he shall be filled with the holy ghost, even in his mother's womb: and many of the children of Israel shall he turn to their Lord God. And he shall go before him in the spirit and power of Elias to turn the hearts* of the fathers to the children, and the unbelievers to the wisdom of the just men: to make the people ready for the Lord.

And Zacharias said unto the angel: Whereby shall I know this? seeing that I am old and my wife well stricken in years. And the angel answered and said

Zacharias.

Elizabeth.

Lev. 11. d.

John.

* To make the children
have such an heart to
God as Abraham and
the Fathers had.

Psa. 131.
Mal. 3. a.
Mal. 4. b.

A sign is asked.

88

Figure 1.1. Tyndale's New Testament

It didn't take long for the experiment to be tried again. Similar new cultural expressions often occur independently yet in close historical proximity. In this case, something seems to have been insisting on coming to expression in the Bible realm, and the turn to modernism was its fullness of time. Close to the heart of modernity is the impulse to segment, in the belief that the path to understanding comes from the exhaustive examination of the constituent pieces of a thing. Sure enough, Robert Estienne, a French printer and classical scholar, gave numbered verse divisions another shot in 1551. What was Estienne's motivation? He wanted to produce a Bible concordance, a tool that would change decisively the answer to the question, what are we supposed to do with the Bible? Estienne introduced his numbered verses to a Greek New Testament, and this time the system caught on. These are the verse numbers we see reflected in most Bibles today. All that was left was to number the older verse markings that already divided the First Testament. Everything was in place for a fully segmented, modernistic Bible. Tyndale's beauty had been escorted to the edge of a cliff.

Just a few short years later in 1557, an edition of the Geneva New Testament turned each verse into a paragraph of its own. In 1560 the Geneva Bible would repeat and enshrine the error. As for Tyndale's clean and readable text? Over she goes. In truth, it was a kind of death, a demolishing of the natural form of the Bible. Of course, literary words would continue to be translated, but words alone do not literature make. King James I of England, unhappy with the strongly Calvinistic notes in the Geneva Bible, would commission a new English translation a generation later. The King James Bible was a literary masterpiece as far as its language was concerned, but it continued the destructive device of indenting and thus isolating each newly-numbered fragment. And it became the new standard for Bible printing. It was the death knell for a certain kind of Bible, a Bible that presented something closer to what the Scriptures inherently were. In this new form an essential part of the literature had withered, expired and disappeared, namely, the form.

It is critical to note here that Estienne's intention was to produce a reference tool (a concordance for a Greek New Testament), but the Geneva Bible took this specialized form intended for a specialized use and transferred it to a Bible for general readers of the English text. The new form f Thy iudgements are most constant against the wicked, and passe our reach.

g Thou wilt strengthen them with all power, & blesse them with all felicitie.

h Though the faithfull seeme to wither, and be cut downe by the wicked, yet they shall grow againe and flourish in the Church of God as the cedars doe in mount Lebanon.

i The children of God shall haue a power aboue nature, and their age shall bring forth most fresh fruits.

foole doeth not vnderstand this,

7 (When the wicked grow as the grasse, and all t the workers of wickednesse doe flourish) that they shalbe destroyed for euer.

8 But thou, O Lord, art f most High for euermore.

9 For loe, thine enemies, O Lord : for loe, thine enemies shall perish: all the workers of iniquitie shalbe destroyed.

10 g But thou shalt exalt mine horne, like the vnicornes, and I shall bee anoynted with fresh oyle.

11 Mine eye also shall see my desire against mine enemies: and mine eares shall heare my wish against the wicked, that rise vp against me.

12 The righteous shall h flourish like a palme tree, and shall grow like a cedar in Lebanon.

13 Such as bee planted in the house of the Lord, shall flourish in the courts of our God.

14 They shall still bring foorth fruit in their i age : they shalbe fat and flourishing.

15 To declare that the Lord my rocke is righteous, and that none iniquity is in him.

PSAL. XCIII.

1 Hee praiseth the power of God in the creation of the world, and beareth downe all people which lift them vp against his maiestie, 5 and promiseth to consider his promises.

THe Lord a reigneth, and is clothed with maiestie : the Lord is clothed, and girded with power, the world also shall be established, that it cannot be mooued.

2 Thy b throne is establish ed of old: thou art from euerlasting.

3 c The floods haue lifted vp, O Lord : the floods haue lifted vp their voyce : the floods lift vp their waues.

4 The waues of the sea are marueilous through the noise of many waters, yet the Lord on high is more mighty.

5 Thy d testimonies are very sure : holinesse becommeth thine House, O Lord, for euer.

a As God by his power and wisedome hath made and gouerneth the world : so must the same be our defence against all enemies and dangers.

b Wherein thou sittest and gouernest the world.

c Gods power appeareth in ruling the furious waters.

d Besides Gods power and wisedome in creating and gouerning, his great mercy also appeareth in that hee hath giuen his people his word and couenant.

PSAL. XCIIII.

1 He prayeth vnto God against the violence and arrogance of tyrants, 10 warning them of Gods iudgements. 12 Then doth he comfort the afflicted by the good issue of their afflictions, as he felt in himselfe, and did see in others, and by the ruine of the wicked, 23 whom the Lord will destroy.

2 Whose office is is to take vengeance on the wicked.

b Shew by effect that y art Iudge of the world to punish the wicked.

c That is, bragge of their cruelty & oppression: or esteeme themselues aboue all other.

d Seeing the Church was then so sore oppressed, it ought not to seeme strange to vs, if we see it so now, and therefore we must call to God, to take our cause in hand.

e He sheweth that they are desperate

O Lord God a the auenger, O God the auenger, shew thy selfe b clearely.

2 Exalt thy selfe, O Iudge of the world, and render a reward to the proud.

3 Lord, how long shall the wicked, how long shall the wicked c triumph?

4 They prate and speake fiercely: all the workers of iniquity vaunt themselues.

5 They d smite downe thy people, O Lord, and trouble thine heritage.

6 They slay the widow and the stranger, and murther the fatherlesse.

7 c Yet they say, The Lord shall not see: neither will the God of Iaakob regard it.

8 Vnderstand, ye vnwise among the people : and ye fooles, when will ye be wise?

9 Hee that f planted the eare , shall hee not heare? or he that formed the eye, shall he not see?

10 Or he that chastiseth the g nations, shall he

in malice, so rasmuch as they feared not God , but gaue themselues wholly to doe wickedly. f He sheweth that it is impossible, but God should heare, see, and vnderstand their wickednesse. g If God punish whole nations for their sinnes, it is mercie folly for any one man, or els a few to thinke that God will spare them.

not correct ? he that teacheth man knowledge, shall he not know?

11 The Lord knoweth the thoughts of man, that they are vanitie.

12 Blessed is the man whom thou h chastisest, O Lord, and teachest him in thy Law,

13 That thou mayest giue him rest from the dayes of euill , whiles the pitte is digged for the wicked.

14 Surely the Lord will not faile his people, neither will he forsake his inheritance.

15 For i iudgement shal returne to iustice, and all the vpright in heart shall follow after it.

16 Who will rise vp with me against the wicked ? or who will take my part against the workers of iniquitie?

17 If the Lord had not k holpen me, my soule had almost dwelt in silence.

18 When I said, l My foot slideth, thy mercy, O Lord, stayed me.

19 In the multitude of my m thoughts in mine heart, thy comforts haue reioced my soule.

20 Hath the throne of iniquitie n fellowship with thee, which forgeth wrong for a Law?

21 They gather them together against the soule of the righteous, and condemne the innocent blood.

22 But the Lord is my refuge, and my God is the rocke of mine hope.

23 And he will recompense them their wickednesse, & o destroy them in their owne malice, yea, the Lord our God shall destroy them.

h God hath care ouer his, and chastiseth them for their weale, albeit they should not perish for euer, with the wicked.

i God will restore the state & gouernment of this garo their right vse, and then the godly shall follow him cheerefully.

k He complaineth of the which would not helpe him to resist the enemies: yet was assured that God helpe would not faile.

l When I thought there was no way but death.

m In my trouble and distresse I set found thy perfect helpe.

n Thoughe the wicked iudges pretend iustice in oppressing the Church, yet they haue not that authority of God.

o It is a great token of Gods iudgement when the purpose of the wicked is broken, but most, when they are destroyed in their owne malice.

PSAL. XCV.

1 An earnest exhortation to praise God 4 for the gouernment of the world and the election of the Church. 8 An admonition not to follow the rebellion of the olde fathers, that tempted God in the wildernesse. 11 For the which they might not enter into the land of promise.

COme , let vs reioyce vnto the Lord : let vs sing a alowde vnto the rocke of our saluation.

2 Let vs come before his face with praise: let vs sing lowd vnto him with Psalmes.

3 For the Lord is a great God, and a great King aboue all b gods.

4 In whose hand are the deepe places of the earth, and the c heights of the mountaines are his.

5 To whom the Sea belongeth, for he made it, and his hands formed the dry land.

6 Come, let vs d worship and fall downe, and kneele before the Lord our maker.

7 For he is our God, and we are the people of his pasture, and the sheepe of his e hand: to day, if ye wil heare his voyce,

8 f Harden not your heart, as in || Meribah, and as in the day of || Massah in the wildernes.

9 When your fathers * tempted mee, prooued me, though they had seene my worke.

10 Fourtie yeeres haue I contended with this generation, and said, They are a people that g erre in heart, for they haue not knowen my wayes.

11 Wherefore I sweare in my wrath, saying, Surely they shall not enter into h my rest.

a Reseruing his Gods seruice from death not in dead ceremonies, but chiefly in the faith certise of praise & thankgiuing.

b Euen the idolatrous and false gods, if any such be.

c By this three words he signifieth one thing, meaning that they most wholly giue themselues to serue God.

e That is, the flocke, whom he gouerneth with his owne hand.

f By these three words he signifieth one thing, meaning that they most wholly giue themselues to serue God.

e That is, the flocke, whom he gouerneth with his owne hand.

f By these three words he signifieth one thing, in they are Gods flocke that it.

if they heare his voice. f By the contemning of Gods word. || Or, in strife: which of the place was so called. || Or, tentation. reade Exod. 17. 9. * Exod. 17. 7. Numb. 14. 22. g They were without iudgement and reason. h That is, into the land of Canaan, where he promised them rest.

PSAL.

Figure 1.2. A page from the Psalms in the Geneva Bible

became standard, and its visual message altered how readers perceived and understood the very nature of the Bible.

At stake here is a key feature of any reader's communication pact with any piece of writing: the recognition of an author's chosen literary type and a subsequent agreement to follow the rules of that choice. Once the Bible is visually fragmented and made uniform, where then is the letter, the poem, the oracle, the story? They are gone with the new modernist wind and replaced by bits and pieces, all numbingly the same, a uniform list bound by two columns on the printed page. The new form actively works at undoing the author's literary intentions as well as the reader's under-standing of their corresponding obligation. As the reader takes in the num-bered list going down the page, the message is clear: these propositions are meant to be read and understood independently as separate statements of spiritual truth. And the Bible, therefore, is the collection of these true, perfect, divine spiritual statements.

This revolution was actually twofold. The new modern reference imprint that was placed on top of the Bible text simultaneously masked the original, natural units of the text while also imposing a new structure of numbered, fragmented micro-units. It was a double loss: the Bible's native form was lost as a foreign one was forced in. This colonization of the Bible text would decisively change the course of the Bible for the next five centuries.

This wind blew in quickly, and the change it brought was momentous indeed. From now on the versified Bible became what almost everyone thought of simply as the Bible. The Bible had gone from being a collection of books—a rich variety of genres, each fulfilling its specified task in the developing overall narrative—to a list of singled-out statements. It was the form that morphed, but this changed what the Bible *was* for people. As Bible historian David Norton says of this crucial period, "The reader is being di-rected to texts rather than to the text."[4] The early modern period thus proved to be a crucial one for the Bible. As we will see, there was a direct link be-tween the new form of the text and new Bible practices.

What does the Bible look like now? How is it presented? What does the format of the Bible tell us it is? Before anyone even says a word, the modern complexification of the Bible has staked out its preemptive position on the issue and has *already shown us* what the Bible is. And given this predetermined answer in the format itself, it should come as no surprise at all what people will then do with this Bible.

Bamboozled by Biblioclutter

In 1707, one hundred and fifty years after the appearance of the Geneva New Testament, philosopher John Locke would write that the Scriptures "are so chop'd and minc'd, and as they are now Printed, stand so broken and divided, that . . . the Common People take the Verses usually for distinct Aphorisms," and "even Men of more advanc'd Knowledge in reading them, lose very much of the strength and force of the Coherence, and the Light that depends on it."[5]

Chop'd and minc'd, the modern Bible has bad complexity. This is not the kind of complexity that science speaks of these days, those intricate patterns of nature—waves, leaves, coastlines—formed by the simplest of small patterns iterated and reiterated over time and space. That kind of complexity is pleasing to us and fitting to the nature of things. But the Bible's newfound complexity is artificial, intrusive and ultimately misleading as to the true nature of what it is.

Granted, the Bible is in and of itself a complex book—diverse literary types, diverse authors, a meandering storyline that can sometime seem completely off track. But this kind of complexity in the Bible does come together over time and space to create a pleasing and fitting pattern. What we've done to the Bible—that's something else entirely. We've created a Bible exoskeleton—a hard outer structure that covers and essentially hides what is beneath. Columns, numbers, headings, footnotes, cross-references, callouts, colored letters, etc., etc., etc. Our overindulged addiction to addition has given us everything we could ask for except the text itself in a clean, natural expression. What we have in our Bibles now is excess. We have effectively buried the text and blinded readers with data smog.[6]

The modernist Bible has the problem of presenting the reader with an imposingly dense and complicated book to digest, and this in an age when reading in general is already under assault. We should rethink how we've presented our holy book, if only for the sake of issuing a decent invitation for people to simply read it. But the form of the modernist Bible has other issues.

will be liberated from its bondage to decay[c] and brought into the freedom and glory of the children of God.

[22] We know that the whole creation has been groaning[d] as in the pains of childbirth right up to the present time. [23] Not only so, but we ourselves, who have the firstfruits of the Spirit,[e] groan[f] inwardly as we wait eagerly[g] for our adoption to sonship, the redemption of our bodies. [24] For in this hope we were saved.[h] But hope that is seen is no hope at all. Who hopes for what they already have? [25] But if we hope for what we do not yet have, we wait for it patiently.

[26] In the same way, the Spirit helps us in our weakness. We do not know what we ought to pray for, but the Spirit himself intercedes for us[i] through wordless groans. [27] And he who searches our hearts[j] knows the mind of the Spirit, because the Spirit intercedes for God's people in accordance with the will of God.

[28] And we know that in all things God works for the good of those who love him, who[a] have been called[k] according to his purpose. [29] For those God foreknew[l] he also predestined[m] to be conformed to the image of his Son,[n] that he might be the firstborn among many brothers and sisters. [30] And those he predestined,[o] he also called; those he called, he also justified;[p] those he justified, he also glorified.[q]

More Than Conquerors

[31] What, then, shall we say in response to these things?[r] If God is for us, who can be against us?[s] [32] He who did not spare his own Son,[t] but gave him up for us all — how will he not also, along with him, graciously give us all things? [33] Who will bring any charge[u] against those whom God has chosen? It is God who justifies. [34] Who then is the one who condemns?

No one. Christ Jesus who died[v] — more than that, who was raised to life — is at the right hand of God[w] and is also interceding for us.[x] [35] Who shall separate us from the love of Christ? Shall trouble or hardship or persecution or famine or nakedness or danger or sword?[y] [36] As it is written:

> "For your sake we face death all day long;
> we are considered as sheep to be slaughtered."[bz]

[37] No, in all these things we are more than conquerors[a] through him who loved us.[b] [38] For I am convinced that neither death nor life, neither angels nor demons,[c] neither the present nor the future, nor any powers,[c] [39] neither height nor depth, nor anything else in all creation, will be able to separate us from the love of God[d] that is in Christ Jesus our Lord.

Paul's Anguish Over Israel

9 I speak the truth in Christ — I am not lying,[e] my conscience confirms[f] it through the Holy Spirit — [2] I have great sorrow and unceasing anguish in my heart. [3] For I could wish that I myself[g] were cursed[h] and cut off from Christ for the sake of my people, those of my own race,[i] [4] the people of Israel. Theirs is the adoption to sonship;[j] theirs the divine glory, the covenants,[k] the receiving of the law,[l] the temple worship[m] and the promises.[n] [5] Theirs are the patriarchs, and from them is traced the human ancestry of the Messiah,[o] who is God over all,[p] forever praised![dq] Amen.

God's Sovereign Choice

[6] It is not as though God's word had failed. For not all who are descended from Israel are Israel.[r] [7] Nor because they are his descendants are they all Abraham's children. On the contrary, "It is through Isaac that your offspring

---

Cross-references (center column):

8:21 c Ac 3:21; 2Pe 3:13; Rev 21:1
8:22 d Jer 12:4
8:23 e 2Co 5:5 f 2Co 5:2, 4 g Gal 5:5
8:24 h 1Th 5:8
8:26 i Eph 6:18
8:27 j Rev 2:23
8:28 k 1Co 1:9; 2Ti 1:9
8:29 l Ro 11:2 m Eph 1:5, 11 n 1Co 15:49; 2Co 3:18; Php 3:21; 1Jn 3:2
8:30 o Eph 1:5, 11 p 1Co 6:11 q Ro 9:23
8:31 r Ro 4:1 s Ps 118:6
8:32 t Jn 3:16; Ro 4:25; 5:8
8:33 u Isa 50:8, 9
8:34 v Ro 5:6-8 w Mk 16:19 x Heb 7:25; 9:24; 1Jn 2:1
8:35 y 1Co 4:11
8:36 z Ps 44:22; 2Co 4:11
8:37 a 1Co 15:57 b Gal 2:20; Rev 1:5; 3:9
8:38 c Eph 1:21; 1Pe 3:22
8:39 d Ro 5:8
9:1 e 2Co 11:10; Gal 1:20; 1Ti 2:7 f Ro 1:9
9:3 g Ex 32:32 h 1Co 12:3; 16:22 i Ro 11:14
9:4 j Ex 4:22 k Ge 17:2; Ac 3:25; Eph 2:12 l Ps 147:19 m Heb 9:1 n Ac 13:32
9:5 o Mt 1:1-16 p Jn 1:1 q Ro 1:25
9:6 r Ro 2:28, 29; Gal 6:16

---

[a] 28 Or *that all things work together for good to those who love God, who;* or *that in all things God works together with those who love him to bring about what is good — with those who*   [b] 36 Psalm 44:22   [c] 38 Or *nor heavenly rulers*   [d] 5 Or *Messiah, who is over all. God be forever praised!* Or *Messiah. God who is over all be forever praised!*

Figure 1.3. A contemporary modernist Bible with two columns, chapter and verse numbering, section headings, translators' footnotes, cross-references, etc.

The Thunderbird problem is known in the automobile industry as the problem of upgrades that backfire. The original Thunderbird was immediately well-received, so much that Thunderbird clubs were formed by the car's enthusiasts. Perceived as smart, sporty and fun, the Thunderbird clearly struck a chord with a dedicated group of drivers. Then, in the usual pattern of well-intentioned tinkering with the goal of improving on the good to make it even better, the Thunderbird somewhere lost its way. No doubt a case could be made for each added feature and new design. But when you added them all up, something else happened. All the enthusiasts rebelled. They claimed they didn't recognize their beloved anymore. Whatever else this big, complicated machine was, it wasn't the car they had fallen for. Feature creep had led to feature fatigue. Upgrades had overwhelmed the original vision. But then in an important, clarifying move, Ford went back to the start and released a new retro version of the Thunderbird, thus winning back the tribe.

Such is the story of the modernist TMI Bible. Every note, every heading, every number, every stop-reading-and-jump-around reference was born with the best of intentions. We were only trying to help. Help make the Good Book easier to understand. Help find things more quickly. Help with a little guidance from the authorized, credentialed experts. Help the very words of Jesus himself find a straight line to our hearts. But these additives too have backfired. We've piled them on. Bible readers now face information overload, leading paradoxically to information anxiety. At some point, serving up more facts, data, interpretation and application about the Bible only serves to make us nervous about all that we apparently don't yet know. The release of every new study Bible only reinforces this anxiety. In all of this, the original has gotten very hard to recognize and we seem to have lost the core thing itself. We have a Thunderbird problem with the Bible. Bible enthusiasts should rebel.

It's worth observing that the modernist Bible has a kind of desperation about it, a frantic nervousness that keeps doing things to the text—cutting and cataloging it, fencing it in with approved commentary, cross-referencing everything to prove some kind of harmony. Perhaps this is due to an underlying feeling of inadequacy in the face of modernity's demand for comprehensive certainty. The bare text makes the modernist nervous, so

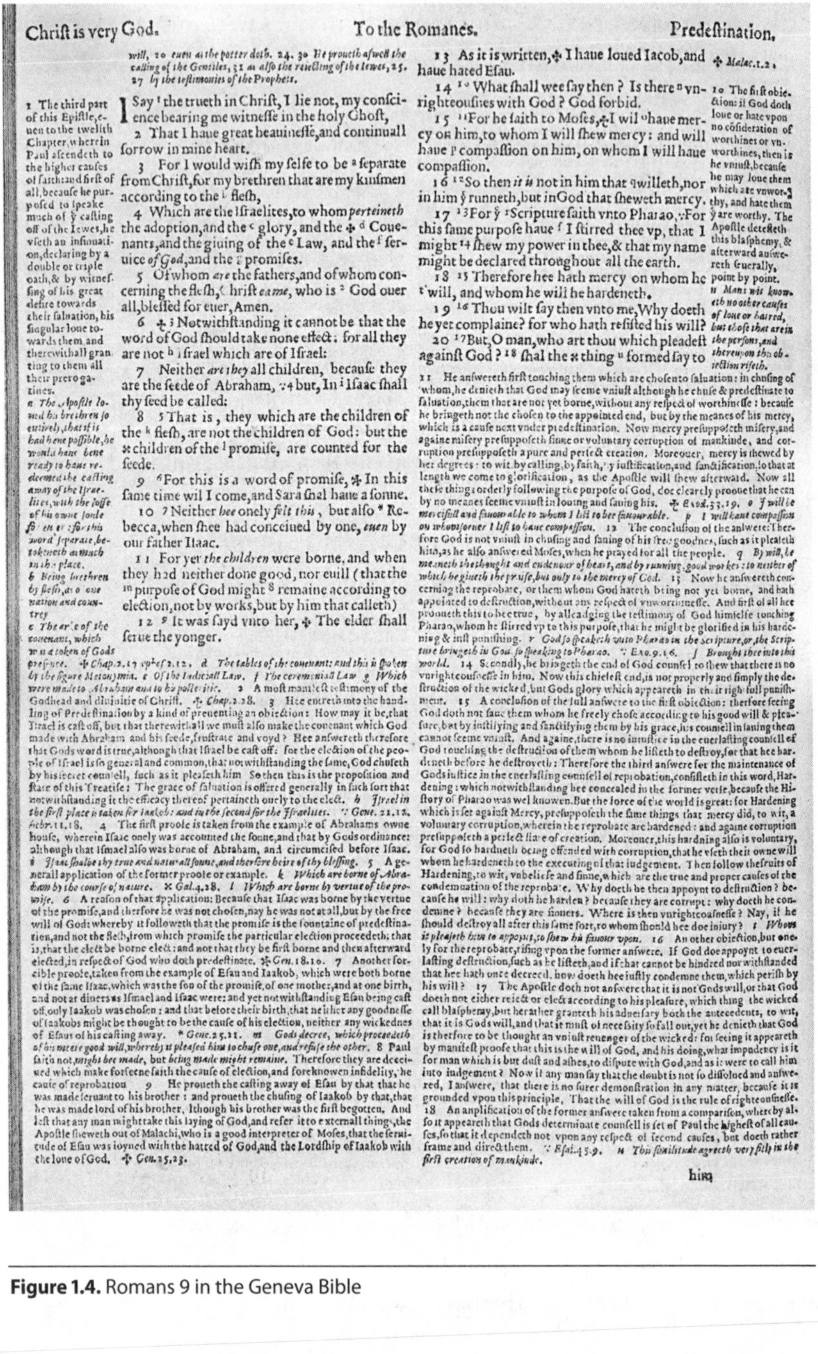

Christ is very God. To the Romanes. Predestination.

will, 20 euen as the potter doth. 24. 30 He prooueth aswell the calling of the Gentiles, 31 as also the reiecting of the Iewes, 25. 27 by the testimonies of the Prophets.

1 I Say [1] the trueth in Christ, I lie not, my conscience bearing me witnesse in the holy Ghost,

2 That I haue great heauinesse, and continuall sorrow in mine heart.

3 For I would wish my selfe to be [a] separate from Christ, for my brethren that are my kinsmen according to the [b] flesh,

4 Which are the Israelites, to whom *perteineth* the adoption, and the [c] glory, and the ✠ [d] Couenants, and the giuing of the [e] Law, and the [f] seruice *of God*, and the [g] promises.

5 Of whom *are* the fathers, and of whom concerning the flesh, Christ *came*, who is [2] God ouer all, blessed for euer, Amen.

6 ✠ [3] Notwithstanding it cannot be that the word of God should take none effect: for all they are not [h] Israel which are of Israel:

7 Neither *are they* all children, because they are the seede of Abraham, ✠ but, In [i] Isaac shall thy seed be called:

8 [5] That is, they which are the children of the [k] flesh, are not the children of God: but the ✠ children of the [l] promise, are counted for the seede.

9 [6] For this is a word of promise, ✠ In this same time wil I come, and Sara shal haue a sonne.

10 [7] Neither *hee* onely *felt this*, but also * Rebecca, when shee had conceiued by one, *euen* by our father Isaac.

11 For yet *the children* were borne, and when they had neither done good, nor euill (that the [m] purpose of God might [8] remaine according to election, not by works, but by him that calleth)

12 [9] It was sayd vnto her, ✠ The elder shall serue the yonger.

13 As it is written, ✠ I haue loued Iacob, and haue hated Esau. ✠ *Malac.1.2.*

14 [10] What shall wee say then? Is there [n] vnrighteousnes with God? God forbid.

15 [11] For he saith to Moses, ✠ I wil [o] haue mercy on him, to whom I will shew mercy: and will haue [p] compassion on him, on whom I will haue compassion.

16 [12] So then *it is* not in him that [q] willeth, nor in him ÿ runneth, but in God that sheweth mercy.

17 [13] For ÿ [r] Scripture saith vnto Pharao, ✠ For this same purpose haue [s] I stirred thee vp, that I might [14] shew my power in thee, & that my name might be declared throughout all the earth.

18 [15] Therefore hee hath mercy on whom he [t] will, and whom he will he hardeneth.

19 [16] Thou wilt say then vnto me, Why doeth he yet complaine? for who hath resisted his will?

20 [17] But, O man, who art thou which pleadest against God? [18] shal the ✠ thing [u] formed say to

1 The third part of this Epistle, euen to the twelfth Chapter, wherein Paul ascendeth to the higher causes of faith: and first of all, because he purposed to speake much of ÿ casting off of the Iewes, he vseth an insinuation, declaring by a double or triple oath, & by witnessing of his great desire towards their saluation, his singular loue towards them and therewithall granting to them all their prerogatiues.

a The Apostle loued his brethren so entirely, that if it had bene possible, he would haue bene ready to haue redeemed the casting away of the Israelites, with the losse of his owne soule for euer: for this word separate, betokeneth as much in this place.

b Being brethren by flesh, as o one nation and country

c The arke of the couenant, which was a token of Gods presence. ✠ *Chap.2.17 ephes.2.12.* *d The tables of the couenant: and this is spoken by the figure Metonymia.* *e Of the Iudiciall Law.* *f The ceremoniall Law* *g Which were made to Abraham and to his posteritie.* 2 A most manifest testimony of the Godhead and diuinitie of Christ. ✠ *Chap.2.28.* 3 Hee entreth into the handling of Predestination by a kind of preuenting an obiection: How may it be, that Israel is cast off, but that therewithall we must also make the couenant which God made with Abraham and his seede, frustrate and voyd? Hee answereth therefore that Gods word is true, although that Israel be cast off: for the election of the people of Israel is so general and common, that notwithstanding the same, God chuseth by his secret counsell, such as it pleaseth him. So then this is the proposition and state of this Treatise: The grace of saluation is offered generally in such sort that notwithstanding it the efficacy thereof pertaineth onely to the elect. *h Israel in the first place is taken for Iaakob: and in the second for the Israelites.* ✠ *Gene.21.12. hebr.11.18.* 4 The first proofe is taken from the example of Abrahams owne house, wherein Isaac onely was accounted the sonne, and that by Gods ordinance: although that Ismael also was borne of Abraham, and circumcised before Isaac. *i Isaac shalbe thy true and naturall sonne, and therfore heire of thy blessing.* 5 A generall application of the former proofe or example. *k Which are borne of Abraham by the course of nature.* ✠ *Gal.4.28.* *l Which are borne by vertue of the promise.* 6 A reason of that application: Because that Isaac was borne by the vertue of the promise, and therfore he was not chosen, nay he was not at all, but by the free will of God: whereby it followeth that the promise is the fountaine of predestination, and not the flesh, from which promise the particular election proceedeth: that is, that the elect be borne elect: and not that they be first borne and then afterward elected, in respect of God who doth predestinate. ✠ *Gen.18.10.* 7 Another forcible proofe, taken from the example of Esau and Iaakob, which were both borne of the same Isaac, which was the son of the promise, of one mother, and at one birth, and not at diuers as Ismael and Isaac were: and yet notwithstanding Esau being cast off, only Iaakob was chosen: and that before their birth, that neither any goodnesse of Iaakobs might be thought to be the cause of his election, neither any wickednes of Esaus of his casting away. * *Gene.25.21.* *m Gods decree, which proceedeth of his meere good will, whereby it pleased him to chuse one, and refuse the other.* 8 Paul saith not, *might bee made*, but *being made might remaine*. Therefore they are deceiued which make forseene faith the cause of election, and foreknowen infidelity, the cause of reprobation. 9 He prooueth the casting away of Esau by that that he was made seruant to his brother: and prooueth the chusing of Iaakob by that, that he was made lord of his brother, although his brother was the first begotten. And lest that any man might take this saying of God, and refer it to externall things, the Apostle sheweth out of Malachi, who is a good interpreter of Moses, that the seruitude of Esau was ioyned with the hatred of God, and the Lordship of Iaakob with the loue of God. ✠ *Gen.25.23.*

10 The first obiection: if God doth loue or hate vpon no consideration of worthines or vnworthines, then is he vniust, because he may loue them which are vnworthy, and hate them ÿ are worthy. The Apostle detesteth this blasphemy, & afterward answereth seuerally, point by point.

n Mans wit knoweth no other causes of loue or hatred, but those that are in the persons, and thereupon this obiection riseth.

11 He answereth first touching them which are chosen to saluation: in chusing of whom, he denieth that God may seeme vniust although he chuse & predestinate to saluation, them that are not yet borne, without any respect of worthinesse: because he bringeth not the chosen to the appointed end, but by the meanes of his mercy, which is a cause next vnder predestination. Now mercy presupposeth misery, and againe misery presupposeth sinne or voluntary corruption of mankinde, and corruption presupposeth a pure and perfect creation. Moreouer, mercy is shewed by her degrees: to wit, by calling, by faith, by iustification, and sanctification, so that at length we come to glorification, as the Apostle will shew afterward. Now all these things orderly following the purpose of God, doe clearely prooue that he can by no meanes seeme vniust in louing and sauing his. ✠ *Exod.33.19.* *o I will be mercifull and fauourable to whom I list to bee fauourable.* *p I will haue compassion on whomsoeuer I list to haue compassion.* 12 The conclusion of the answere: Therefore God is not vniust in chusing and sauing of his free goodnes, such as it pleaseth him, as he also answered Moses, when he prayed for all the people. *q By will, he meaneth the thought and endeuour of heart, and by running, good workes: to neither of which he giueth the praise, but only to the mercy of God.* 13 Now he answereth concerning the reprobate, or them whom God hateth being not yet borne, and hath appointed to destruction, without any respect of vnworthinesse. And first of all hee prooueth this to bee true, by alleadging the testimony of God himselfe touching Pharao, whom he stirred vp to this purpose, that he might be glorified in his hardening & iust punishing. *r God so speaketh vnto Pharao in the scripture, or, the Scripture bringeth in God so speaking to Pharao.* ✠ *Exo.9.16.* *s Brought thee into this world.* 14 Secondly, he bringeth the end of God counsel to shew that there is no vnrighteousnesse in him. Now this chiefest end, is not properly and simply the destruction of the wicked, but Gods glory which appeareth in their rightfull punishment. 15 A conclusion of the full answere to the first obiection: therfore seeing God doth not saue them whom he freely chose according to his good will & pleasure, but by iustifying and sanctifying them by his grace, his counsell in sauing them cannot seeme vniust. And againe, there is no iniustice in the euerlasting counsell of God touching the destruction of them whom he listeth to destroy, for that hee hardeneth before he destroyeth: Therefore the third answere for the maintenance of Gods iustice in the euerlasting counsell of reprobation, consisteth in this word, Hardening: which notwithstanding hee concealed in the former verse, because the History of Pharao was wel knowen. But the force of the world is great: for Hardening which is set against Mercy, presupposeth the same things that mercy did, to wit, a voluntary corruption, wherein the reprobate are hardened: and againe corruption presupposeth a perfect state of creation. Moreouer, this hardning also is voluntary, for God so hardneth being offended with corruption, that he vseth their owne will whom he hardeneth to the executing of that iudgement. Then follow the fruits of Hardening, to wit, vnbeliefe and sinne, which are the true and proper causes of the condemnation of the reprobate. Why doeth he then appoynt to destruction? because he will: why doth he harden? because they are corrupt: why doeth he condemne? because they are sinners. Where is then vnrighteousnesse? Nay, if he should destroy all after this same sort, to whom should hee doe iniury? *t Whom it pleaseth him to appoynt, to shew his fauour vpon.* 16 An other obiection, but onely for the reprobate, rising vpon the former answere. If God doe appoynt to euerlasting destruction, such as he listeth, and if that cannot be hindred nor withstanded that hee hath once decreed, how doeth hee iustly condemne them, which perish by his will? 17 The Apostle doth not answere that it is not Gods will, or that God doeth not either reiect or elect according to his pleasure, which thing the wicked call blasphemy, but he rather granteth his aduersary both the antecedents, to wit, that it is Gods will, and that it must of necessity so fall out, yet he denieth that God is therfore to be thought an vniust reuenger of the wicked: for seeing it appeareth by manifest proofe that this is the will of God, and his doing, what impudency is it for man which is but dust and ashes, to dispute with God, and as it were to call him into iudgement? Now if any man say that the doubt is not so dissolued and answered, I answere, that there is no surer demonstration in any matter, because it is grounded vpon this principle, That the will of God is the rule of righteousnesse. 18 An amplification of the former answere taken from a comparison, whereby also it appeareth that Gods determinate counsell is set of Paul the highest of all causes, so that it dependeth not vpon any respect of second causes, but doeth rather frame and direct them. ✠ *Esai.45.9.* *u This similitude agreeth very fitly in the first creation of mankinde.*

him

Figure 1.4. Romans 9 in the Geneva Bible

he won't leave the text alone. The bare text has too many possibilities—mysteries even. The bare text is difficult to control. The modernist turn in culture led the keepers of the Bible to transform it into something "precise, punctual, calculable, standard, bureaucratic, rigid, invariant, finely coordinated, and routine."[7]

This nervousness emerges clearly in that template of all modern Bibles, the Geneva Bible. In the book of Romans, wherein so much was at stake for Reformation Christians, the interpreters could take no chances. The framing notes dwarf Paul's own portrait of Jesus and the meaning of his gospel, scarcely leaving the apostle any room on the page. God's system of salvation is presented as precise, standard, invariant and finely coordinated. All those carefully divided and numbered particles of what was once a letter to a church are addressed and explained one by one. Perhaps all the boundaries, explanations and controls issued by the Geneva divines are correct—I'm not here to take issue with their theology right now. But there is virtually no chance that a reader of this Bible will engage first of all, and freely, with the sacred text itself and on its own terms. This is a Bible that needs to be saved.

What do we see when we see a Bible? What if we saw something completely different? Would we then envision a different answer to the question of what the Bible is?

- two -

UNVEILING THE
ELEGANT BIBLE

*Elegance is "far-side" simplicity that is artfully crafted,
emotionally engaging, profoundly intelligent.*

MATTHEW MAY

In his insightful book *In Pursuit of Elegance: Why the Best Ideas Have Something Missing*, Matthew May relates the story of Laweiplein, the name of a busy intersection in the heart of Drachten in northern Holland.[1] Laweiplein was the brainchild of Hans Monderman, a Dutch traffic engineer, or perhaps we should say, a Dutchman engaged in the art of reverse engineering. Monderman had a firm commitment in the opposite direction of modern traffic control. Monderman began his career as an accident investigator, and he eventually connected some dots. He saw that most traffic accidents happen because motorists are given far too much of the wrong information. What Monderman saw was that traffic engineers, attempting to account for every mistake or wrong choice a motorist might make, seek to direct, manage, control and regulate all those choices. Motorists respond by disengaging and bringing less of themselves into their driving. Assuming that the signs and road markings are doing all the work, they stop thinking.

So Monderman mounted a long-term war on what he considered overbearing and counterproductive traffic regulation. As May puts it, "To Monderman, the problem wasn't one of engineering, but rather one of context."[2]

Laweiplein is a red brick square in the center of the city, and since 2004 has been completely unregulated. Every day some 22,000 cars and trucks plus thousands more cyclists and pedestrians pass through this intersection. When people come to the intersection, they are completely engaged, taking full account of everything the situation presents at the moment they arrive. They slow down, account for others, blend in and go through. The result is a smooth, natural flow of traffic in which each participant is expected to participate appropriately, rather than being expected to be a problem that has be told what to do in every respect. As Monderman says, "The trouble with traffic engineers is that when there's a problem with a road, they always try to add something."[3] Monderman believes that every road tells a story, and if we simply listen attentively to that story, we will intuitively know what to do on that particular road.

The Geneva Bible introduced the same philosophy behind overwrought traffic control to the Bible. It filled the Bible with the equivalent of traffic signs, road markings, white lines and arrows. But as the people of Drachten came to see when they removed all the regulations and formal control mechanisms from Laweiplein, the number of accidents—and all the attendant frustration, anger and social tension—went down. Can we similarly reverse engineer the modern study Bible? If we were to remove our imposed, regulatory-like certainty, predictability and control, would Bible engagement and awareness rise? Would people start bringing more of themselves to the Bible?

We have created a Bible with an imposing, off-putting surface of bad complexity, while pretending the Bible is a directly-accessible list of simple propositions. This is backwards on both counts. What we need is a Bible with an elegant surface simplicity that will open up for us the inherent and immensely interesting good complexity that lies deep within.

An Elegant Bible that breaks free from the nearly five-hundred-year stranglehold of the cluttered modernist Bible will be a Bible that respects what we should have known all along. The Elegant Bible will reflect the wisdom that form and content always belong together in God's good creation. Form is part of the content of things. If you change the form, you change the content. If you change the form of the Bible, you have already answered the question of what it is.

Careful observers have for some time detected a semi-gnostic bent in much of modernistic Christianity, and this is reflected in how we often think about the Bible.[4] Naively believing that the Bible is essentially a collection of ideas, we've convinced ourselves that the form, structure and visual appearance of the text is irrelevant and concerned ourselves only with the content. If the words are there, we presume the rest of it doesn't really matter—as if reading the book of Romans in the Geneva Bible is like reading a letter from a Christian leader to a first-century church.

We need the Elegant Bible because we are creational monotheists. A healthy, well-functioning biblical doctrine of creation entails a thoughtful attention to form. For too long we have merely affirmed the bare fact that God is Creator, but have not attended to the implications of what this means for our understanding and good functioning in this Creator's world. The Bible is not magically communicated to our minds through some kind of mental telepathy. We always apprehend the Bible by means of some physical form. Every Bible is an artifact in the physical world, and the kind of artifact the Bible is can serve it well, or it can grossly distort what it essentially is. Whatever form the Bible takes matters to our understanding and shapes what we think we're doing. Immensely.

A crucial shift will have to take place in order for us to break off our love affair with the fragmented Bible. We will have to commit to focusing first on the rich tapestry of the Bible itself, rather than beginning with our overriding desire to use and manipulate the Bible in certain ways. Stephen Langton wanted short, easy-to-find sections for commentaries, so he developed a chapter system. Robert Estienne wanted a Bible concordance as a tool to study the Bible in a new way, so he added numbered verses to the text. The Complicated Bible begins with the question, how can we do what we want with the Bible? The Elegant Bible begins with the question, what is the Bible and how can we honor what it is?

It is time to turn our attention to a Laweiplein Bible, a Bible in which people can immerse themselves—fully present, fully attentive—without being overdirected about what to believe or misled as to the nature of what it is they are encountering.

A Centuries Overdue Extreme Bible Makeover
The Bible has never stayed the same. Its journey has already been extensive, from the people gathered at the New Gate of the temple in Jerusalem to hear

Jeremiah's thundered oracles, to churches around the Mediterranean reading the scrolls sent to them by Paul, to early Christian scribes copying and gathering the books into codex form, to gifted artists illuminating the text with brilliant colors and precious gold, to presses rolling out pages after pages, and all the way up to electronic screens glowing with the sacred words. The Bible has always been an artifact in our world, and the journey will continue. One way or another, the Bible of the future will be shaped, and we are the ones who will shape it.

If, as I have argued, the current popular form of the Bible is problematic, the first step seems clear enough. We need a bit of cultural unmaking, a dismantling of the modernist overlay on the Bible. Its fractured format demonstrably leads to fractured readings. Deconstructing the Bible of the Reformation is the first step toward saving the Bible. The Langton-Estienne dynasty has had its day, but it's time for the rule of chapter-and-verse to end.

Of course, given the extensive infrastructure we've built around this modernistic system of slicing and dicing the Bible, at this point we likely can't dispense with it completely. The use of the numbered pieces of the modernist Bible is a practice deeply embedded in modernistic Christianity. (Now that we're stuck with it to some degree, one wishes its creators had been more attuned to the natural flow of the writings themselves.) We'll need to keep a chapter-and-verse copy around as a book on our shelves or a setting in our ebooks. The system was created to enable certain reference works in the first place—commentaries and concordances—and as the occasional reference tool it will remain helpful. But if we wish to hear the Scriptures sing to us again, this tone-deaf intrusion need not be the Bible we live with daily. We can read, study, meditate on and preach from a holistic Bible. The use of a better form will help reform our diminished Bible engagement habits.

Also, contrary to what most people think, a chapter-and-verse Bible is not essential for referring to a particular passage. It would be healthier and show a greater knowledge of the Bible itself if we were to adopt the practice of referencing by context and content.[5] People in book clubs do it all the time, the Bible itself does it when quoting from other books in the Bible and the whole church had to do it for most of its history. The rather rigid de facto requirement that every mention of a Bible passage be accompanied by a numbered reference is somewhat about precision, and useful in reference tool contexts, but it seems mostly to reflect an issue of trust and potential verification. We first employed proof-texting for doctrinal squabbles, and apparently now it's needed for every devotional use of each fragment as well.

The bookcleaning will commence with the removal of the artificial additives—chapters and verses to be sure, but also all the other helps we've boxed in this text with. It's the cumulative effect of all the additives that produces the modern Bible's downfall. Just as when we clean out the garage, we have to pick up each item and ask, what is this and why is it here? Then we can decide what to do with it.

Chapter and verse numbers. These are intrusions that fail to reflect authorial intent and so divide up the text in unnatural ways. Both are rather inattentively placed. They signal readers to take as appropriate units sections of text that are often not appropriate units. Chapter divisions can break up larger units of thought—the very first chapter marker in the Bible, between Genesis 1 and 2, cuts off the opening song of creation by several lines; the servant song of Isaiah 53 actually starts in Isaiah 52, etc. They can also throw several smaller units of thought together in a single chapter. Chapters miss natural units of thought that are both bigger and smaller than the typical chapter size. Verse divisions are similarly misplaced, often dividing what should be held together or combining what should be separated. But verses are particularly pernicious because they positively encourage the reader to take each numbered thought out of context as a standalone statement of truth. And to take the bad news and drop it to the level of devastating, verses have now become the primary way millions of people approach the Bible. Verses read in isolation, selected by topic, arranged in groups, sent out in kitschy-decorated Facebook updates—this is what passes for Bible knowledge in our era. The point here is that the format of the Bible is where this trouble begins. The word *Scripture* has even been transformed. Rather than using the word in its original sense of a complete writing—a book of the Bible—people now commonly use it to refer to a single one of these artificially created fragments: "Let me share a scripture with you." If we were to do nothing but take the verse numbers out of our Bibles and refuse to use them as references in our Bible practices, this alone might spark a Bible re-engagement movement.[6]

Section headings. These are interpretive signs that tell the reader in advance what the next few paragraphs are about. They are both directive and limiting. Because they are printed right in among the Bible text itself, it is very easy for readers to take them as part of the Bible, just as authoritative and inspired as the rest of it. But in reality they are the literary equivalent of watching a movie and having someone sitting next to you constantly saying, "This is the part where . . ." After a while it's best to let the person know you'd like to watch the movie for yourself and see what unfolds. These section headings also incorrectly send the signal to readers that the Bible is essentially made up of short, topical portions meant to be read independently, like entries in an encyclopedia.

Cross references. These attempt to take the free-standing verses of the modern Bible and point you to other free-standing verses that ostensibly address the same topic. The very live danger here is that by following the thread of cross references and adding them up, we believe we've arrived at the Bible's teaching on that particular point. Sadly, the crucial step of determining the meaning of these various free-standing statements in their full context (immediate, literary, historical, location in the overall biblical narrative, etc.) is simply overlooked. Cross references are the print equivalent of hyperlinks in electronic texts. Both function especially well as a steady stream of distractions, temptations to break our concentration and leave the text we are reading and jump to somewhere else. A cross-referenced Bible is not a deep reading, immersive Bible.

Study Bibles. These have developed the fine art of designing the Bible page to reverse the relative importance of the divinely inspired words and our attempted commentary. All the color borders, shaded backgrounds, and fancy bold and italic fonts surround and uphold the chaff, not the wheat. Readers are strongly directed by the visual cues to prioritize the material and shouldn't be blamed for doing what they're told. Neither should it surprise us when readers actually use study Bible notes not to enhance their reading of the text, but to replace it.

Page layout. Finally, our bookcleaning project must address the overall layout of the text on the page. The common two-column setting of the Bible is an understandable phenomenon. (We won't even speak here of the brief but distressing appearance of three-column Bibles a few years ago.) The

Bible is a very large book, and it isn't easy to fit into a reasonable size. Using two columns per page helps save valuable space and makes for a more efficient typesetting that reduces costs. But the deeper price paid is considerable. It is nearly impossible to show literary form in a two-column Bible. The short length of each line effectively cuts off the use of white space and lining to reveal genre or the natural structure of biblical texts. In a two-column Bible everything appears relentlessly the same. Israel's ancient song lyrics, pithy proverbs, lengthy narratives, first-century letters—one wouldn't know about any of this from the looks of it.

So let's say we have this Scripture scrubbing, once-every-half-a-millennium Bible bath. What would we be left with? A mass of unnumbered, undivided, undifferentiated texts? Something like the *scriptio continua* of the old manuscripts? No, because the bookcleaning is merely the necessary but negative first step of our extreme Bible makeover. On my Accordance Bible software program the options under "Display" include "Turn off verse references." Hit it and all the numbers disappear from the text, but the program is at a loss for what to do next. The natural form of the text hasn't been programmed in. Deconstruction is always the easy part, but re-envisioning the Bible is what we're after. We have every reason to hold out for a true Bible apocalypse, an unveiling, a pulling back of the curtain to see what's really been there all along. Step two is based on giving the Scriptures our full, careful and loving attention so that we can faithfully produce Bible artifacts (whether in print, on screen or audio) that authentically reveal the Bible as it is.

REINTRODUCING THE HOLY SCRIPTURES

What is the Bible? The Bible is a collection, not of verses, but of books. The locus of meaning in the Bible is the individual book. A scripture is a book, or sacred writing, and the central intentional unit of the biblical authors and editors. Each book has a unique purpose and point of view, addresses a unique situation or need, and employs a definite literary type, or genre. These books have long been hidden from view and it's past time they were revealed in all their rich, diverse and complex-yet-simple glory.

The first job of a Bible dedicated to simplicity and beauty is to declare the glory of the books. The Elegant Bible accomplishes this by first taking literary analysis and Bible design with utmost seriousness. The goal is an intelligent yet accessible, almost intuitive, literary presentation that honors the books the authors actually wrote. Believing the Bible is a mass of "content" leaves us free to put easy-to-use chapter and verse numbers just about anywhere. Believing the Bible is made up of intentionally crafted and unique books demands an attention to its natural forms and structures. Good Bible literary study will diligently unearth the hidden treasures of the Bible's inherent structures. Good Bible design will enable the reader to see these structures even before they read a word of the content.

Christopher R. Smith has written about the prospects we have for finding the biblical authors' expressed literary-structural intentions:

> Ancient writers didn't have the freedom to add spacing and headings that abundant, affordable publishing materials now permit modern authors to use to indicate their outlines. Moreover, in many cases ancient works were intended to be delivered orally, and were written down only for trans-mission to their recipients. . . . For both of these reasons, it has long seemed reasonable to me that ancient authors would have embedded recognizable literary-structural signals directly within their works. I became convinced, after many years of research and reflection, that within the pages of the Bible these signals characteristically take the form of recurring phrases that have been placed intentionally at the seams of literary structures.[7]

Smith's comments indicate the kind of diligence and reflection that should regularly be brought to bear in Bible publishing, but has not been. We have inherited a modern Bible format. It is a cultural creation, a tradition. It is not original to the Bible but was developed for very narrow reasons over a thousand years after the last biblical book was written. Yet it has become the default for us, our unthinking form for presenting the Scriptures despite the disservice that it does to those very Scriptures. Bible publishers should con-sider taking the Hippocratic oath and applying it to the sacred writings in their care: first, do no harm.

A newly conceived, elegant Bible will instead follow Smith's advice. It will find and format for easy recognition these signals, signs and structures that the biblical authors themselves have indicated. Unique books will be uniquely formatted, helped along by a generous single-column setting. The New Testament's letters will look like letters, with their characteristic three-part pattern, the opening identification of sender and recipients along with greetings, the main body, and the closing good wishes and instructions. Collections of song lyrics (Psalms, Lamentations and Song of Songs) and the prophetic oracles in the First Testament will visually reflect the underlying parallelism characteristic of Hebrew poetry, and stanza breaks will be subtly noted with line breaks. Narratives will be invitingly presented as the uninterrupted stories they are. Collections of short wisdom sayings and reflections (Proverbs, Ecclesiastes, James) will embody the wisdom of allowing their form to serve their content. Lists will look like lists, genealogies like genealogies, speeches like speeches.

Imagine all this variety in the Bible, formatted to look like what it is, and then consider this: a steady succession of modern English Bibles presented the entire text of the Bible—from Genesis to Revelation—as a numbered list. The Geneva Bible, the Bishops' Bible, the King James Bible and their myriad children in the following centuries all succumbed to this revolutionary and disastrous formatting innovation of the sixteenth century. Never mind the king, God save the Bible!

So what would Smith's vision look like in practice? Consider the book of Matthew.[8] The casual reader might be excused for thinking that all four of the gospels are simple collections of a number of short episodes in the life of Jesus. But actually, each of the four has its own unique way of shaping the story of Israel's promised king.

Matthew organizes his work as a whole in a pattern of five, reflecting, no doubt, the strong Jewish attachment to the five books of Moses. (Long before Matthew, the book of Psalms had been similarly structured into five books.) Matthew collects the teachings of Jesus into five long speeches and then inserts them into the story at key intervals. For the first one, revealingly, Jesus goes up on a mountain as Moses did before him. As Smith explains, "To show how important these five speeches are, the author marks them all in the same way. Each one begins with the disciples coming to Jesus for teaching. Each one ends with a variation of the phrase, *When Jesus had finished saying these things . . .*"[9] Here we see an example of Smith's proposal that recurring phrases often mark the seams of literary structures. Matthew thus presents five story and speech pairs that are introduced by an intentionally arranged genealogy and concluded with the passion narrative of Jesus' new exodus. The formatting point that Smith makes about all this is that the pened, they were outraged and went and told their master everything that had happened.

"Then the master called the servant in. 'You wicked servant,' he said, 'I canceled all that debt of yours because you begged me to. Shouldn't you have had mercy on your fellow servant just as I had on you?' In anger his master handed him over to the jailers to be tortured, until he should pay back all he owed.

"This is how my heavenly Father will treat each of you unless you forgive your brother or sister from your heart."

W hen Jesus had finished saying these things, he left Galilee and went into the region of Judea to the other side of the Jordan. Large crowds followed him, and he healed them there.

Some Pharisees came to him to test him. They asked, "Is it lawful for a man to divorce his wife for any and every reason?"

"Haven't you read," he replied, "that at the beginning the Creator 'made them male and female,' and said, 'For this reason a man will leave his father and mother and be united to his wife, and the two will become one flesh'? So they are no longer two, but one flesh. Therefore what God has joined together, let no one separate."

"Why then," they asked, "did Moses command that a man give his wife a certificate of divorce and send her away?"

Jesus replied, "Moses permitted you to divorce your wives because your hearts were hard. But it was not this way from the beginning. I tell you that anyone who divorces his wife, except for sexual immorality, and marries another woman commits adultery."

The disciples said to him, "If this is the situation between a husband and wife, it is better not to marry."

Jesus replied, "Not everyone can accept this word, but only those to whom it has been given. For there are eunuchs who were born that way, and there are eunuchs who have been made eunuchs by others — and there are those who choose to live like eunuchs for the sake of the kingdom of heaven. The one who can accept this should accept it."

Then people brought little children to Jesus for him to place his hands on them and pray for them. But the disciples rebuked them.

Jesus said, "Let the little children come to me, and do not hinder them, for the kingdom of heaven belongs to such as these." When he had placed his hands on them, he went on from there.

Figure 2.1. *The Books of the Bible: New Testament* from Biblica

modern Bible's presentation of twenty eight chapters, oblivious as it is to this actual structure, removes the possibility that the reader will see what Matthew is doing.[10] Matthew not only *tells us with his words* that Jesus is the fulfillment of Israel's story, he *shows us with his structure*. But if we don't pick up on and reflect his cues, part of Matthew's message is lost on the Bible's readers.

You can see in the sample case of Matthew presented above how the Elegant Bible will approach the formatting of individual books and their natural sections. Think for a moment about all the variety of books in the Bible. These books are indeed made up of smaller elements, not our traditional chapters, but smaller elements nonetheless. In the Elegant Bible these elements below the full book level will find their meaning as one of the building blocks of a book, not with blaring numbers, but merely as they are simply and pleasingly set apart. Such things as Jeremiah's collection of oracles against the nations, the assembled sayings of King Lemuel in Proverbs, one of the dramatic scenes in the book of Ruth, a speech of Eliphaz the Temanite in Job, or the gathering of journey stories in Luke's gospel—all these and more will be recognized, acknowledged and clearly presented in simple, obvious form as a gift to the reader.

As part of this interest of promoting a healthy understanding of the books themselves, it's worth pointing out that even our typical division of book boundaries is not entirely correct. Several whole books that were later divided (only because they couldn't fit completely on a single scroll) have remained divided in our contemporary codex form. Though both were originally unified works, Samuel-Kings and Chronicles-Ezra-Nehemiah are now presented as separated books. Scribes would often attempt to stitch them together again by overlapping their copy of the text at the ending of one scroll with that at the beginning of text in another. In our current Bibles we can find this feature in the text that ends with Chronicles and begins Ezra. But since we're no longer reading off of papyrus scrolls, it would seem reasonable to reunify these books. The same goes for Luke's divided two-volume history of the early Christian movement, Luke–Acts. The two volumes work together in significant ways, both structurally and in terms of content. They are best read in tandem. Even given the ancient status of the collection of the four gospels, I have to doubt that Luke himself would appreciate having John's book divide his two volumes.

Finally, the Bible is more than a single collection of books. In fact, the whole collection is made up of smaller groupings of books. We're used to a standardized collection and ordering of books in the Bible, but it wasn't always so. In the history of the development of the Bible there was actually a lot of variation in how the books were collected and in what order they were presented. In the First Testament we're used to Law, History, Poetry and Prophets, while in the New it's Gospels, History, Letters (Paul's and then the others), and then Revelation. But our grouping of the First Testament came from a later Greek translation (the Septuagint), not the Hebrew Bible. The Bible Jesus knew was Law, Prophets and Writings (see Luke's account of what Jesus said to the disciples after his resurrection). And as for the New Testament, while the overall groupings have long been fairly standard, there has been a lot of variety within them.

The point is that it is not necessary that there be a single, permanently set order of books. There is diversity within the history of the Bible. There are important things to think about in relation to the order of books. Why should the Prophets simply have the big ones first and the smaller ones next? Would a chronological order perhaps be more helpful to readers? The same goes for Paul's letters; why largest to smallest? Why should the Gospels be bunched together? Perhaps their distinctive points of view would be better realized if they were separated. The meaning of a book is related to its surroundings. The rabbis of old used to debate why this or that order was better, why certain connections between books made sense. We might be more engaged in our Bibles if we began to have the same kinds of discussions.

RECLAIMING SIMPLICITY

Overall, the vision of the Elegant Bible is a vision for recovering the smart simplicity of the Bible itself. The Elegant Bible has no desire to be precise, punctual, calculable, standard, bureaucratic, rigid, invariant, finely coordinated and routine. The Bible was not born in modernity and was not written by moderns. It speaks to modernity as it speaks to every age, but we have allowed our current historical period to transform our Bible into something it is not. William Thompson, Lord Kelvin once said:

> When you can measure what you are speaking about, and express it in
> numbers, you know something about it; but when you cannot measure it,

when you cannot express it in numbers, your knowledge is of a meagre and unsatisfactory kind.[11]

We have unfortunately been taken in by this deception (in many different cultural realms). In the case of the Bible we have desperately tried to turn it into something that can be counted—its truths added up—in order to validate its claim to knowledge. To save the Bible from ourselves, we must begin to trust once again its ancient ways of saying things.

In a word, the Elegant Bible is a clean Bible. It has unencumbered words on a page, pleasingly set, easy to read. There is no feeling of nervousness or desperation brooding over the book, no trying to protect from every error, rebut every potential interpretive mistake, tell you every application or force a hard harmony from verse to verse. Instead there is a calm confidence in the text alone, the text on its own terms. Oh, all the challenges of the Bible are still there—the Elegant Bible doesn't make the Bible easy. But it leaves these challenges where they belong, in the tensions and surprises and hard words themselves, not in struggling to get past all the flotsam and jetsam of the modernist concoction.

The story is told that when asked how he sculpted his statue of David, Michelangelo replied, "I saw David through the stone, and I simply chipped away everything that was not David." The path to restoring our Bible begins with chipping away at everything that doesn't belong there. There is a masterpiece buried under the modernist Bible. The Elegant Bible seeks to rediscover it.

The saving of the Bible begins with a simple, clean and natural presentation of the text of the Bible, giving us a much better chance to start engaging the Scriptures well. Because form and function always work together in God's good creation, the Elegant Bible naturally introduces us to the Feasting Bible.

three

OUR SNACKING BIBLE

I do not like your Bible verse,
It makes no sense,
It is too terse;
It is devoid of all context,
What will your Holy Book say next?
I do not like your Bible verse,
It seems to go from bad to worse.

NIALL MCAULEY

We do have our favorites. They tend to fall into the general category of Scripture Encouragement. There are many sacred words and they say many things, but it's the Bible Balm that has caught our eye. With a partitioned Bible preparing so many options for us, you might think it would be hard to choose. But no. The people have voted. The customers know what they want.

- Jeremiah 29:11

- John 10:10

- Philippians 4:13

- Joshua 1:9

If you didn't already know, the addresses direct us to these:

- "'For I know the plans I have for you,' declares the LORD, 'plans to prosper you and not to harm you, plans to give you hope and a future.'"

- "I have come that they may have life, and have it to the full."

- "I can do everything through him who gives me strength."

- "Be strong and courageous. Do not be afraid; do not be discouraged, for the Lord your God will be with you wherever you go."

Good, positive verses all. But the shocking news to most people is that there is a parallel universe Bible. It is rarely talked about and almost never explored. In that other world every positive and negative is reversed. Every verse has its anti-verse. In the parallel universe Bible, the favorite anti-verses are:

- Deuteronomy 28:29

- 2 Corinthians 2:16

- Isaiah 49:4

- Deuteronomy 28:65

What? You don't know these? You've never seen them on a scenic piece of Christian framed art? OK, well, here's what they say:

- "You will be unsuccessful in everything you do; day after day you will be oppressed and robbed, with no one to rescue you."

- "We are an aroma that brings death."

- "I have labored in vain; I have spent my strength for nothing at all."

- "The Lord will give you an anxious mind, eyes weary with longing, and a despairing heart."

The real revelation may be that these anti-verses too are in the Bible (our Bible, in this universe). They are set apart, numbered and included in the lineup just like all the rest. It's just that nobody ever wants to use them. They aren't ever selected. They are more like bombs than balm. But there they are. Why? If they are unusable, why are they there? Do we need them for anything at all? (And why do I have a suspicion that anyone being confronted with *these* verses will suddenly develop a strong interest in the original context, so as to nicely distance themselves from any unpleasant implications?)

What is the Bible?

What are we supposed to do with it?

FROM JUSTIFICATION TO PROPHECY AND
PIETY: A SHORT HISTORY OF SNACKING

Small readings. They were the inevitable result of the formatting innovation of the modern Bible. The new form positively demanded to be read and used in a particular way. Historian David Norton says of the early modern period, "The presentation of the text is broken up, and literary reading effectively discouraged. Moreover a specific kind of religious reading is encouraged, fragmentary study."[1] Jaroslav Pelikan describes how "the heaping up of proof-texts became the standard method of verifying the scriptural character of a teaching about doctrine or life."[2] And indeed, dueling over doctrine was a chief purpose of the innovation in the first place. It wasn't an accident that the production of the Geneva Bible was overseen by an exiled English reformer, William Whittingham. It was Whittingham, with some dueling on his to-do list, who seized on Estienne's scholarly reference-tool format (numbered verses that were first added to a Greek New Testament) and said, *Now that's the kind of Bible I need.* Poof! Proof-texting was born. Whittingham and the divines could fire off one-liners on justification from Romans and Galatians like canons of right interpretation, obliterating the ecclesiastical opposition.

But others would come to realize all the possibilities of a Bible like this. If the Bible is filled with these little pieces of spiritual truth, then finding the right ones for arguing with Catholics is only the beginning. Doctrinal debate was the first step, then theologians picked up on the practice and the newly parsed text became the basis for developing systematic theologies. One of the heirs of Reformed orthodoxy, Charles Hodge of Princeton Seminary, could explain in 1873 how the theological task is rooted in using the Bible in a particular way:

> The Bible is to the theologian what nature is to the man of science. It is his storehouse of facts, and his method of ascertaining what the Bible teaches is the same as that which the natural philosopher adopts to ascertain what nature teaches. . . . The duty of the Christian theologian is to ascertain, collect, and combine all the facts which God has revealed concerning Himself and our relation to Him. These facts are all in the Bible.[3]

There should be no question as to the degree Hodge's comments depended on a form of the Bible already broken down into fact-sized pieces. A Bible divided into chapters and verses is perfectly ripe for this particular type of analysis. The modernist format served up a Bible fully prepared for proper modernist dissection. And thus, the cutting commenced.

In his well-known 1994 exploration on the failures of the evangelical mind, Mark Noll explores the biblical practices that undergird some expressions of fundamentalism:

> For decades a much-practiced fundamentalist liturgy was the "Bible Reading,"
> in which leaders selected verses from throughout the Scripture to illustrate a
> particular truth. James Brookes, one of the founders of the Niagara Prophecy
> Conferences, provided a codified instruction for this very common practice:
> "Have your leader select some word, as faith, repentance, love, hope, justifi-
> cation, sanctification, and with the aide of a good Concordance, mark down
> before the time of the meeting the references to the subject under discussion.
> These can be read as called for, thus presenting all the Holy Ghost has been
> pleased to reveal on the topic."[4]

One of the problems for fundamentalists, Noll clearly notes, is that they claimed to be a "Bible only" movement. Yet their Bible method was completely dependent on the very human-shaped versification of the Scriptures and the use of concordances. Not exactly the Bible alone in the form the Holy Ghost had given it. Noll explains:

> That ordinary human beings not inspired by the Holy Spirit had cut up the
> Bible into verses and that other ordinary human beings not inspired by the
> Holy Spirit were rearranging those verses to extract large-scale truths from
> the Scriptures meant that both the fundamentalist Bible Reading and the most
> important fundamentalist theological books partook fully in thoroughly
> natural and thoroughly human activity, even as they attempted to understand
> divine truth.[5]

It may seem strange to identify the method that produces seemingly serious and weighty theological systems of thought, or highly detailed charts and blueprints of end-times prophecy, as "snacking" on the Bible. But if these particular arrangements don't ground their collections of selections on the full contextual settings of each and every one of those bits, then snacking is what it is. Feasting, as we shall see, is something different entirely.

Noll concludes that this new use of the Bible was, "the worse kind of intellectual legacy for later evangelicals."[6] But a legacy it was, and the method in many ways became the standard one for evangelicals. Evangelicals are children of the Reformation. One of the effects of the Reformation was an increasing democratization of Christianity. The invention of the printing press in the 1450s and the explosion of vernacular translations and then study Bibles a century later made it possible for many more people to have their own Bible. Before this, the Scriptures were widely known, but in a different form.

The story is sometimes told that before the time of the Reformation most common people were completely biblically illiterate, but as Lori Anne Ferrell tells it, "the vast majority of medieval folk were both illiterate and deeply familiar with Holy Writ."[7] Through such means as popular street theater with cycles of plays following the biblical narratives, to the explosion in the 1300s of small and compact though still hand-written "Psalters" and devotional books, many people were regularly immersed in the Scriptures. But these were largely communal events and largely based on more holistic forms of the Bible—townspeople gathering to watch a Bible play or individuals following the daily Psalms readings together with others in the church. The change the next couple of centuries would bring was that the Bible was now being directed to private, individual study of the bits.

The Reformation thrust a question upon all those newly-commissioned lay priests with the fresh form of the Scriptures in their hands for the first time: What are we supposed to do with the Bible? The truth is that the modernist form hand fed them the answer. Because it had already spoken to the prior question of what the Bible is—emphatically not a gathering of literary forms that come together to tell a saving story, but rather a collection of short statements of propositional truth—the form instructed them: find the fragments you need at the moment. If you are looking for your daily inspiration, then find a devotional fragment. If you are arguing with the local heretic, find a doctrinal fragment. If you are facing an ethical question, find a moral fragment. They're all in there, already neatly numbered for you. You just have to find the good ones. Many of the fragments won't fit your predetermined needs and they can be (and for the most part are) safely ignored. But you needn't worry about all those unusable ones. There are plenty of gems hidden among all that dross.

This characterization may seem overly harsh. But the picture I paint here is based on my own decades-long experience in researching and publishing Bibles and the reality I encountered there about what people want in their Bibles and how they use them. My perception matches the bigger picture that emerges from pollsters about the level of Bible knowledge among our population, and the actual role the Bible plays in American life.

We can see that the modernist Bible's effectiveness wasn't for rationalistic Christianity alone. It also allowed for feeding on highly selective, small, bite-sized pieces for one's own personal edification. The reconfiguration of the text led first to the doctrinalist Bible but then also to the pietist Bible: a Bible for arguing, and then a Bible for feeling better. Both approaches are built on the small readings made available by the new format. Both types continue to have well-developed expressions in the preeminent Bible of our day—the niche study Bible.

Thus the modernist Bible sparked a revolution in new Bible practices. And these practices are not what people did with the Bible in the centuries pre-dating the Reformation. But these new Bible practices redefined for us what the word *biblical* means. Philip Yancey has said we've essentially reduced our engagement with the Scriptures to eating Bible McNuggets. And snacking, once you've begun to indulge it, is an unhealthy but hard habit to break.

Falling in Love with (Parts of) the Bible

With the onset of Bibles designed for decontextualized random access as well as the growth and spread of Protestantism, the stage was set for the rapid rise of the new Bible-snacking paradigm. There are plenty of exhibits in the gallery as evidence to this rise. We live in a highly commodified Bible world in which the producers of retail religious goods reflect the popularity of, and constantly extend in new directions, the expression of out-of-context, snack-sized Bible bits. Luckily for retailers, the newly-minted Bible pieces fit comfortably onto a multitude of spiritual gewgaw—refrigerator magnets, coffee cups, t-shirts, greeting cards, inspirational scenic plaques and the wrappers of Scripture-sharing Testamints.

But two more substantial contemporary Bible expressions will make the point more seriously. It's already been noted that the Bible is the best-selling book in the world. That is interesting and significant in its own right. But the popularity of a unique form of the Bible in the contemporary marketplace—the specialty study Bible—tells a story by itself. The second example is found not only in how the Bible was refashioned, but also in the books we publish about the Bible—what's known as the "handbook model" of engagement.

The template for themed study Bibles is by now familiar to most of us. The base is the typical versified format of the Bible, which is now combined with all manner of introductions, callouts, study notes, maps, charts, special headings and more. The Geneva Bible incorporated most of these features nearly five hundred years ago, but we've continued to improve and expand the model.

Theoretically, study Bibles have the potential to give plenty of help to Bible readers. But interpretation is often dictated, and they generally direct people to more meager-sized segments as stand-alone units. It's certainly not a small thing that the additives that at first served like-minded doctrinal groups are now increasingly customized for individuals. The search for perceived contemporary relevance for me, right here and right now, is the god to which the material most often bows. Immediacy of application is the demand. There's no time for slowing down and receiving the Bible on its own terms. The highly-targeted nature of the add-ons leaves out whole swaths of biblical teaching and narrative. The specialty study Bible model can have the effect of turning Bibles into mirrors. The material focuses more on us and our own pre-understanding of our needs than it does on genuinely opening the gates to the world of the Bible. There are always extremes, and maybe the whole category of specialty Bibles shouldn't be judged by the most ridiculous, but the appearance of the Bible as a glossy teen self-help magazine was not really a complete anomaly. It was simply a stronger, more radical expression of the basic idea of most themed Bibles.

In a more confessional mode, I should admit here that my own Bible publishing work in the nonprofit arena has for many years freely provided what people have expected from low-cost, give-away Bibles. A standard feature of these "Bible helps" (hurts?) has been the *What should I read when I feel . . . ?* list of Bible bits. Here the reader is directed toward fragments that supposedly speak directly to immediate emotional needs. Again, the premise is that an immediate shot of a little piece of Bible medicine will make things better, completely independent of the embedded and original meaning of the words on the page. And woe to anyone who tries to take the medicine away, as I've discovered. This model of minimalistic Bible engagement has been absorbed at a deep level and forms a clear answer in readers' minds to our basic questions: *What is the Bible?* and *What are we supposed to do with it?* People seem to have no clear idea of an alternative set of answers.

The handbook model of the Bible is our second example of how the snacking approach has multiplied. In a recent book, sociologist Christian Smith set his sights on "biblicism," a theory about the Bible that he says can be identified by its emphasis on the Bible's "exclusive authority, infallibility, perspicuity, self-sufficiency, internal consistency, self-evident meaning, and universal applicability."[8] Smith identifies nine assumptions or beliefs (things like "Commonsense Hermeneutics," "Complete Coverage," "Internal Harmony," "Inductive Method," etc.) that then generate a tenth: the "Handbook Model," about which he writes,

> The Bible teaches doctrine and morals with every affirmation that it makes, so that together those affirmations comprise something like a handbook or textbook for Christian belief and living, a compendium of divine and therefore inerrant teachings on a full array of subjects—including science, economics, health, politics, and romance.[9]

Smith goes on to note that this perspective "pervades the evangelical book-publishing market" and lists over fifty current book titles reflecting this view of what the Bible is *(Bible Answers for Every Need*, etc. and etc.).[10] I would add that the handbook model is overwhelmingly the view expressed in electronic Bible software programs and websites, whose default answer to the question "How does one engage the Bible?" is to offer nanosecond topical search options based on verses. The implication is that the Bible's teaching on any topic can be found by simply collecting statements and adding them up.

The fact is there are many people who want the Bible to be such a guidebook. It may indeed be the predominant picture that people have of the Bible. It's such a practical vision—isn't the Bible meant to be useful? On one level, the appeal of this model is understandable, but the Bible is what it is, and it just isn't that kind of book. Is the Bible useful? Immensely—but not in a handbook kind of way. I suppose God could have given us such a thing, but the implications would be troubling. Do we really want our relationship with God and our understanding of the Christ-following life to be reduced to a handbook? Looking up answers in a how-to manual? Have you ever actually read a how-to manual? God has so much more in mind for us as significant, thinking, fully human, divine-image–bearing creatures. We can be thankful he doesn't think so little of us as to give us merely a handbook.

A review of Timothy Beal's book *The Rise and Fall of the Bible* by Jewish writer Adam Kirsch includes these lines:

> What explains this disparity between Americans' absolute faith in the Bible and their evident ignorance of it? To Beal, the problem lies with the notion that the Bible is a divine guidebook, a map for getting through the terra incognita of life. For as soon as you open it and start reading, it becomes troublingly apparent that the Bible is no such thing. It does not offer answers to problems, especially not to twenty-first-century problems. Only in a few places does it even offer straight-forward moral counsel. Depending on where you read in it, the Bible might give the impression that it is mainly composed of genealogies and agricultural regulations. The gulf between what readers expect to find in the Bible and what they are actually given produces a kind of paralysis, Beal explains. "For many Christians, this experience of feeling flummoxed by the Bible [produces] not only frustration but also guilt for doubting the Bible's integrity." The Bible-publishing industry feeds on this anxiety, he argues, by endlessly repackaging the Biblical text in evermore watered-down and over-explained forms.[11]

When we direct people to use the Bible like this kind of "how-to" book, we are being disingenuous. We are concealing what the Bible really is and falsely telling them it is something else. It's a setup for failure. And once people experience the disconnect themselves—when the Bible doesn't deliver—it leads directly to the "flummoxed" feeling that Beal describes. And, if the research numbers are to be believed, this feeling of dislocation and confusion apparently leads to widespread Bible abandonment.

WHY SNACKING IS NO WAY TO LIVE

It's worth addressing the snacking phenomena at length because it's such a pervasive practice among Bible users. Snacking on the Bible is addictive for all the usual reasons something becomes addictive: it's easy, it feels good at the moment and the alternative seems complex and difficult. But why should we worry about it? It may involve taking in only small pieces, but it's still the Bible, right? Isn't it better than not reading the Bible at all?

I worry because the small readings that follow inexorably from the modernist Bible have become, perhaps, our most common way of encountering the Scriptures, and the result is a deeply damaged set of Bible practices. Our visually fragmented presentation of the Bible induces a noetically fragmented comprehension. Because we see the Bible in little pieces, we come to know it in little pieces. Even if you call your Bible snack a Bible vitamin, the bite-sized piece too easily ends up being a replacement for a full meal. Such a thing is not the same and can never be the same as eating a full Bible course. Bible snacking is highly selective. It filters the Bible into predetermined categories of things we already know we want to hear.

We live in a time when the late-modern form of capitalism shapes our self-understanding in deep and powerful ways. There is necessarily a profound and difficult spiritual struggle involved in following King Jesus in such a world. Who am I? What am I supposed to be doing? Who or what do I worship? What captures my imagination? Turning the Bible into a collection of fragments that I preselect according to my own desires—snacks that I pick and choose from an inspired vending machine— can only feed the disease of capitalistic modernism in my life. I am already constantly shaped and pulled by this culture in the direction of obsessive self-preoccupation. To chop the Bible into my favorite pieces prevents the Bible from being an alternative voice in my life. I need a whole Bible. I need the hard parts. I need words of judgment. I need to read of the consequences of ignoring the good way that God has laid before us all.

There is apparently no end to the making of personalized, niche Bibles. But what I need most in a world like ours, which is relentlessly tempting me to place myself first anyway, is not another Bible selling the idea that the Bible is truly, honestly relevant to me and my needs, but something that will gently but firmly turn my gaze away from the looking glass and into what Karl Barth called the strange new world of the Bible.[12] Merely reflective glass will not do. I need to see *into* and therefore *through* the Bible to discern the contours of new creation, this coming age that has somehow, strangely, already burst in among us.

Modern consumers are individuals first and foremost, centered on their ability to make choices as independent, self-determining entities. Since most people don't buy what they don't want to hear, this filter prevents our constant searches for pleasant verses and favorite passages from ever introducing us to the real Bible. We too easily end up seeing a Cheshire-cat Bible—all smiles and no body. We find encouragement, but not correction, we heap blessing upon blessing and promise upon promise, but we fail to be challenged. This fragmented Snacking Bible fails us, because we have prevented the Bible from being what it is, and turned the Bible into something it is not. How can the Bible possibly do its work?

The fatal flaw of the modernist Bible is how it dictates our relationship to the Bible. It makes us believe we have mastered the Bible. We can use it to either defend what we already believe or feed us the things we already think we need. But instead, our constant stance should be one of willing submission. We should be ever open to hearing things we were deaf to, seeing things we were blind to, and this cannot happen with a Bible that has been prepackaged just for us and that appeals to us on the basis of what we already believe and know. The only Bible that can function as a corrective for us, as an ongoing guide for our life together in Christ, is a Bible that is free and that speaks to us on its own terms. That alone is a compelling reason to rescue the Bible from its current captivity. We need to save the Bible so that the Bible can save us—from ourselves.

Snacking, in spite of the high-pitched protests of its practitioners, betrays a low view of the Scriptures. It rejects the Bible as it is received from the inspired authors and instead decides for itself what the Bible is supposed to be: *I need the Bible to be a quick-and-easy access point for inspirational or doctrinal verses.* But God did not choose to give us this kind of Bible. Christian Smith wisely counsels us,

> If American evangelical biblicists are to learn to move beyond biblicism, they must step back from biblicism's highly demanding theory and move toward a humble, trusting acceptance of the Bible as it actually is, as God actually saw fit to deliver it to his church. They will have to learn to start with the scriptures that they actually hold in their hands.[13]

Snacking is based on the presumption that the Bible is a flat book. The modernist Bible contains page after page of small, numbered statements there for the picking. This Bible is flat in the sense that all the literary variety has been leveled out and covered over. It is a monotonous Bible, made up of two-column lists of propositions that go on and on. We've taken away crucial visual cues and the meaningful use of space, which should point us in the direction of more nuanced reading, treating the different kinds of books as the different kinds of literature that they are. In the modernist Bible we can't see that there are letters, stories, poetry and proverbs. And the Snacking Bible accepts the premise that the Bible is a collection of statements that all function similarly and attempts to treat it accordingly. Of course, in reality the pieces are not all equally useful. They are not all simple, straightforward, literal statements of spiritual truth of equal value. Nobody uses them this way consistently. The form has lied to us. Even as we accept the lie and try to use the Bible this way, we find that we can't. Those alternate reality anti-verses are there in great numbers: *You will be unsuccessful in everything you do* (Deuteronomy 28:29). The only alternative is rampant cherry-picking. And by its very nature, cherry-picking Bible verses is a confession, an open admission that the Bible really isn't what we want it to be.

Snacking hides things to be sure, but it also distorts the things it does show us. For example, the Snacking Bible is not great news. It has gospel verses, but no gospel, because the gospel is the announcement of a particular turn of events within an ongoing story. The gospel is not a sentence about justification by faith or a verse reference on the forgiveness of my sins. The gospel is not the Romans Road. The gospel is not John 3:16. What the apostles Paul and John wrote—what God's Spirit enkindled in them—was something entirely different than these boiled-down reductions. Evangelist D. L. Moody said he could write the gospel on a dime. Well, Paul and John couldn't, and didn't.

Romans is a carefully crafted letter to a congregation of believers asking for their support for further missionary work. It makes the case for God's faithfulness to his covenant through the saving, though surprising victory of Messiah Jesus. Paul's gospel is no timeless and disembodied series of soterian steps.[14] His gospel is rooted in history and is embedded in a story that can only be told with a bit of work and some time. As for John, his description of the encounter between Jesus and Nicodemus is one piece of the case he is building that Jesus is the light of the world, with all the new creation implications of that phrase. He notes that Nicodemus came to Jesus at night and is in fact in the dark about some key things. So Jesus carefully explains the Spirit's ways and the work of the Son. These are both richly descriptive, fully grounded explorations of the depths of the gospel message. Knowing the gospel means becoming familiar with these explorations. You can't possibly know the gospel if you don't know the story. And you can't know the story in all its texture and richness if you don't read the Bible at length, becoming familiar with all of its territory.

So I conclude that the Snacking Bible should be done away with. The practice must be named for what it is: verse jacking.[15] To hijack something is to seize control of it to impose a purpose other than its originally intended one. As we see in other uses of the word (like carjacking), it is an aggressive action, a breaking in and taking over to force one's own will upon something. Taking isolated verses out of context and using them for other, extraneous purposes is a form of hijacking. It is a misuse of the Bible.[16] And I should be clear: verse jacking is not limited to kitschy displays of Christian trinkets. Pastors, professors and all manner of would-be serious students of the Bible are drawn into this debacle. As I've said, it's our common form of the Bible that has compelled us to engage in this all-too-common yet ill-begotten practice. Our complicated, piecemeal form hands out Bible snacks like a vending machine.

But we don't have to live this way. There's a better way, a way that is honest to what the Bible is. There are Bible practices that honor and accept the Bible God actually saw fit to give us. The second crucial step to saving the Bible will be to rediscover what it means to eat a book. What we'll find is that it's possible to replace fragmentary hope, out-of-context encouragement and snippets of the gospel with whole, healthy, well-rounded meals. When we take away individual verses, we don't get less Bible—we get more. More and better Bible eating. It *is* possible for our Bible formats to set the table for feasting on the Scriptures.

- four -

*My appetite is hearty and when I sit down
to read I like a square meal.*

C. S. Lewis

From Normal to New Normal: Assumptions and Anomalies

Perhaps *The Structure of Scientific Revolutions* by Thomas Kuhn is a classic
in a Mark Twain sense: a book that people praise but don't read. Kuhn is the
one who coined the much-used phrase that has become untethered from
the book itself: paradigm shift. But there is much more in Kuhn's book than
a useful phrase or two. Kuhn describes how cognitive, explanatory, big-
picture transformations happen. Though Kuhn's focus is on the scientific
community, his explanation of the process is helpfully applicable to other
cultural settings. In particular, Kuhn's ideas can assist us in understanding
how a Bible revolution could happen.

Kuhn begins by noting that for a long time people thought of the history
of science as simply an ongoing process of incremental increases in pieces
of knowledge about how the world works. In contrast, Kuhn posits that the
history of science is marked by a series of significant, revolutionary turning
points, like those associated with the names of Copernicus, Newton,
Lavoisier and Einstein. These major leaps in scientific development were all
based on fundamental reorientations of the basic, shared assumptions that

had guided science up to that point. These revolutions, in other words, upset what was known at the time as normal science. Normal science is the collection of assumptions and beliefs that form the foundation upon which ongoing scientific work is done.

Normal science, says Kuhn, "often suppresses fundamental novelties because they are necessarily subversive of its basic commitments."[1] If novelties are regularly suppressed, then how do revolutions happen? How does normal science change? The answer is found in the existence of anomalies, those test results, observations or ongoing problems that form intractable glitches in the ongoing process of normal science. Anomalies arise because the theory can't account for what is actually found to be. The current paradigm's explanatory power is discovered to be lacking in some crucial respect. The persistence of these rough spots, marring the smooth surface of normal science, eventually leads to a crisis that confronts the entire scientific community. It's actually the existence of anomalies within current paradigms that propel the imaginative creation of new paradigms. New paradigms "gain their status because they are more successful than their competitors in solving a few problems that the group of practitioners has come to recognize as acute."[2]

My premise is that the world of normal Bible practices is due for a revolution. We need a new Bible paradigm because the combined effect of the modernist Bible and the practices that we have built around it have resulted in a crisis. We have anomalies—intractable problems that are increasingly rising to the surface. Christian Smith's *The Bible Made Impossible*, Rachel Held Evans's *A Year of Biblical Womanhood*, Richard Schultz's *Out of Context*, Peter Enns's *Inspiration and Incarnation* and others are forming a cadre of books pointing out the existence of the rough spots in our current modernistic Bible paradigm.[3] These authors refuse to let us continue the strategy of denial when it comes to the current problems of the Snacking Bible.

Kuhn tells us that the birth of a new theory "implies a change in the rules governing the prior practice of normal science."[4] With the Elegant Bible in our hands, we are free to rediscover the Bible that's been hiding beneath the artificial and off-putting complexity of the modernist Bible. The inviting simplicity of the new form will help us begin exercising new rules for Bible engagement.

It is crucial at this point to see the community-based nature of things like paradigms.[5] The rules we follow for our Bible practices are by and large shared rules. The Snacking Bible phenomena demonstrates how widespread the modernistic assumptions and beliefs about the Bible are. The nature of our Bible studies, our preaching, our devotional life, our Bible teaching and our use of the Bible in virtual spaces such as social media, websites and mobile Bible apps, all reveal the currently shared assumptions of normal Bible. We have functioning answers to the questions *What is the Bible?* and *What are we supposed to do with it?* They're just not consistent or healthy answers. Combine this with the glaring absence of one key practice—Bible reading at length—and we get a pretty clear picture of our current life with the Bible. Kuhn's story of paradigm shifts suggests that if all of this is going to change, we're going to have to change together.

Following Kuhn's model, this would begin with a community-wide acknowledgment of the extent and seriousness of our current Bible breakdowns. This would be difficult, but paradigm shifts have always been difficult. In every scientific revolution there have been those whose strength of commitment to the old paradigm has prevented them from ever accepting the new one. No doubt many people have a long and deep history with modernism's Bible, and to lose the shared understandings and practices may feel like losing the Bible itself. That's why the distinction between the Bible in and of itself and any particular, historical Bible artifact is crucial. We aren't ultimately obligated to defend a certain cultural form or expression of the Bible. Our focus is rightfully on the Bible behind or within that form. The goal is a form that serves the Bible itself well. Better practices will follow from a truer form.

In the interest of this goal, all I can do at this point is extend an invitation, first to admit the state of our current brokenness, and second to encourage people to try on the new paradigm for size. As for me and my household, we've seen and experienced the anomalies of normal Bible practices. I believe it has too many acute difficulties to continue. To begin feasting on the Bible will not cause us to lose the Bible, but it will challenge the dominance of the Snacking Bible. A paradigm shift is needed in order to return the Bible to us in all its fullness and power.

On Not Bringing Your Own Fast Food to the Feast

Martin Luther was hungry. Tutored in a late-medieval piety and theology focused on personal holiness and introspection, the Augustinian monk struggled deeply with his plagued conscience. The well-established system of Penance and Indulgence (a not unnatural development from Augustine's inwardly oriented *Confessions*) only fed his tortured preoccupation with his own status before a perfection-demanding God. So it was that Luther came to the Scriptures with his own very pointed questions. In a sense, he already knew what kind of food he needed there, and in his mind it didn't have very much to do with the question of the relations between Jews and Gentiles. He had read his penitentials and needed an answer for the darkness he found within himself. And so Luther had difficulty reading texts about justification in any sense other than the one that soothed his own soul.

Krister Stendahl's groundbreaking essay "The Apostle Paul and the Introspective Conscience of the West" summarizes Luther's situation this way:

> The manuals for self-examination among the Irish monks and missionaries became a treasured legacy in wide circles of Western Christianity. The Black Death may have been significant in the development of the climate of faith and life. Penetrating self-examination reached a hitherto unknown intensity. For those who took this practice seriously—and they were more numerous than many Protestants are accustomed to think—the pressure was great. It is as one of those—and for them—that Luther carries out his mission as a great pioneer. It is in response to *their* question, "How can I find a gracious God?" that Paul's words about a justification in Christ by faith, and without the works of the Law, appears as the liberating and saving answer.[6]

Stendahl goes on to note that from this time on the standard reading of passages about justification were decisively altered: "Where Paul was concerned about the possibility for Gentiles to be included in the messianic community, his statements are now read as answers to the quest for assurance about man's salvation out of a common human predicament." And then comes the crux of the matter for our purposes here: "Sayings which originally meant one thing later on were interpreted to mean something else, something which was felt to be more relevant to human conditions of later times."[7]

This is precisely the perennial danger we face with the Bible, namely, that our urgent and well-meaning desire to find something that speaks immediately and directly to our own situation will derail the intention and meaning first placed there by the Bible's authors. The quest for a "more relevant" Bible tempts us beyond our ability to resist, and we take the shortcuts: reading out of context, reading only carefully selected portions, reading quick and dirty.

Here someone from the next generation of New Testament scholars takes up the cause and urges us into better encounters with the Bible. N. T. Wright's book *Justification* jumps into the very debate that Stendahl's article did so much to start, but along the way he addresses directly the matter of how to read the Bible. His second chapter, titled "Rules of Engagement," is a primer of sorts on what Bible feasting looks like. First things first, says Wright: "Scripture . . . does not exist to give authoritative answers to questions other than those it addresses."[8] Eating the Bible means giving primary attention to the Bible's own cause, its own concerns, the flow of its own arguments. The Scriptures have prepared their own feast, and it is rather rude to show up at the door with our own preconceived ideas about what we have to find there.

> If you read your own questions into the text, and try to get an answer from it, when the text itself is talking about something else, you run the risk not only of hearing only the echo of your own voice rather than the word of God but also of missing the key point that the text was actually eager to tell you, and which you have brushed aside in your relentless quest for your own meaning.[9]

A double loss. Snacking on the Bible costs us dearly in both ways: we seek and find only what we already want, and we miss all that God was trying to communicate.

So why are we so tempted to snack? Why do we bring so much of our own agenda to our would-be Bible engagement? I believe the answer is that we're afraid we won't end up being fed at all. We're told the Scriptures are a banquet, but the process of eating this meal seems challenging. Turning the Bible into a slow food experience is difficult for us. We don't have the time, the background knowledge, or even the interest in all those academic-sounding requirements: cultural setting, historical background, literary genre and on and on. Is the Bible only for scholars? And then there's this: sitting down to read, uninterrupted by the constant buzz our world presents is a countercultural act in our time. If that's what it takes to partake of the Bible's feast, who will do it?

Even if these slightly heroic steps are taken, who's to say that this long way around will satisfy us in the end? We're too hungry. The verse-of-the day, the one-minute Bible, the nanosecond topical search on the e-Bible—at least give the impression of providing spot-on, helpful, encouraging, useful bites of the Bible.

Part of our conversion process, our adoption of a new Bible engagement paradigm, will be to come to terms with the fact that the Bible was written for us, but not directly to us. Believing this will encourage us to begin to be virtuous readers of the Bible. Without having to become seminarians, we will become lifelong learners, willing to listen to those who know more than we do. We will give the Bible the honor of our time. Such things as trust, patience and submission to the Bible and its concerns will mark our reading. Rather than demanding instant satisfaction, we will give ourselves over to the Bible. With faith ultimately in the Spirit whom we believe inspired it to be the kind of book it is, we will believe that over time it will do for us all we need and more. It will feed us. It will speak to our lives now. It will be relevant. But we will come by these gifts honestly, in the dining room, not cheaply through those drive-thru windows that both distort and demean the Bible.

David Ulin captures what this kind of reading means in our cultural moment:

> This is the burden of technology, that we are never disconnected, never out of touch. And yet, reading is, by its very nature, a strategy for displacement, for pulling back from the circumstances of the present and immersing in the textures of a different life. . . . Reading, after all, is an act of resistance in a landscape of distraction, a matter of engagement in a society that seems to want nothing more than for us to disengage. It connects us at the deepest levels; it is slow, rather than fast. . . . In the midst of a book, we have no choice but to be patient, to take each thing in its moment, to let the narrative prevail.[10]

FALLING IN LOVE WITH (ALL OF) THE BIBLE

God had all the options open to him. He could have given us any kind of Bible he wanted. And he chose to root his revelation in the real history of a particular nation (see chapters five and six) and bring it all together to tell a redemptive story (see chapters seven through nine), a drama that is already in the process of transforming the world. But the building blocks of all this are the individual books that make up the Bible. These are the Scriptures, unique writings shaped by authors and editors to do a special duty in God's overall purpose.

The place to begin with feasting on the Bible is with reorienting our eating habits. Eat an individual book and eat it whole. Some are short, some are long—regardless, eat them whole. Some relatively simple, others are built in complex ways. Either way, sit down and dine. As I said in chapter two, the central intentional unit of the inspired authors and editors of the Bible is the book.[11] Accepting the Bible God gave us means adapting our habits so we can interact with it on its own terms, and the first term the Bible presents to us in this covenant is that it is a collection of distinct literary units.

Once we begin with whole books, we can work our way both up (to collections of books and on to the entire story) and down (to the parts that make up a book—a single story, parable, oracle, vision, or one of the points in the body of an instructive letter). But both of these secondary steps are dependent on getting this first step right. When we read whole books we will be equipped for looking more broadly at other levels of meaning.

For some reason (likely a predisposition related to the broader cultural turn toward modernity) we have elevated Bible study over Bible reading. This has been a crucial mistake. There is a place for looking at how a particular topic develops over the course of several books. There is a place for the finer study of the smaller parts of the Bible—sections, sentences, phrases, even single words. But Bible study is a specialized activity, subservient to a larger goal. Frogs were not given their place in the creation to serve as specimens for dissection. And if I am unfamiliar with frogs as they jump and croak in the wider world, taking up their role in the ecosystem of my backyard pond, cutting them open in a laboratory will not enable me to know and understand them. So it is with the books of the Bible. Read and understand them as whole things functioning in their own world, and then you can study their parts as contributing members of that whole.

Reading any book of the Bible, from the first to the last, will immediately put the reader into the midst of a hermeneutical circle. My understanding of any one of the books will be limited without a comprehension of the shape and movement of the whole collection. (For example, what sense can I make of the controversy addressed in the letter to the Galatians without a background knowledge of Israel's bigger story and the dramatic turn of events surrounding Jesus of Nazareth?) And I won't understand the complete Bible without comprehending the building blocks of its individual books. This is the quandary we face if we are to accept the Bible as it is. We can attempt to circumvent this by imagining it to be a book of principles or fragmentary, stand-alone statements of spiritual truth—we can try to flatten the Bible, to imagine there is no circle. But we've already seen that this attempt is fatally flawed and dishonest to the book we have.

What do you do with the circle? Simply jump in. Eat books and eat them whole. As you go it will be important to keep clearly in mind the books you've read before. As you go you will find that your own ability to understand will grow the more books you've read. Having read *The Fellowship of the Ring*, you will have a much better time with *The Two Towers*, after which you will be prepared for *The Return of the King*. Read Genesis, Jeremiah and Daniel, and then read Revelation. And to clarify that this is not merely about reading in chronological sequence, if you read Tolkien's whole trilogy and then go back to *The Hobbit*, you will find much that is enriched and deepened from your knowledge of the later turns of the story. Read Revelation, and then re-read Daniel, Jeremiah and Genesis. All this is to say that the books of the Bible are mutually explanatory and enriching, going both forward and backward in the story. Jump in and keep reading and you will find connections both coming and going.[12]

But this isn't a task for individuals alone—the Bible is inherently a community book (see chapters twelve and thirteen). We have been led off the path by a modern emphasis on the free, independent and self-determining individual. We've been told that individualistic interpretation and application is the right pattern of our work with the Bible. We've confused *personal* with *individualistic*. One important part of the recovery of the Bible will involve a rediscovery of community-based engagement. The circle was always meant to be navigated with others. Eating alone is sometimes a necessity, but meals are best enjoyed with company.

Rather than spending our time on extraction techniques—finding ways to isolate and take out the little pieces we find useful—we can begin to learn those things that will help us enter the world of the Bible. What literary form is this book? What are the normal conventions of this form? What is the right way to read and interpret a writing like this? To whom was this book first addressed? What is this book trying to do? Where does this book fit into the big narrative of the Bible? What unique contribution might it be making?

When we begin to eat our Bibles like this, we will indeed discover a whole new meal. Without the pressure to instantly apply every fragment to my daily life, Barth's strange and startling world will soon appear. Snacking stays in the present and merely takes from the Bible. Feasting on the Bible means going back and going in. This requires tabling my personal agenda. For example, if I read whole books I will discover soon enough that if I'm interested in the Bible I will have to gain an interest in Israel and her place in the story. No one in and among these books can stop talking about Israel. If the story of Israel seems limited and ancient and merely tribal to me, then, if I'm honest, I'll have to admit I'm not particularly drawn to the choice God made for how he would reveal himself to the world.

But if I persist and submit to this book, I will slowly digest the story of Israel. I'll gain an interest in how she fares. Perhaps it will begin to dawn on me how my destiny and everyone's destiny is involved in what happens in this ongoing struggle between God and the family of Jacob. I will no longer have to be driven by the frenetic search for an application of every piece of the Bible to my daily life. I can relax and commit to learning Israel's covenant history by reading its books as the long-form narrative they are. I can trust that the history is worth delving into. I will care about Israel's song book, which is not just my song book. I will read a gospel with intense curiosity about how this author thinks the prophet from Galilee is making sense of the whole convoluted history of this people.

This narrative of Israel's journey is built in the Bible book by book, all the way to its culmination in the story of Jesus, and then to its outworking in the story of the world. Going book by book I will sit with broken people in the ashes of a fallen Jerusalem, and I will confront the pain and anguish of five full songs of loss. I will not cheat by picking out Lamentations 3:22-23, and begin singing too easily of God's great faithfulness while refusing to be crushed with all the other prisoners of the land. I will observe with interest how the prophet Habakkuk challenges the ways of God, and perhaps I will decipher how questioning and answering seems to go both ways in the story of this deity and this particular people. I will be perplexed with Ecclesiastes over the crooked, indecipherable and frequently unfair twists of life in this crooked, indecipherable and frequently unfair world. I will read straight through Esther and then consider how it is that God simply will not act alone in this drama. He is uncompromising in his determination that humans act like humans and play their parts.

Going book by book, I will see how the last words of Moses to Israel (Deuteronomy) lay out the terms and conditions for living as the people of the Great King in the new land. These, in turn, will reveal themselves to be crucial for understanding Matthew's portrait of a Jesus who becomes Israel for Israel after it's clear that the nation can't seem to be itself.

Going book by book I will take a few minutes and read through Paul's letter to the Philippians in one sitting. I will reflect on the fact that Paul's joyous tone in the letter sits side by side with his talk of being in chains under Caesar's thumb, with his friend Epaphroditus's near-fatal illness, with his continuing frustration with those "dogs" who are undermining his teaching in the churches he's founded. In short, I will begin to enter the world of Paul and the community of believers in Philippi. I won't settle for a couple lines of "rejoice always" and "I can do all things."

All this and many times more I will gain if I reorient my fundamental stance toward the Bible—book by book. This is what it looks like to accept the Bible God gave us. This is what it means to begin feasting on the Bible. Much more must be said about how this feasting then feeds us, how it does its work, what it does to us, how the books come together and do more than any of them could alone, and how we bring the story of our own lives into this rather strange assemblage of texts. But our first answer to the question *What are we supposed to do with the Bible?* is to accept it on its own terms by reading its own discrete literary units—not verses, not chapters, not topically headed sections, but whole books.

The simple and pleasing format of the Elegant Bible, stripped of all the modernist additives, encourages us to move beyond our minimalist Bible practices and rediscover the Feasting Bible. The opening steps for saving the Bible are thus set. Even with only these first two moves, the Bible has a much better chance of achieving its mission of transforming lives. Once we begin to savor the full and healthy meals of whole books again, we can't help but begin to appreciate the Historical Bible. By no longer self-selecting those seemingly ahistorical bits of timeless truth, we will fully confront the fact that the Bible is embedded in time and does all of its work in the midst of our ongoing human saga. The Historical Bible is a challenging Bible, but it promises us that God's story is truly and fully intertwined with our story, here and now.

- five -

*But supposing history remains
one of the father's true sons?*

N. T. Wright

The whole thing started one day when Xi was out walking and the strangely-shaped object fell from the sky and landed very near him. Xi and his fellow bushmen lived far out in the desert away from any civilization. The gods had given the little people of the Kalahari a gift. They had never seen anything quite like it and they weren't quite sure what to do with it. But soon they found ways to make it useful. Because it was smooth, it was very good for curing snake skins. Because it was hard, it was very good for breaking open plant tubers and getting the moisture out. They even discovered that by blowing gently over the opening on one end, soft musical notes would come out. At first, it really did seem like a useful gift.

The gods must have been absent-minded, however, because they only sent one. Since everyone seemed to need it at the same time for their very important chores, soon disagreements broke out and harsh words were spoken over who should get it first. It wasn't long before someone even used the strange gift to strike someone else. The gift had become a weapon. Xi grabbed the gift and threw it back up into the sky, returning it to the gods. But the gods didn't want it, and the gift fell back to earth once again (hitting someone on the head).

Xi talked it over with the clan that night around the fire. He decided that although it rarely happens, the gods had made a mistake. In this case, they were crazy. Because the gift, although useful in some ways, was destroying the good life the tribe had known and was causing harm, Xi would carry the gift to the end of the earth and get rid of it. It was a long and complicated journey, but when Xi finally got there he gently tossed the Coke bottle over the edge.[1]

OF RAINBOWS, COKE BOTTLES AND THE BIBLE

I can still feel the shock. I was in the fourth grade at Van Dellen Christian Elementary school in Denver, Colorado, and I remember the emotion distinctly. The topic that day was rainbows, and the explanation I heard for how light is refracted through the moisture in the air immediately caused a crisis for me. I think there may have even been a demonstration with some spraying water, or maybe it was just an illustration in a book. Either way, the idea hit me like a splash of cold water in the face. But it was my soul that was stunned. My still-young faith had somewhere along the line determined that if the Bible said God did something, that meant he did it and he did it alone and no other cause was involved or necessary or even possible. If there was another explanation for rainbows, then the Bible's account for the existence of rainbows as placed by God in the sky as a sign of a promise wasn't true. It had to be one or the other, not both. I didn't know what to do about this: the evidence was right there in front of me, and my Christian school teacher was the one explaining it after all, but I also knew what the Bible story said. God puts rainbows in the sky.

That crisis can happen in the fourth grade, in the fourth semester in graduate school pursuing Old Testament studies or in lots of places in between. This category of "things from God that come from the sky"—whether rainbows, Coke bottles or the Bible itself—is really just a smaller subset of a much larger category of issues having to do with how God chooses to interact with his world. This larger category includes the doctrine of providence, the question of the relationship between the divine and human natures of Jesus Christ, and, of course, the nature of the Bible's books as divine revelation in the midst of human writing.

I don't remember exactly how or when I came to reconcile the two truths that rainbows are a sign from God and rainbows have a natural explanation.

But it strikes me now that there are a number of things my community believed about the Bible that were never explicitly addressed or taught as I was growing up. I was certainly taught a lot of "Bible," but some very key things *about* the Bible (what it is exactly, how it works, what we believe about it) were never really brought up. I mostly picked up on bits and pieces of what I saw and heard and tried to make up my own working hypothesis of the Bible as I went. The main thing for sure, the thing that was unmistakable, was that the Bible is the Word of God. Anything else I may have placed in my cobbled-together doctrine of the Bible was clearly subservient to this big thing. If I picked up anything about the Bible also being a human book, it was incidental and never explained.

The Word of God. The connotations of this phrase all carry great weight. It means the Bible is truth, authoritative, unique, powerful. The Word of God—it *is* things and *does* things that only the Word of God can be and do. We easily refer to the Bible as the Word of God—it seems natural and automatic for us. But would we just as easily call it "the book of human words" or "the words of people"? An orthodox view of the Bible will say the Bible is both, human and divine. But it's the uniqueness of the divine aspect that we want to emphasize. There are lots and lots of human words in existence, but Bible folk understandably want to highlight the one-and-only inspired status of the Scriptures relative to other human writings. It's the Word of God designation that sets the Bible apart.

But what is the consequence of this constant reinforcement of only half of our confession about the Bible? The consequence is the Bible-falling-from-the-sky syndrome, which doesn't mean that there are lots of people who literally believe the Bible came down from heaven as a complete book. (If that were the case, however, it would most certainly have been in the King James Version.) The problem is that there are many people who in their ongoing interaction with the Bible and efforts to understand it minimize the essentially historical nature of the Bible. It's as if the Bible came straight to us, a direct word from the Lord, unmediated. The Bible is seen as mostly an otherworldly book.

The historical aspect of the Bible (or the lack of it) has repercussions for our two big questions: *What is the Bible?* and *What are we supposed to do with it?* The implications of the fact that the whole collection of writings is fully human—embedded in real history and in ancient cultures, using particular languages, addressing specific issues, reflecting habits, customs and ways of thinking unfamiliar to us—have not deeply registered with these readers. The difference that history makes to the Bible has not been appreciated. The challenges of a this-worldly Bible have not been faced. The gifts of a historical Bible have not been received.

There is a fair bit of serious distrust of the historical nature of the Bible. Just as we've inherited a modern format of the Bible and many of the fragmented Bible practices that go with that format, we've also inherited a suspicion that too much history (that is, too much attention to the human side of the Bible) is bad for the Bible and for our faith.

A Short History of History as a Tool of the Devil

Hermann Samuel Reimarus (1694–1768) deserves a fair amount of the credit for discrediting the study of history in relation to the Bible. A German Enlightenment philosopher and deist, he wrote a life of Jesus that used history as part of an attack on Christianity as a revealed religion. His sinister idea was to claim that a more honest look at the real history of Jesus (or, we might say, the real Jesus of history) would unveil a different story than that being told by the established Christian church. Thus by showing the foundation of the whole thing to be untrue, he hoped to help topple traditional Christianity.

In typical Enlightenment fashion Reimarus preferred a rational over a revealed basis for understanding God and the world. And the word *rational* at the time meant that God would not, could not, interfere with the operations of his world. Miracles and other wonders ascribed to supernaturalism were out of the question. The time of light had come, and humanity now saw that Jewish or Christian stories that grew out of primitive and naive mindsets were inadequate for a catholic religion. Our hope lay in something truly universal—reason—not in something so parochial as ancient Near Eastern tribalism. So the Bible's account of Jesus was parsed and sifted to sort the true from the legend. Historical study became the means by which Christianity was discredited. The picture of Jesus that emerged from this process in Reimarus's case was of a Jewish revolutionary who hoped to reform the religion of his day, but whose movement never caught on. In a kind of desperate panic and despair, Jesus died on the cross, realizing his failure.

Reimarus introduced a turning point of sorts. His foray into the historical study of Jesus started a movement that's lasted for hundreds of years now. Many have followed in his footsteps and found that one surefire way of getting published is to write a book on the life of Jesus. The core plot of this storyline at its founding, as N. T. Wright explains, is that

> history leads away from theology. . . . The "Quest" [for the Historical Jesus] began as an explicitly anti-theological, anti-Christian, anti-dogmatic movement. Its initial agenda was not to find a Jesus upon whom Christian faith might be based, but to show that the faith of the church (as it is was then conceived) could not in fact be based on the real Jesus of Nazareth.[2]

Others who contributed later chapters in this ongoing Book of Jesus do attempt to offer up a Jesus worth worshiping, or at least emulating, but almost always the historical blade is used to cut away this or that from the Gospel's telling of the events. And so we've seen a parade of people right up to our own day, some serious researchers and scholars, some merely pundits and agitators, offering up their portraits of the supposedly real Galilean who walked the earth in the first century.

On top of all of this, there have been parallel developments that only heighten the fear that a Bible believer might have toward the whole modern business of science, history and investigation. It's one thing to apply science to technology in the interest of improving our lives in a multitude of ways. But when science and history turn their sights on the Bible and start poking around in the things we believe in, that's another matter. But sure enough, right alongside the time when Reimarus and his ilk were spilling their ink on tracing Jesus' footsteps, others were taking up different positions in what was perceived as a battle against the faith. Charles Darwin shared his thoughts on the gradual development of biological beings, seemingly undermining the Bible's creation account. New scientific explanations for how the world works came day by day and more and more people began openly questioning the stories of miracles, healings, suns standing still and waters parting and dead people rising. The rainbows of the covenant were falling left and right. *It's not a promise, it's just light and water.*

Then a new investigative department was formed with the dangerous name "Higher Criticism of the Bible." The poking around made its way over to the Scriptures. Who really wrote these books? Or who pulled all these different parts together and tried to smooth it all out? And when? Have you noticed that other ancient peoples had their own creation stories and flood tales? Which of these things did Jesus likely say, and which ones did the early church put in his mouth? Now that we know that God doesn't break in to our world and intervene, what can we say about this or that event described in the Bible? Perhaps we can reconstruct what "really happened" and get the truth behind what the Bible itself says. If we don't go in assuming that everything in the Bible is true, good and beautiful, what will we really find there?

It all had an aggressive and unsavory scent to it, often made worse by academic arrogance. The pressure on traditional beliefs was relentless during this period. So it's hard to get too angry with the fundamentalists for reacting strongly. It must have felt like their world was falling apart. In some very real ways it was. A new, modern world was being born. Traditionalist Protestant Christians had grown used to being ascendant in America and suddenly they were being culturally sidelined in all kinds of ways. The pendulum had swung strongly to one side. It doesn't take modern science to predict what would happen next.

If history and science and investigations into all manner of human realities in the Bible lead to *this*, then why do we need them at all? And so for a large number of Christians in the late nineteenth and early twentieth centuries, the door was effectively closed to historical considerations of the Bible. Having seen historical study used so negatively, there was little appetite for more of it. History? Be careful, here there be monsters.

Rather than embark on further exploration of what were already known to be treacherous waters, fundamentalists retreated to the firm and solid ground of traditional faith. Simple biblical truth was all that mattered. Supernatural explanations would suffice. The world's learning can only lead you astray, so the way to be spiritual is to shun that learning. As applied to the Bible, this retreat meant a focus on the straightforward, plain teaching of the Bible and taking it at its word. Here a strong doctrine of the Bible's inerrancy was developed. As Mark Noll describes it, "This belief had the practical effect of rendering the experience of the biblical writers nearly meaningless. It was the Word of God pure and simple, not the Word of God as mediated through the life experiences and cultural settings of the biblical authors, that was important."[3] A hard wedge was driven between grace and the world, between the spiritual and the natural. The way to read the Bible was *directly*, as a word from God to you, and not worry about all that background noise and those distracting matters of the original historical setting. What was not considered, however, was the possibility that historical studies of the Bible might be undertaken *but without the antagonistic modernist assumptions and agenda*. Every historian of the Bible need not share the malice of Reimarus.

One bit of irony in this tale is that it was a strongly modernist form of the Bible that these anti-modernist fundamentalists were reading. And it was largely this chopped up and numbered form that allowed them to focus on those simple spiritual statements and clear Bible facts they so dearly valued. But ironic or not, the elements of this picture did all seem to fit together for them at the time. A not-of-this-world Bible cut up into small readings, plainly read and directly understood, became a well-established pattern of thinking about the Bible. The pull was toward a supernatural Bible, untainted with the merely human, the earthly, the historical. The classical dual truths of Christian orthodoxy—human and divine together—transitioned in fundamentalism to an either/or: human or divine. The more human the Bible became in modernism, the less divine it appeared to be. So the reaction was naturally to reassert the divine and submerge the human.

But perhaps at this point you're thinking, *That's all very interesting about those fundamentalists back there and then, but what has all that got to do with Bible readers today?* Most people have moved on, no? In his chapter called "The Intellectual Disaster of Fundamentalism" Noll concludes by facing exactly this objection: "But surely the author doth protest too much. Surely we are flogging a dead horse by being so preoccupied with beliefs and practices from the early twentieth century that must now exert only a residual effect on the evangelical community."[4] Not so fast, says Noll. He responds by noting that "fundamentalist intellectual habits, however, have been more resilient than fundamentalism itself."[5] The ongoing problem, he says, is that these strong reactions to modernist trends formed deeply embedded "patterns of thought" and "habits of mind" that evangelicals have not been able to break. N. T. Wright identifies this as the "magic book" syndrome, "whose 'meaning' has little to do with what the first-century authors intended, and a lot to do with how some particular contemporary group has been accustomed to hear it in a call to a particular sort of spirituality or lifestyle."[6]

Many today continue to operate as if a supernatural book can't really be a fully human book at the same time. The either/or has taken hold and doesn't let go easily. Even for non-fundamentalists there is the remnant of belief that too much talk of the humanity of the Bible serves mostly to undermine it, not illuminate it. The continuing afterlife of the fundamentalist distrust of natural means keeps many Bible readers even now from receiving the Bible God has seen fit to give us. As Eugene Peterson says, "What is surprising today is how many people treat the Bible as a collection of Sibylline Oracles, verses or phrases without context or connections. This is nothing less than astonishing. The Scriptures are the revelation of a personal, relational, incarnational God to actual human communities of men and women with names in history."[7]

WHEN SUPERNATURALISM ISN'T SO SUPER

Believing and using the Bible as if it is only a divine book, exclusively a collection of supernatural words, supernaturally given, hurts the work of the Bible in the mission of God. It is important for me to say that none of this should be taken as denying a strong sense of divine inspiration of the Scriptures. The issue is whether we will have a view of inspiration that operates almost independently, negating the real human marks on the Bible. A non-historical Bible distorts what we think the Bible is, what we think we're supposed to do with it and what we think God is doing with it.

Here are some of the specific ways an otherworldly view of the Bible can misguide readers:

• A non-historical Bible discounts the way God uses our human "stuff" to serve his purpose. Because this view minimizes the human role in the Bible, it is prone to ignore things like *literary genre* and *ancient ways of using language* (ancient authors chose specific literary forms common to their time period for their writing and followed the conventions of those forms, expecting their audiences to do the same when reading—if we are uninterested in those forms and conventions we will easily misread their writings), *ancient worldviews* (ancient authors viewed the world and thought like ancient people—certainly God in his word was challenging some aspects of those worldviews, but he didn't simply and instantly override them all in his inspiration of the Scriptures) and *original issues and concerns* (God's people faced specific issues in relating God's new revealed way of life to their own ancient cultures—a non-historical reading will tend to overlook and discount those original issues if they are not perceived as being immediately relevant to our concerns today).

- A non-historical Bible leads to a misleading directness of Bible application. Non-historical views of how we got the Bible lead to non-historical attempts at interpretation and application. If I'm not too concerned about the original setting of the Bible, then I won't tend to worry too much about what the meaning of the Bible was to its first audience. I will jump straight to me and my concerns and what the Holy Spirit is saying to me today. This approach can only be done selectively, since so many statements in the Bible obviously don't have direct applicability to us.

- Closely related to this is the issue of chronocentrism, the biased belief that it is our time in history that is the most important. A non-historical reading of the Bible increases the chance that I will operate as if we are unique in all of human history, so certainly the Bible had us and our time in view when it was speaking. This view is especially common in end-times prophecy circles, and it is fascinating to see how this perspective fluidly adapts what any particular biblical prophecy is about as current global social-political situations change over time, without apology. In these circles there is little attention given to the significance of the prophecies and perspectives of Jeremiah, Ezekiel, Daniel and Revelation for their original ancient audiences. The real audience is always us as we constantly scan cable news channels for world events.

- A non-historical Bible leads to misunderstandings of what the Bible is actually saying, and replacing its intention with our own meaning instead. Krister Stendahl tells the story of Martin Luther accusing the Catholic church of reading its own meaning of medieval-style penance onto the Gospel word *repent*,[8] while N. T. Wright tells the story of Martin Luther reading his own meaning of individualistic and interior repentance onto a word that included a much bigger, national meaning in a first-century Israel still suffering the effects of ongoing exile.[9]

- Perhaps most seriously, a non-historical Bible is in the end unreal and dualistic. To deny, ignore or minimize the fact that God purposefully entered fully into our story and firmly grounded his revelation right in the midst of our language, culture and lives is in essence a kind of denial of the doctrine of creation. This is God's world, the place he intended for us to work out our lives in relationship with him. It is the context in which we find meaning and pursue our human vocation. God makes full use of his world for his own purposes. A non-historical Bible would have us believe that this world and all its ways are best avoided so we can focus on another, different realm where we really belong. The heresy of Docetism can be found not only in one's views of Jesus (he only *seemed* to be human, he wasn't really), but also in the realm of the Bible.

As in that satisfying moment when Xi dispenses with the strange gift from the gods, it's time to throw the Coke-Bottle-from-Heaven Bible over the edge of the end of the earth. The defensive posture of fundamentalism that bled over into evangelicalism has harmed our interaction with the Bible. Because others have abused the gift of God's historically and culturally situated revelation, we have turned away in disgust and acted as if the Bible is not that kind of book at all. We've found ways to navigate the Bible as if its groundedness in history isn't there. As with the Snacking Bible, so with "The Gods Must Be Crazy Bible"—it's superficially easier to take the Bible in little decontextualized pieces and think that they dropped from heaven as God's simple supernatural words just for me. We've tried to find a way to live off these morsels, but it just doesn't work. We're biblically underfed.

Feasting on the Historical Bible is slower and seems harder. But it's the Historical Bible that is the real Bible. So whatever it is that God had in mind when he gave us a Bible that is fully immersed in our human stories and cultures and lives, this intention will not be served if we go on pretending the Bible is something else. And so a third critical way we can save the Bible from ourselves is to repent, turn around and take seriously our responsibility to wrestle with the Historical Bible, and then happily receive its remarkable benefits.

six

FINDING GOD IN THE HISTORICAL BIBLE

People and other creatures would be known by their names and histories, not by their numbers or percentages. History would be handed down in songs and stories, not reduced to evolutionary or technological trends.

WENDELL BERRY,
STANDING BY WORDS

In some cases we know exactly how the books of the Bible were produced—for example, an early Christian missionary leader sat down and wrote a letter to a congregation under his care. In other cases we can only vaguely trace the backstory of the biblical text—someone started collecting the songs from Israel's temple worship. But regardless of the inconsistency of our knowledge of the birth of the Bible, the final form again and again insists on one thing: the stories, laws, covenants, songs, letters, visions—all of it—emerged because God willingly and intentionally immersed himself in the lives and times of his people. God is not the distant god of deism or typical civil religion. God has wed his story to ours, and ours to his. He is intimately involved. God is a God of history. Therefore the Bible is a book intertwined with history, and understanding it aright includes the good, hard work of historical investigation.

THE ORGANIC WORD: GOD'S PEOPLE SINGING, WRITING, LISTENING, SHARING

The Bible is no dry narration of the facts of the case. To know the Bible is to learn the texture of the story: the tip-toe anticipation of long-awaited good news or the deep dread of certain disaster, moments of exuberant joy on seeing oppressors finally overthrown or the dull weariness of too-long-endured injustice. All of this and more is given to us. The Bible has the feel of real life, with all its attendant ambiguity and multiple levels of meaning, with moral confusion and partial victories, heroes with feet of clay and whores who save the day. The Bible is no whitewashed tale of clear-cut good guys and bad guys and easy moralistic lessons. It's hard sometimes to even tell what's going on and what the thread really is. That's because the Bible is history, and history is like that. Yes, to be sure, there's divine revelation and the history has a direction, but this is not just a story about God. This is God with us, and the us part makes it inevitably messy.

We too often read right over the grain and feel of the Bible's history, or we miss it altogether because our preselected heavenly tidbits don't cover these parts. But it's all there. The Bible itself pervasively testifies to its own embeddedness in history.

- When Pharaoh's horses, chariots and horsemen were washed away by the chaotic sea, the Bible bothers to elaborate on how the women led Israel's celebration in song and dance. The moment is presented as spontaneous and buoyant, an embodied outbreak of human emotion upon seeing God come down from heaven to act on their behalf:

  Then Miriam the prophet, Aaron's sister, took a timbrel in her hand, and all the women followed her, with timbrels and dancing. Miriam sang to them:

  > "Sing to the LORD,
  >   for he is highly exalted.
  >
  >   Both horse and driver
  >   he has hurled into the sea." (From the book of Exodus)[1]

- When Deborah and Barak sang their victory duet after subduing the Canaanite king, we get a glimpse into the ancient way stories were preserved in song as people congregated in the usual places. This is no doubt how

Israel's narratives became the stuff of legend—stories worth remembering—and thus were given a chance to make it into our Bibles:

You who ride on white donkeys,
sitting on your saddle blankets,
and you who walk along the road,
consider the voice of the singers at the watering places.
They recite the victories of the LORD,
the victories of his villagers in Israel.
Then the people of the LORD
went down to the city gates.
"Wake up, wake up, Deborah!
Wake up, wake up, break out in song!
Arise, Barak!
Take captive your captives, son of Abinoam." (From the book of Judges)

- When the wicked Jehoiakim, son of the righteous Josiah, succeeded his father as king over Judah, the Lord told the prophet Jeremiah to "take a scroll and write on it all the words I have spoken to you concerning Israel, Judah and all the other nations from the time I began speaking to you in the reign of Josiah till now." It makes you realize Jeremiah hadn't been sitting up in some white tower writing poetry while sipping tea. The prophets, as Gregory Mobley reminds us, were street performers, not authors.[2] Jeremiah had been out mixing it up with the people, speaking truth to power and bearing the consequences by facing rejection, punishment and the threat of death. It fell to Baruch the scribe to actually write down the prophet's mostly depressing oracles as Jeremiah remembered and recited the words to him. And when Jehoiakim later got his hands on the scroll and felt the sting of its rebukes, he sliced it into pieces and threw them into his firepot (the text tells us that after listening to three or four columns being read he would start cutting again). From this we get a more realistic sense of how fragile the birth of the Word of God really was as it came into the world, not unlike the birth of the Word of God in Bethlehem later in the story. So Jeremiah and Baruch had to get together and do the whole thing over again.

- When the apostle Paul wrote to the holy and faithful brothers and sisters in Colossae, he closed his letter with the kind of historical and human particulars that inescapably refute the idea that Paul's writings are abstract theological treatises sharing general religious teaching. He shared personal notes about Tychicus, who was carrying the letter, the runaway slave Onesimus, his fellow prisoner Aristarchus, Mark the cousin of Barnabas, Jesus called Justus, Epaphras who first brought the news of Jesus' victory to the Colossians, Luke the doctor, Demas who sends greetings, Nympha who hosts a church in her home, and then Archippus, the leader of the church there that Paul urges to fulfill his calling and ministry. In other words, Paul wasn't writing to us. The letter to the Colossians was written to a gathering of Jesus-followers in first-century Asia Minor. But just before signing off with a greeting written in his own hand (implying the rest of the letter was dictated), Paul includes a final instruction that gives us a hint that even historically particular writings can find a usefulness outside their original audience: "After this letter has been read to you, see that it is also read in the church of the Laodiceans and that you in turn read the letter from Laodicea." Paul wanted his letters to the churches circulated and shared with others. This no doubt was how collections of Paul's letters began to be formed, a crucial step in the overall development of what became our New Testament.

It would have been easier for God to simply drop The Book of Jeremiah's Oracles from heaven, ready-made, but that would not be taking us and our place in the world seriously. God inspired the Bible's authors, but he also suffered with the authors in the ups and downs and the give and take of real life once that word was given. God tenaciously remains as committed as ever to the partnership with humans he established at the beginning. He has his own image bearers in the world and he will continue to work through them come hell or high water, both of which actually do show up. The progress of the partnership is slow, and for anyone invested in it as the hope of the world, it can seem tedious and even agonizing. It was undoubtedly painful for God, as it was for his servants the prophets, to see what happened when the divine word began to interact with the human world. Mark's Gospel depicts a Jesus who gets angry and deeply distressed at the poor response to his ministry of the word of God. He sighs in frustration more than once, and asks even his own disciples, "Are you so dull?" Apparently even stellar presentations of divine revelation can be met with dumb stares. But the word of God did not arrive here in a hermetically sealed container, untouchable by unworthy recipients. The word of God entered the fray of a fallen world.

God once directly wrote his covenant words onto stone tablets and gave them to Moses. It was a remarkable, unmediated presentation of the word of God. But soon after, when Moses saw the faithless behavior of the people, he threw the tablets down in disgust and shattered them into pieces. So Moses had to trudge back up the mountain and God engraved the words again. As we've already seen, later it was Baruch who twice had to write out his assigned portion of the Bible by hand. It's a risky thing to bring this divine word of God into contact with these less-than-receptive people and this less-than-secure historical process. Jesus preached and healed and was accused of colluding with Beelzebul, the prince of demons. The original ending of Mark's Gospel apparently got lost. The story of Jesus and the woman caught in adultery was clearly circulated among the early followers of Jesus, but no one was quite sure where to put it, if anywhere (it shows up in various locations in John's Gospel and in Luke's, but not at all in the earliest manuscripts). To enter history really is to give it a go in the rough-and-tumble. Even for God.

How to Read the Bible Both-And Rather Than Either-Or

The various books of the Bible were all birthed from organic historical processes. God worked in and through the regular ways people communicated in antiquity to bring his particular message into the world. The Bible is also historical in its subject matter—it all revolves around what God has done and is continuing to do in history. So reading the material in a non-historical way radically deconstructs the text at more than one level. Virtuous Bible readers will receive the books as historical documents, taking onboard everything that this recognition entails. Having an Elegant Bible and a Feasting Bible already take us well down the road to a Historical Bible. Both acknowledge the reality that the Bible was given in the midst of our story, tied to a particular time and place and using the natural material of that setting. If we can clearly see the natural forms of the books, reflecting their authors' and editors' chosen literary genres, the first steps to reading the Bible historically are easier to take. And a commitment to engage the Bible via its fundamental literary units (primarily eating whole books) will further open the door to good contextual understanding.

Along with this we must actively embrace the dual nature of the Bible as simultaneously human and divine. In this regard historian Mark Noll references B. B. Warfield's reflections on the Bible as concursively human writings and God's revelation.[3] The alternative, which Warfield saw already in his day (the late nineteenth century) was a zero sum conception in which the Bible was either human or divine, but not both. In this view people try to divide the Bible between the two characterizations, conceiving them as "striving against and excluding each other, so that where one enters the other is pushed out." Some, seeing plenty of evidence for the humanity of the Bible, presume it can thereby have no divine voice. Others, determined to protect the status of God's word, minimize or eliminate the human element.

A third option is better, and also in line with historic Christian orthodoxy. God has chosen to use existing human forms and elements—language, culture, history and literature—as his means to communicate. Thus our good reading will mean accepting, learning and accounting for these human elements. At the same time, since these are God's inspired, authoritative writings, we are assured the Scriptures will express his intentions for us, reveal our salvation, guide our living and give birth to our hope. We believe that these human-shaped writings are simultaneously enveloped with God's presence and that they will impart that presence to us by giving us his word. We have confidence that God will be "with us" in the Bible—to instruct us, direct us, change us. The written Word of God will be seen as closely aligned with the living Word of God who also came to be among us, uniting human and divine in a similar way.

Once this rich, profound and mysterious view of the Bible is welcomed, it will be incumbent on us to fully accept the Bible we actually find. Having refused to refashion the Bible into something we find more useful or accessible (but something it really isn't), we will squarely face the Bible as it is and receive it. And what is it we will find there? Many things, but at the center is the narrative of God's people Israel *as they lived in the ancient world*. Here we may immediately hesitate, since the authors, the audience and the subject of the Bible are all on the face of it rather foreign to us. Thus it is a crucial step to authentic Bible engagement to willingly immerse ourselves in the Bible as a crosscultural and even transhistorical experience. Which means that it's not necessarily easy.

We have to resist the impulse to anachronistic reading at every step. What does the Bible say about marriage? Economics? The creation of the world? Anything else we're interested in? In all these cases and more we intuitively want the Bible to speak directly to us. But it doesn't. It spoke directly to its original audience (and not as an easily-indexed handbook of religious topics either). It speaks indirectly to us. What it says about anything and everything it says in the language, literary forms and patterns of thought common to ancient worldviews and cultures. Does it challenge and transform many of these things even as it uses and reflects them? Most certainly. Ancient views of marriage, economics, creation and all the rest are both reflected and changed by the word of God in the sacred writings. But they are manifestly not addressed from our present-day point of view. Reading our questions, expectations, science and ways of viewing the world into the Bible is to reject the revelation God has chosen to give us. The way God has chosen to speak to these and all human struggles is not to give us answers lifted out of time, place, culture and historical setting. That would be something closer to the goals of Greek philosophy or the European Enlightenment. The Bible has something universal to say, but it will only say it through the very down-to-earth story of one particular tribe of people struggling to make its way in an old Mediterranean world.

The whole Bible is for us, even if it wasn't written to us. But appropriating the message for ourselves, now, means first doing the necessary due diligence on what the message was for others, then. The temptation is ever before us to short-circuit this step. We're eager to make the connection to our lives and our concerns. And of course this is appropriately our goal—few of us read the Bible merely because of our passionate interest in history for its own sake. But if we skip the crucial first step of historical understanding, the connection we find will be the wrong one. Accepting the Historical Bible means reading the Bible its own way. There is a promise that the Bible will speak to more than its original audience, but the promise is best realized when we honor what God's Spirit has inspired in the first place.

CAN GOD REALLY BE FOUND IN THIS KIND OF BOOK?

If the Bible is this kind of historical book, and we are called to respect the historical nature of the Bible, how is it that we can expect to find God revealed in such a thing? A historically honest reading of the Bible can start to sound more like an academic exercise than a spiritual journey. But the Bible claims to have a continuing voice, and the promise still holds. It's worth noting that since the collection of books in the Bible covers such a large expanse of time, we can see others face this issue within the Bible itself. At several points within the story we see people looking back and struggling to understand and apply what had already become foreign territory to them. When Ezra stood on a high platform and read publically from the Book of the Law of God to the returned exiles gathered there, the Levites had to circulate among the people "making it clear and giving the meaning so that the people understood what was being read" (The book of Nehemiah in the section on the reading of the law, right before Nehemiah's great prayer of repentance and just following the genealogical lists.) The point is that the promise will be made good when we attend well to the true nature of the writings.

We have to be honest at this point and acknowledge that a full embrace of the Historical Bible will present us with new challenges. Ancient historiography operated by different rules than our history writing today. We are regularly tempted to read our history-writing standards back into the Bible as if the ancients thought about history the same way we do. But it is not so. Anachronism is a constant danger with our Bible reading. But it also remains possible to use historical readings to create such a distance that the Bible becomes a book we can't even recognize, or to use them to so radically deconstruct the books that essential elements of the story disappear completely. There may have been an overblown fear of historical study of the Bible in our past, but that doesn't mean there aren't real dangers here. Historical study, like any other approach to the Bible, can be misplayed.

However, we shouldn't underestimate the gifts of the Historical Bible. First Testament scholar Peter Enns rightly claims that it is a positive thing that the Bible is so connected to our world. "How *else* would you have expected God to speak?" he asks. "In ways wholly *disconnected* to the ancient world? Who would have understood him?"[4] It is a measure of God's commitment to us that he expresses his voice through the means by which the world regularly communicates. Here is some of what we stand to gain from a steady appreciation of and commitment to a historical reading of the Scriptures:

First, the Historical Bible highlights for us the progressive nature of God's revelation. It is through history that we learn to avoid reading the Bible as a flat book as if it's all the same and all its truth is equally distributed throughout. In fact, as Geerhardus Vos describes in an address he gave upon becoming the inaugural professor of biblical theology at Princeton Seminary, "The elements of truth, far from being mechanically added one to the other in lifeless succession, are seen to grow out of each other, each richer and fuller disclosure of the knowledge of God having been prepared for by what preceded, and being in its turn preparatory for what follows."[5] As the Bible progresses book by book, the intentions of God are slowly unveiled. For Vos this helps us grasp the multifaceted wisdom of God in a more organic way, as opposed to some collection of "abstract propositions logically correlated and systematized."[6] It is the Historical Bible that teaches us to read and interpret the Scriptures in a way true to its ever-increasing light.

Second, the Historical Bible can serve as a major corrective when our theology gets off track. I've already argued that non-historical readings—in which we put our own concerns first and then go searching for the answers in the text—are our constant temptation. Fall to them and it's possible to massively misunderstand the meaning of the text. If someone is determined to ignore the first steps of historical understanding and carry on as if the choice of literary form by the Bible's authors doesn't matter, everything from that point on can go wrong, crazy wrong.

At a particular point in Israel's history apocalyptic literature came to be well known and regularly used. These apocalypses followed certain well-defined conventions that those who wrote and those who read both agreed to follow. To write all this off today as esoteric academic nitpicking is to invite disaster. Carefully constructed and highly symbolic visions of first-century struggles with government-sponsored persecution will be read straight off the page as accurate and literal descriptions of modern weaponry and the latest political news. Or the details of the visionary descriptions of the New Jerusalem will be taken as the wrong kind of gospel truth, and preachers, teachers and even gone-there-and-back-from-the-dead travelers will regale us with tales of pearly gates and streets of gold. Meanwhile, the actual point of what the Bible is trying to say will be missed. Good historical diligence will help spare us these and other false readings of the Bible.

It's not only supposed prophetic words about our future that need vetting. Core theological questions sometimes get skewed because we're not used to reading biblical texts according to their patterns of thought. The burning issues of biblical times don't always immediately align with what we think should be important in the text. For example, we have placed front and center the question of how individual sinners gain a right standing before a holy God. Some passages we thought were talking about this turned out to be struggling with how Jews and Gentiles can get together to become the new family of God.

Or, to take another case, we have long thought that salvation meant going to heaven when we die and that this is what Jesus was referring to in his teaching on the kingdom of heaven. But historical study of the setting and language of first-century Judaism helped us learn that biblical salvation has a much richer and broader redemption of the whole cosmos in mind, and that the kingdom is a hope for God's will to invade the earth, and not for flying away to some other place.

New Testament historian N. T. Wright reminds us that "we cannot assume that by saying the word *Jesus*, still less the word *Christ*, we are automatically in touch with the real Jesus who walked and talked in first-century Palestine, the Jesus who, according to the letter to the Hebrews, is the same yesterday, today and forever. We are not at liberty to manufacture a different Jesus."[7] Wright's impressive multivolume series Christian Origins and the Question of God can be taken as an extended, passionate argument that if we wish to be true to the vision of "a reformed church ever reforming," there is no better aid than constantly testing our would-be orthodox and evangelical biblical interpretations by the Historical Bible.[8]

Finally, the Historical Bible definitively shows us that God is right here with us, talking to us in our own place in the way we usually talk. He does not make us go somewhere else or learn some otherworldly heavenly language in order to understand his message. That message and the salvation it aids and announces both happen in and through our history, our story, our world. Trying to avoid history is to turn away from what God is doing in the world. Not taking seriously the historical nature of the Bible allows us to embrace a view of salvation that puts off God's redemption to another time and another place. But it is *our story here* that he is working to restore, therefore his communication to us is also through *our story here.*

Vos reminds us that in the Bible's story God has already planted the seeds of new creation within this world. "God's method is . . . that of creating within the organism of the present world the center of the world of redemption, and then organically building up the new order of things around this center."[9] So we must attend to the Historical Bible lest we misunderstand those seeds of the new world in our midst, or even miss seeing them altogether. Without the Historical Bible we don't have the word made flesh—we have only a mere idea in our minds (that we get from somewhere else). A Bible rooted in history matters because it happens in the place God created for us and in the story he has written for us.

The miraculous imposition of rainbows in the sky by some kind of magical zapping procedure would perhaps produce a certain kind of wonder, but it is an entirely different thing to realize that God is present and working, not from outside this world, but from within it; that God is there as the light hits the molecules of water and scatters into all the colors of the world, and that right in the midst of all that scattering and all that color God is making promises—this is the bigger wonder. We don't need magic or surprises from other realms falling from the sky into our laps. At the end of the day, we need to know that God is at work in our story, right here where we live.

> No one will be able to handle the Word of God more effectually than he to whom the treasure-chambers of its historic meaning have been opened up. It is this that brings the divine truth so near to us, makes it as it were bone of our bone and flesh of our flesh, that humanizes it in the same sense that the highest revelation in Christ was rendered most human by the incarnation. To this historical character of revelation we owe the fullness and variety which enable the Scriptures to mete out new treasures to all ages without becoming exhausted or even fully explored.[10]

With these words Geerhardus Vos encourages us to embrace the depth of God's "treasure-chambers" in the Historical Bible. God has humanized his truth. He doesn't want it to appear ultimately alien to us, but rather as "bone of our bone and flesh of our flesh." Historical truth is a truth we can touch, a truth we can know. This is what it means to effectively handle the Bible.

CONCLUSION

Timeless is not a word that captures the meaning of the Historical Bible. It's not really timeless truth that we need or should seek. What will really speak to us and reveal a God who has determined to be with us in the world is time-*full* truth. We need a Word of God that's full and overflowing with time, including the time we live in. Timelessness is not a human language. Timelessness speaks of leaving our story and of merely escaping this often-tortured time rather than healing it. We should be more interested in what God is interested in, that is, in what's happening in this age as God's new world has come ashore and staked a claim to the whole land, and in the world-age to come, when God will be all in all.

The Bible bypasses any idea of static, unchanging "eternity" in favor of the more robust, interesting and creational language of "ages"—past, present and future. The Bible presents a vision of life full of time, life with all the time in the world. It is a vision of history redeemed.

The three Bibles we have explored so far bring us to the center of our chiasm and the heart of this book. An elegant, accessible, and uncomplicated format of the Bible enables us to reengage with all of the content of the Bible holistically. When we do so, we discover the Historical Bible. God speaks to us within time through the events of the ongoing narrative of his people. What is this story the Bible tells? To find out, we must recover the Storiented Bible. A narrative orientation will help us learn where history has been, where it's going and how we can come along for the ride. This, first and foremost, is what the Scriptures are trying to do: they are inviting us to take up our own roles within the community of the new creation. We are being called to enter the story. We will know the Bible is being saved when more and more people understand this and respond to the Bible accordingly.

seven

OUR DE-DRAMATIZED BIBLE

*Metaphysical systems have not been able to maintain
the intellectual life of our community and abstract systems
of morality have not conveyed devotion and the power
of obedience with their ideals and imperatives.*

H. RICHARD NIEBUHR

The Teacher was the Son of David, king in Jerusalem, and he spoke to the
people about what it's like to run in circles, chasing the wind and expending
a lot of effort to no avail:

> What do people gain from all their labors
> at which they toil under the sun?
> Generations come and generations go,
> but the earth remains forever.
> The sun rises and the sun sets,
> and hurries back to where it rises.
> The wind blows to the south
> and turns to the north;
> round and round it goes,
> ever returning on its course.
> All streams flow into the sea,
> yet the sea is never full.
> To the place the streams come from,

there they return again.
All things are wearisome,
more than one can say.
The eye never has enough of seeing,
nor the ear its fill of hearing.
What has been will be again,
what has been done will be done again;
there is nothing new under the sun.
Is there anything of which one can say,
"Look! This is something new"?
It was here already, long ago;
it was here before our time.
No one remembers the former generations,
and even those yet to come
will not be remembered
by those who follow them.
(The opening reflection of the book of Ecclesiastes)

The Teacher was Jewish, and his book of musings about our vaporous lives is ultimately reflective of a Jewish point of view. In the end he tells us that someone is watching everything carefully, and that we will all be called to account for our efforts, wearisome or not. But this poem that launches the book sounds more like what the rest of the ancient world thought of things. Here, in what Thomas Cahill calls "the world of the Wheel," the philosophies, worldviews and religions found uniformly across the globe determined that there isn't really any meaningful history.[1] There is only the ever-turning and returning biological cycle of birth and aging, growth and decline. This is the circle of life, which could just as well be called the circle of death, since each returns as frequently as the other. This is why sacred copulation rites were so common: whatever forces in heaven or on earth were responsible for generation and regeneration had to be coaxed and cajoled and even modeled into doing their part once more. The tribe had to eat and the tribe had to be constantly reborn. Fertility was the key to the Great Circle.

What people everywhere consistently saw was the world-go-round going by again and again. Sun to moon, day to night, back and forth, forth and back. Rainy seasons, dry seasons, crops coming, harvests collected, and on and on. Ever it had been, and ever it will be ever the same.

Until. As Cahill tells the tale of how tales came to be in the first place, it was the Jews who broke the cycle, disrupted the circle and began to tell real stories. Linear narrative. Movement beyond mere repetition. This event connected with that event in a way that didn't merely turn back on itself in the Wheel, but began to genuinely move forward. Speaking of the way the very old-world Sumerians tried to tell even little everyday dramas, Cahill says "their stories miss a sense of development: they begin in the middle and end in the middle."[2] So this is the gift of the Jews to the world: a timeline of history that said it was all going somewhere it had never been before. Not just back again to the same old place, but somewhere *new*. This is a fine gift indeed, and it is a gift contained in our Bible. It offers a reading of the events of the world and of our lives as a genuine story. A series of "and thens" connect in a meaningful way, headed toward a purpose, a goal, a *telos*.

But as often happens with fine gifts, this one has been underappreciated and at times, sadly, its value even completely unrecognized. How did we manage to untell the story of the Bible?

How to Memento the Bible

Leonard Shelby had lost his way for the simple reason that he could no longer remember his own story. In the film *Memento* (2000), Leonard suffers from anterograde amnesia, which blocks his ability to register and record the continuing events of his life. Without new memories being added to and connecting with his intact older memories, Leonard forgets who he is on an ongoing basis. The only way he maintains some sense of a thread is to fill his life with mementos—Post-it notes affixed to walls and mirrors, Polaroid photos of people he is supposed to know, tattoos with numbers and messages stamped all over his body. They are always there to remind him of who he is and what he's trying to do with his life (avenge his wife's murder). Every new day, several times a day, he studies them in the attempt to keep his life anchored to some kind of meaning.

But mementos can only do so much. They function best as symbols or stand-ins of well-remembered events and grand occasions. Alone and out of context, they can easily fail to do their job. And so it was for Leonard.

His mementos give him slices of a story, but not the real thing. Imagine walking into a stranger's bedroom and seeing the stub of a concert ticket on a bulletin board, a photo of a young woman, a newspaper clipping about someone receiving an award from the local sheriff's office. Do you know these people? What do these things mean? Are they tied together somehow? Why are they significant?

It is the gaps between mementos that make all the difference between sense and chaos. It is only the full story with all its texture and detail and glue that can fill in the gaps and transform mementos into meaning. Stand-alone mementos are subject to varying interpretations, and Leonard has various people in his life trying to sway his understanding of his own story. The single thread that should be Leonard's life is now frayed and nearly impossible to follow. It all ends up confused, and people get hurt. How could it not end up confused? Mementos are not stories, and they cannot function independently of them. As free-standing bits of information they are as likely to mislead as to reveal.

And so it is that a Memento Bible misleads and confuses so many of us. We too function with ongoing memory loss, though it is not our own stories we've misplaced but rather the Bible's. We seek to compensate for this loss with well-intentioned reminders scattered around the places of our lives. We wake up to discover these small ornamental samplings of Scripture instructing and encouraging us through our day. No doubt each individual sacred memento can be packed with individual significance for us. We manage to assemble them in such a way that we can create a kind of personal meaning from them. We gather these keepsakes and souvenirs, pinning them up on our walls (both physical and virtual) so we won't forget their importance.

But the kind of Bible memory we really need is not so much the short Post-it notes variety of this verse or that, inspirational Polaroids, or tattoos of Bible references, but rather the deep, connected narrative remembrance born of long immersion in the world of the text. Only the story that weaves through the whole canon will fill in the gaps between our Bible mementos: What do these pieces of information mean? Are they connected? Why are they significant? A de-dramatized Bible takes away the opportunity to find the full answers to these questions. The pieces are subject to varying interpretations most often taken directly from our own setting and context as replacements for the story they actually came from.

In many ways this is the same story we saw of how the Complicated Bible unsurprisingly introduces the Snacking Bible. When the form of the Bible is piecemealed, it is to pieces that we naturally turn. It takes an intentional effort to read right over the embedded visual signals and stop signs of a traffic-control Bible and then transform its collection of rules, directions and propositions into a grand narrative. Our antifeasting formats do double duty as antistory presentations, just as our antifeasting practices diminish the chance that we will appreciate the whole drama. Distracted, impatient, disjointed and self-oriented ventures into the Bible do not unveil the big things God has done, is doing and has in store for us. Small readings deconstruct the metanarrative, leaving us with mere smatterings of the record of God's mighty acts and surprising ways.

In his book *The Eclipse of Biblical Narrative*, Hans Frei has detailed how academic and philosophical views of the Bible in the eighteenth and nineteenth centuries turned away from realistic readings based in the world of the text and so lost the ability to take seriously the narrative of the Scriptures.[3] This move among scholars was mirrored in the life of the Bible within the church. With the standardization of a chapter and verse Bible and the spread of a modernist mindset focused on dissection and detailed analysis as the path to both knowledge and inspiration, small readings became the norm. These small readings could be doctrinal or pietistic, systematized as theologies or serialized as daily devotions, but either way the turn was away from reading the collection as a coherent and compelling narration of God and his world. And so for many, theologian and lay reader alike, the Bible's larger plot was lost. The gift of the Jews was squandered and replaced by Sumerian-like scraps that "begin in the middle and end in the middle."

The swerve in modern cultural history was toward atomistic thinking.[4] Close analysis of the pieces was seen as the gateway to new understanding. Immediately after the Reformation and the appearance of the Reformation's Bible, this trend was applied to the holy writings by splitting and separating the recently demarcated verses from each other and reconstructing them into new systems of religious truth. As we have moved in some ways from a modern to a postmodern (hypermodern?) way of imagining things, the ongoing atomistic impulse is rarely expressed anymore by cutting out Bible building blocks and stacking them into massive doctrinal structures. The predominant interest is now to apply the small readings to me and my interior world. The focus is personal benefit–centered rather than doctrinal system–centered.

Frei describes how "emphasis" became a technical term in pietism for "a way of seeing a meaning of scriptural words quite beyond what they appear to have in ordinary usage or in their immediate context."[5] The desire was to discover the spiritual sense beyond the grammatical-historical, a sense revealed to the reader now by the same Spirit who inspired the Bible in the first place. In this way of Bible reading "what the text says to me" became preeminent. It's important to note that this isn't a discernment of the first meaning of the words followed by an effort to have them speak today also. No, this well-intentioned and warm-hearted procedure is an attempt to go directly, without mediation, from the text to me. This pietistic approach only works when you're taking in very short readings. The more you read, the harder it is to pretend the message was written directly to you today. This and other common techniques for extracting meaning from the Bible represent failures to understand what the Bible essentially is.

It's clear that inspirational, moralistic and even doctrinal Bible keepsakes and snapshots will continue to be mined from the text with the hope that these scraps of meaning will be enough to live on yet another day. It is doubtful, however, that when God gave us the Bible his intention was for us to cut and paste sacred souvenirs from it while leaving the story itself far behind.

LOSING OUR WAW

Without connections there are no stories. Stories essentially make the claim that one experience, one event, one thing, is related to the next one that follows it. Stories are series of links that posit meaning. Good storytelling can build these links in ways that expectantly and pleasingly move from what is to what could be. Good storytelling follows well-worn paths from introductions and settings to tension and conflict to rising action and climax to peace-extending resolutions. Good stories rise and fall and rise again. Our stories are built on these journeys from daylight through darkest nights into new dawns. We want these stories. We live off of these stories. Whatever new media we invent we immediately populate with these stories. These stories are our sine qua non.

The Bible gives us significant and meaningful links beyond anything ever imagined in the world. Rather than nameless, faceless, soon-to-be-fertilizer people taking up temporary space in the circle of life, the Bible gives us Avram and Sara, their son Yitzhak and grandson Yaakov who becomes Yisrael. YHWH appeared once to Avram, making promises about a storied future. YHWH's presence passed between the split halves of a heifer, a goat and a ram, saying, in essence, *If I don't do what I said I would do for you, let me become like these sliced-up animals.* A deity who makes self-maledictory oaths contingent on his yet-to-be actions is a deity who is serious about story. A little later Yaakov had his name changed because he struggled with God— and then God made more promises. In fact, YHWH tells each and every one of them to look over the horizon for what is to come. That is what story does. It gives us promises. And this is something the Wheel knows nothing about. We need a "relentlessly narratival" Bible because that is the only Bible that can give people like us hope.[6]

In his lively and remarkably insightful little book *The Return of the Chaos Monsters*, Gregory Mobley relates that the first battle in the Bible—and one good way to view the entire master narrative in the Bible—is the struggle against chaos.[7] This battle is introduced in the very first words of the Bible, before any human characters even appear on stage. There YHWH takes on the powers of *tohu wa bohu* ("formlessness and emptiness") and begins to shape and fill the creation so that it will function and flourish. Chaos is not completely eliminated, however, but pushed to the edges of the world's borders, ever threatening to return and wreak its havoc. Later, when humans show up, God immediately enlists them to partner with him in the management of chaos, giving them the tough love of moral cause and effect and eventually Torah and then prophets.[8]

Profoundly, Mobley claims that the first powerful weapon against chaos is story itself:

> Narratives create chains of events bound by cause and effect along a timeline, allowing us to pin down a story before it slips away. Once a story is told, the chaos of experience assumes shape, direction, motive, and episodes. *This led*

to that which led to this which led to that.... We no longer have chaos; we have meaning and order.[9]

Hebrew stories are built, says Mobley, on the rather plain element of syntax known as the *waw consecutive*, translated "and then." This *and then* that *and then* something new *and then . . .* lo and behold, a story is born.[10] This simple connector is the genesis of what turned out to be our biggest dreams and most moving visions. We want to believe in life beyond the Wheel, something more substantial than come and go, come and go, ad infinitum nauseam. The *waw consecutive* gave us the future.

That is why losing the Bible as a narrative was in a very real sense losing not only our *waw* but our way. To lose story, to try and read the Bible in some other, lesser manner is to lose the connections between things. Pieces of teaching and wisdom and law and praise and lament and the telling of individual events were never meant to stand aloof, disconnected from each other. A de-dramatized Bible is a static Bible, and static is not alive. Our popular "timeless truth" language completely fails to capture the sense of story that is central for the Bible, as well as its embeddedness in real history. A de-dramatized Bible, because it ignores or severs links of meaning that story provides, can open the door to chaos. We may have all these pieces of truth, but how do they fit together into a coherent life? Where are these pieces of truth going?

This is why so many of our contemporary strategies for engaging the Bible fail. Looking things up in the Bible like a handbook, as if it were all the same anywhere you look, is to delete all those "and thens." A true "and then" gives real movement to the story. Everything that comes before is an earlier part of the story and contextualized differently. Everything after an "and then" is genuinely later and therefore different in myriad ways. Are there threads of connection in the story and characteristics of faithfulness and continuity over time? Yes. Is the Bible a flat and lifeless list of *what forever is* from the divine point of view? No. The story of the Bible is the ongoing interplay between a faithful God and his unstable children. This is what used to be called progressive revelation, but can be even more helpfully identified as the dramatic movement of a story.

We can't be biblicists and treat the Bible like a handy reference book for looking up infallible answers to all our questions because as we go from

Numbers to Isaiah to Luke to Titus things change and we get to new places. The "and then" doesn't only work within particular narratives to get us from this event to the next one, it also works between the books of the Bible. Genesis *and then* Exodus. As the story unfolds, new twists and turns become clear and some of them supersede and negate what came before. There are both recurring patterns and genuine surprises. Because God created our world and always intended to interact with us meaningfully within it, the record of his revelation in the Bible *moves along with us*. If the Bible came to us within human history and wants ultimately to change the course of that history, it has no choice but to be story. Because story is where we live.

Several authors who've written about the importance of reading the Bible as a story have made the sobering point that because we ourselves are "relentlessly narratival," if we don't get our story from the Bible, we will end up fitting pieces of the Bible into a story we've picked up from somewhere else. We have no choice but to live our lives as a narrative that fits into some bigger narrative that we believe makes sense of the world. We know well enough the nationalist, consumerist, narcissist and many other stories that vie for our imaginations and seek to colonize our desires. It is imperative that we be intentional about the kind of overall story we seek to live out.

Regarding theology, its connection to story and how we go about developing it, N. T. Wright says, "To be truly Christian, [theology] must show that it includes the story which the Bible tells, and the sub-stories within it. Without this, it lapses into a mere ad hoc use of the Bible, finding bits and pieces to fit into a scheme derived from somewhere else."[11] Craig Bartholomew and Michael Goheen make a similar point:

> Many of us have read the Bible as if it were merely a mosaic of little bits—theological bits, moral bits, historical-critical bits, sermon bits, devotional bits. But when we read the Bible in such a fragmented way, we ignore its divine author's intention to shape our lives through its story. All human communities live out of some story that provides a context for understanding the meaning of history and gives shape and direction to their lives. If we allow the Bible to become fragmented, it is in danger of being absorbed into whatever *other* story is shaping our culture, and it will thus cease to shape our lives as it should.[12]

If we don't allow the divine drama to provide meaningful links between the various elements of our lives—events, experiences, actions, beliefs, longings—then some other narrative will gladly take its place and the Bible will be relegated to a lesser, subservient role. It is crucial that we knowingly and intentionally find our connections in God's own story.

HERE WE STAND, AS STORIED CREATURES WE CAN DO NO OTHER

Story is our home, the place we always want to be. If someone tries to take away our story, or we lose it through brain trauma, we will immediately begin to reconstruct a new one. There is nothing quite so disconcerting to human creatures as a feeling of ongoing randomness or true chaos. We relentlessly try to connect the dots of our experiences. We want to make sense, and if necessary we will manufacture significance. It may not always be a good, healthy or life-affirming meaning we find in our stories, but it is meaning that we unavoidably seek. Whether we ultimately believe we are living a comedy or a tragedy, we will necessarily construct a narrative of our lives. British literary scholar Barbara Hardy tells us that "we dream in narrative, day-dream in narrative, remember, anticipate, hope, despair, believe, doubt, plan, revise, criticize, construct, gossip, learn, hate and love by narrative."[13] We just can't help ourselves.

That story is our real home and at the core of what it means to be human should have been all the clue we needed that of course God would speak to us in it. Why would he have hidden his purpose in the chaff of all these narratives in the Bible if what he really wanted us to do was fundamentally reconfigure the character of the Bible into something different? To skip the story and find the doctrinal truths buried here and there? Merely obey the commands and follow the instructions? Reduce the Bible to a topical reference book? Scan the Bible for the small readings that seem to speak directly to me and my needs today without all that intervening bother of those strange people and their strange lives way back then? We should have known better. The abandonment of story in the modernist attempt to make sense of the Bible is one of the biggest mistakes God's people have made with the Scriptures in the entire history of the church. As we will see, it is precisely the narrative character of the Bible that allows us to make an authentic connection between these ancient writings and our own lives.

The Bible's story welcomes us to be true human beings—creatures, yes, but creatures who image the divine and who have received from God the gift of this earth. We learn early on in the Bible that the world is ours to run, to shape, to manage, to rule. And we learn later on in the story that we are to do so as servant-leaders in the pattern of our self-sacrificing King Jesus. This is where the power for transformation in the Bible really lies. The Scriptures change us by giving us a new understanding of what all our "and thens" are supposed to be about. The Scriptures change us because the story they tell is infused with the power of Jesus and the Spirit, who bring renewal. This is what we should mean when we say that the Word of God has power. It's not that each little scrap is a kind of magic rune or potent piece of juju. The power is in the drama as it witnesses to Christ and invites us to enter into his journey of new life.

We are lords of creation and when we read the Bible well we start to see the world in fresh perspective. We ourselves become new creations, and then we become agents of new creation. We begin to live a completely different story. This is manifestly a better story than our own attempts to discover or impose meaning on the events of our lives. It's a story that never ceases to surprise, even as we see how fittingly it unfolds. But all of this is defeated and lost if we deconstruct and de-dramatize the Bible. That is why we must decisively reject subpar piecemealing presentations and understandings of the Bible. The saving narrative of the Bible with all of its intentions to subvert and unravel its rivals to world-rule is at stake.

The centerpiece of our recovery of the Bible, and the heart of the chiasm of this book, is the rejection of the rejection of narrative. We need to re-orient ourselves, set aside our insistence that the Bible be what we have predetermined it must be in order to be useful for us, and inhabit the more humble stance that will patiently receive whatever it is that the Bible offers. And what it offers in its totality as a collection of unique literary compositions is the Story. The words of the Word create a new world. These words break in and deconstruct in order to reconstruct. Not all at once (that would be creation-rejecting timeless intervention), but slowly and deliberately as God unveils within the present order of things what the new order of things will look like. The kingdom grows like a seed. This new Story of stories does not reject the world because it has become crooked, but comes into the distorted places of human lives and our various lies and mistellings so it can set the record straight.

Our sore temptation has been to change the Bible in order to make it of more practical help, which has lead us into all kinds of Bible debacles. We've shown a determined insistence to impose on the text when what we were asked to do was sit still and listen attentively. We've been trying for several centuries now to make Christianity work as something other than a story. The recent return to narrative theology should be seen not as one more scholarly fad or passing theory, but as a crucial recovery of the fundamental nature of the Scriptures. A story orientation toward the Bible is one of the ways we humbly receive the Bible as the kind of gift God chose to give us.

- eight -

REDISCOVERING THE STORIENTED BIBLE

*There is no "world" for us until we have named
and languaged and storied whatever is.*

AMOS WILDER

N. T. Wright positively insists that the New Testament "must be read so that the stories, and the Story, which it tells can be heard *as* stories, not as rambling ways of declaring unstoried 'ideas.' . . . And, for full appropriateness, it must be read in such a way as to set in motion the drama which it suggests."[1] This is the center of our journey to saving the Bible, the great alternative to our long-term attempt to escape from narrative and force fit the Bible into some other mold. Wright advises us to read the Bible as a story and then set it in motion as a drama. Story, then drama. These must be taken up in order.

I have made the case that the first thing to do with the Bible is to read its books as the unique compositions they are and fully engage the unique message each brings. Reading holistically like this is best and most easily done with an Elegant Bible that uses good design to simply and pleasingly present the books in their natural form. But whether cooperatively with the Elegant Bible or in tension with the cluttered Complicated Bible, we must begin our Bible forays by reading well the whole books that are the central intentional units of the Bible's inspired authors. This kind of Bible feasting will indeed feed us well. For one thing, it's almost impossible to read whole books without facing squarely the fact that the Bible is rooted in real history. Reading whole books immerses us in the very thing that verse-jacking pretends doesn't exist—the Bible's "strange new world" and the "alternative world of the text."[2]

READING WELL: FROM BITS TO BOOKS TO STORY

Reading whole books of the Bible functions as the preliminary act to the main event. This is because the biggest thing to do with the Bible is to read its overall story as *the Story*, and to do so with such regularity and in such depth that we can begin to reimagine our personal and community stories as part of its world-restoring drama. This has little to do with the patchwork assemblage of Bible verses we've been attempting to survive on. This has much to do with rediscovering the narrative that's been waiting to be set free to do its work of subverting all the other metanarratives trying to run the world. Those buckets of Scripture McNuggets we've been snacking on find their rightful meaning as contributors to the messages of books, and books in turn progressively reveal the grand story. Through this story the Bible comes into its own to confront, judge, invite, redeem, save and transform. As we continually feast on whole books, the story will emerge with greater and greater clarity. And with clarity comes both understanding and invitation. We will begin to understand what God is doing, and we will be invited to join him.

This is the path to rediscovering the Storiented Bible. We eat whole books and then intentionally read them *together*. That is, we read them as unique contributors to a growing narrative. To be sure, there are many voices in the Scriptures, and sometimes they seem to say, "Yes, but . . ." to one another. The reason the assembly of Christ-followers brought them together into the canon is that they found in them a witness to Jesus that legitimately binds them to each other. It's not a superficial or forced connection, but a deep narrative bond that holds the books of the Bible in relationship. The narrative prepares the way for Jesus, reveals him and then unveils the vision of the cosmic, peace-extending implications of his great work. So as we read the books we pay attention to how later ones build on earlier ones, expanding or nuancing or sharpening our understanding of God's mission to the world as it develops through Israel's history. We listen closely to how the books dialogue with each other. The more we read the more attuned we become to echoes and allusions, the deep repeating patterns in the story. We don't think of these books as standalone manifestos but as escalating acts in a drama.

There are several ways to find connections that hold the books together. There is, first of all, the way we structure groups of books together. This arrangement has not had much influence lately, given the piecemeal nature of our interaction with the Bible: Who cares about the order or grouping of the books if the ongoing business of the day is looking up verses? But as we recover big readings of the Bible, we will likewise rediscover the importance of book order for reading in context.[3] Second, we will also recognize that the Bible ties its own pieces together by reference to a set of increasingly focused covenants between God and humanity. These move progressively from the universal to the more specific, ultimately in the service of regaining the universal. When this all comes together as a single story, we can identify the decisive, major movements of the narrative, allowing us to helpfully name the key acts of the overall drama.

Although we're used to thinking of the order of the books as a fixture, the history of the Bible reveals a great variety of books orders. The pattern, in the case of both the First Testament and the New, was to settle the major groupings of books pretty early on, even as there continued to be significant variety of individual book orders within those larger sets. Thus, the First Testament quickly became a three-part set of Torah, Prophets and Writings. The New Testament came together as a collection of Gospels, Paul's letters and then General Epistles. Following this overall pattern and thinking about the relations between the groups can be our first guide to discovering the shape of the emerging narrative.

THE BIG STORY OF THE BIBLE

The great covenant history that extends from Genesis all the way to Samuel-Kings is bookended with accounts of the people of God exiled from his presence and his paradise, first Eden and then the garden-temple land of Israel. It's here we discover the great foundations of the story that the author has put in place. The setting of the drama and the focal point of the action is in God's good creation. The story will be won or lost here, in our realm.

In the beginning of the biblical narrative, Genesis presents the creation itself as God's temple, his intended dwelling place, and also as a home for all creatures, including humans.[4] These creatures have their appropriate roles and places within God's world. The divine image–bearing humans, however, are given the unique position of reflecting God's own care and rule over the creation. But they open the door to the darkness and throw the world back into chaos. The rebellion comes early in the story, so the greater portion of the Bible is taken up with presenting God's response—his plan, his struggle, his saving restoration of all that he had in mind when he launched the production in the first place.

The name of this divine response is Israel. The foundational history of the Bible quickly shows us that God is relentless in his intention to partner with humans in managing the world, and for this particular project he will focus on the descendants of Avram. And so the establishment, the rescue, the vocation, the failures and the restoration of Israel become the focus of this opening section of the Bible. God promises that the decisive turning point of the story for everyone will somehow come through this special tribe, reluctant as they are to step into their calling. God binds himself to them in a series of covenants, each one propelling the story forward while also narrowing God's focus and revealing more about how the great restoration will actually take place. The covenants move from God's relationship with the earth to establishing the people of Israel to making promises to Israel's royal line, until there finally seems to be a word about a particular king who is to come.

The point of all this choosing and favoring should never be forgotten (though it seems to be forgotten precisely by the chosen ones throughout the whole story): election is a means of regaining the life of the world. The overall Israel shape of the Bible's founding narrative compels me to say that anyone who talks about the message of the Bible for any length of time without talking about Israel is not taking the narrative of the Bible seriously. But legion are the number who try to negate or ignore this and turn the Bible into a general treatise on the divine-human relationship. The various expressions of the well-known evangelical "plan of salvation" are perhaps the clearest example. Amid all the steps to personal repentance, Israel has vanished. But gospel, covenant, kingdom, and indeed, salvation itself—none of these or other key biblical terms can be properly understood without reference to Avram's descendants. For God has determined that it is through Israel that the entire narrative will do its work.

Next in the canon come the words of YHWH's prophets, presented as a form of divine commentary on the history that preceded them.[5] Mobley reminds us that as covenant caseworkers, the prophets were YHWH's attempt at an intervention with Israel when the people have balked at the standard methods of chaos management—regular Torah observance and authentic, prescribed worship.[6] The prophets' role in the developing story is dual: as Israel's story degenerated, the prophets urged the people back to shalom-producing obedience and warned of the dire consequences of continued failure, and then, when that failure was assured, they announced that God was not yet done with the story. In a series of future mighty acts he would not only judge but also rescue and restore according to the model of his earlier salvation in the exodus. In this way the collection of the prophets sets up the story to come. It teaches us the crucial point that later movements will echo earlier key events.

The group of writings that follow in the canon might seem like an oddball kind of collection. There are gatherings of songs, a variety of wisdom books, the strange and wonderful book of Daniel and even an alternative telling of Israel's history that emphasizes not the rule of kings but rather worship in the temple. How does all this fit into the storyline? Most importantly, the Writings add color and texture to this narrative. While not narrative in form for the most part, the Writings keep the story grounded in the realities of daily life. They find their proper meaning as expressions of the ongoing story and contributors to the story in other ways. They reveal what it's like to live this story in action. Wedding songs and celebrations of the delight of physical beauty and lovemaking sit next to wails of lament when the story goes way wrong. Exclamations of temple praise and worship combine with earthy words of wisdom about hard work and difficult neighbors. There is even some serious questioning of the core covenant premise (both Ecclesiastes and Job wonder out loud how those who do good can end up on the wrong side of things). In case we were tempted to believe this drama was somehow above it all, a nice and tidy tale of God's good work and the unwavering progress of the coming salvation, or some kind of merely theoretical narrative, the Writings keep it honest.

The Bible's three-part Covenant History (the Torah and Former Prophets), Prophets and Writings combine to tell us what we need to know about the launch of the story of God and the world. Whatever else we do with the Bible, we cannot cut off the First Testament foundation from the rest of the building. Insufficient comprehension of the connection and continuity of the two major sections of the story (for example, to read the New as only a word of no to the First) puts the narrative in jeopardy. Some in the early Christian era tried this approach, but they were condemned as heretics. Today, few are so bold as to openly announce that they have no use for the First Testament, but an almost complete avoidance is a widespread practice.

Turning to the groups of books in the New Testament, the nature of the unbreakable bond between the two major parts of the Bible is made clear. All four of the ancient tellings of the life and work of Jesus begin by tying his appearance to the promises, events and patterns of what came before. *De novo* they aren't. The significance of what's new in the New is precisely the surprise by which God overcame the obstacles to obtaining what had been his longstanding creational intention.

The New Testament's three-part Gospels, Letters of Paul and General Epistles perform the task of bringing the story to its climax.[7] The power of darkness has waylaid God's world and even prevented God's chosen agent (Israel) from playing its rightful role. The new thing in the story is that a radical new agent is sent—from within Israel—to fight the key battle. Following the presentation of King Jesus, the rest of the New Testament lays out the implications of God's victory for the now-renewed Israel and the rest of the world. Crucially, *it is the same story* that continues in these fresh developments.

One of the biggest losses in our bits-and-pieces approach to the Bible is the disappearance of the fourfold witness to the gospel of Jesus the Messiah. Our constant jumping around for "daily manna" here and there prevents us from hearing how each of the four Gospels presents a unique way of understanding the vital meaning of Jesus' identity and work. We may act as if there are worthwhile messages in only the small pieces of the Bible, but whole books have their own messages, revelations and perspectives that can only be gained by reading the entire work.

So as we learn to read whole Gospels we will begin to see the deep connections they make to the story that came before. With our eyes opened, we will see the Second Adam reliving temptation stories and producing a new outcome. We will see Israel's lawgiver sitting on a mountainside presenting a new Torah and being baptized in the Jordan to initiate the renewal of the people of God. We will see the Son of David engaging evil on behalf of his people, this time winning a completely different and deeper kind of victory. With Jesus it will be like it was "in the beginning," except now it's a new beginning that satisfies and fulfills what God had in mind all along. Reading big will bring about the rebirth of what has been too-long dormant in our modern expression of the Christian faith—the big story that is the point of all the smaller parts of the Bible.

The rest of the New Testament is focused on showing concretely how the announcement of God's victory over sin and death through King Jesus plays itself out in new communities of Jesus' followers spread throughout a world now reclaimed by God. Paul plays a special role in the New Testament, and indeed in the whole Bible, as the author of a significant number of books. As a "Hebrew of Hebrews" and yet also the designated "apostle to the Gentiles," Paul plays a major bridging role in the overall drama. It took a radical reorientation of his own understanding of the narrative of what God is doing in and through Israel. Yet he made the transition and dedicated his life to fulfilling Israel's founding vocation: "I have made you a light for the Gentiles, that you may bring salvation to the ends of the earth" (Paul, in the book of Acts, quoting from one of Isaiah's servant songs while teaching at the synagogue in Pisidian Antioch). It should be deeply instructive to us when Paul makes it clear in his letters that he expected Gentile believers in Jesus to become familiar with the earlier story of Israel and to view it as their own story.[8]

Paul's correspondence in the New Testament consists of ongoing, contextualized instruction and encouragement to the new outposts for the kingdom of God. The Gospels end with the claim that with the triumph of Jesus, the kingdom has been inaugurated, and that it is time for God's will to be done on earth as it is in heaven. The rest of the New Testament reveals what this begins to look like in practice. In the Messiah, God is creating one new humanity, and this newly unified people must take shape in tangible ways in God's world. It all remains a very messy affair, because, as N. T. Wright puts it, "the actors remain fallible."[9] Paul's letters reveal the ongoing struggle in real congregations between the powers of the two ages, the present evil one that continues for now and the newly arrived world-age of the enthroned Messiah.

In the early ordering of the New Testament, the set of catholic epistles conveniently came out to the number seven, thus representing the sense of a complete revelation for the church universal. Of course, these seven "letters" (James is more like wisdom writing) are actually quite situation specific, with several addressed to believers in specific places and addressing specific people and problems in local congregations. As with Paul's letters, these seven also help new covenant people make first covenant narrative connections. Peter says Christian believers are Israel-like in their new situation: "a chosen people, a royal priesthood, a holy nation." John emphasizes new creation themes like light and darkness, employs the language of atoning sacrifice and firmly opposes gnostic-leaning, anti-creation voices that were heard in the early churches. All of this is grounded in the foundation of the First Testament. And our tail-end book, Revelation, is incomprehensible without reference to the deep themes and patterns and language of Israel's earlier story.

Throughout the groups of books of the Bible, we see narrative threads that make the story whole. It is a testament to the Bible's depth and comprehensiveness that the story can be described through so many different lenses. It's appropriate to characterize the Bible overall as a temple and dwelling place story, a liberation and exodus story, a forgiveness and reconciliation story, a kingdom-rebellion-reclamation story, an account of the creation, distortion and restoration of God's image in humanity, a narrative of overcoming chaos and bringing peace and order, and many more such descriptions. What all of these have in common is the sense that something significant of God's intention for creation was lost and God has been working through the ages to recover it, with the decisive moment coming in the accomplishment of King Jesus. The history of the world after Jesus is an outworking and implementation of what he has already done.

THE DRAMA OF SCRIPTURE

A canonical survey of the major book groups reveals several key points about the big story of the Bible:

- It's vast in its overall scope, including everything from the beginning of the world to God's final purpose for us and the rest of his creation.

- It's comprehensive and fundamental, the true story of God and the world that gives ultimate meaning to all the smaller, individual stories in our world.

- It's complex, intricate and textured as it moves along, book by book, with the realistic ups and downs of actual people over an extended period of time.

- It's rooted in the historical journey of a particular people—the nation of Israel—as God works with and through them to bring his purposes to the wider world.

- It has a redemptive and saving goal, centered in the life, death and resurrection of Jesus, Israel's Messiah and the world's true Lord, leading to the renewal of life that God always intended.

With the Bible's metanarrative acknowledged and given its due, we're almost ready to explore what it means for the Bible to become the controlling story of our lives today. But one more step remains: Is there a way to helpfully outline the major acts in the biblical narrative? In their book on the drama of Scripture, Craig Bartholomew and Michael Goheen recall that the second-century BC Roman dramatist Terence gave our Western culture the gift of the five-act structure as a means of telling an important story. They describe the function of the five acts this way:

> (1) The first act gives us essential background information, introduces the important characters, and establishes the stable situation that will be disrupted by the events about to unfold. (2) The first action begins, usually with the introduction of a significant conflict. The middle of the play (3) is where the main action of the drama takes place. Here the initial conflict intensifies and grows ever more complicated until (4) the climax, or the point of highest tension, after which that conflict *must* be resolved, one way or another. After the climax comes (5) the resolution, in which the implications of the climactic act are worked out for all the characters of the drama, and stability is restored.[10]

N. T. Wright takes up this five-act structure as a way to understand the big story of the Scriptures.[11] The narrative of the Bible contains all the standard elements of the classic five-act drama, which Wright defines succinctly as Creation, Fall, Israel, Jesus and Church. Variations on this are possible: Bartholomew and Goheen expand on Wright's scheme and add a sixth act while incorporating kingdom language throughout all the acts: "God Establishes His Kingdom: Creation," "Rebellion in the Kingdom: Fall," "The King Chooses Israel: Redemption Initiated," "The Coming of the King: Redemption Accomplished," "Spreading the News of the King: The Mission of the Church," and "The Return of the King: Redemption Completed." Regardless of how we might nuance the structure of the acts, the energizing point is that we have a reasonable model for making sense of the overarching storyline of the Bible.

The value of this should not be underestimated: it reconnects us to the gift of the narrative of the Bible that we received from the ancient Jews. It's a way of showing that the Bible's "and thens" make sense together. In my twenty-five years as a Bible publisher one of the things I have heard repeatedly is that people have difficulty grasping how all the disparate parts of the Bible fit together into something coherent. It's significant that so many people don't know that there is an identifiable story and believe instead that the Bible is primarily a sourcebook for ad hoc picking and choosing. Even those who do believe there is a master story are often working with a seriously distorted view of what that storyline actually is. So having a shorthand, accurate way of referring to the Bible's grand narrative is helpful indeed, and some version of it should become widely known among those claiming the Bible as their guide to Christian living.

Here we have an emerging model for what it means to read the Bible well. All the previous steps are intended to build up to this great drama, for it's here that we most truly have the opportunity to enter into God's story. We don't live in lists or handbooks or principles or mementos of inspiration or systems of thought. We live in stories. The preeminent way to view the Bible overall is as a story. The Bible comes to us in the form of a collection of literary compositions, but the Bible becomes what it was always meant to be when we see that these strange and ancient books are creating a new world. Stories create worlds, and that is what the Bible does most of all. We haven't read well until we've seen the Bible's new world emerging from the text right before our eyes.

READING WITH CHRIST AT THE CENTER

There is a saving story in the world—a story grounded in real events, true to the things we ourselves know about life under the sun, and authored by the God and Father of us all. But our account is not complete without a highlighted word about the place of Jesus the Messiah within this story. Jesus is not merely one of the characters within the drama—he is the centerpiece, the only way for us to make good sense of the entire narrative. There is a crucial point to be made here, because it is possible (and in fact done all the time even by would-be orthodox readers of the Bible) to try and make sense of the various parts of the Bible apart from the supreme revelation of God in Christ. It's not just that Jesus is important to the story, which is obvious, but that he conditions, relativizes, summarizes and clarifies every other thing that happens in the story. Too often, however, our ventures into understanding or applying the Bible are undertaken in isolation from what we see and learn from the Center of the story.

Reading the Bible well must include reading by the overarching light of Christ. This means reading the Bible as a progressive revelation where more and more light shines as the story moves forward toward Jesus. For Jesus Christ himself is the Word of God that stands over all other words. The enscripturated word of God serves as a means for pointing us to the truest and fullest embodiment of the Word of God himself. The Bible must be read in this way, because the saving work of Jesus is the narrative core, the interpretive key that unlocks all the rest. And because the Bible is a Christocentric set of books, we cannot merely pick up fragments from just anywhere and presume they are God's final answer. The Spirit-empowered and kingdom-inaugurating life, teaching, death and resurrection of Jesus reveals God and his will for the world most clearly.

An example from the book of Hebrews may help us here. The author was writing to a group of Jewish believers in Jesus who were under pressure and in danger of turning away from Christ. So this collection of exhortations on the supremacy of the Messiah reveals how the earlier chapters in the story find their satisfaction in the work that Jesus did. Strikingly, the book opens with a decisive statement on the superiority of the revelatory power of the Son over and above all previous divine communications:

In the past God spoke to our ancestors through the prophets at many times and in various ways, but in these last days he has spoken to us by his Son, whom he appointed heir of all things, and through whom also he made the universe. The Son is the radiance of God's glory and the exact representation of his being, sustaining all things by his powerful word.

"In these last days" has the force of "in this final and climactic moment." God has given us his clearest Word, and we know him as the Son. The collected messages of Hebrews will go on to show that the Son is superior to the angels and the message they spoke (the Torah), superior to the earlier apostles Moses and Joshua ("apostles" here means those sent on a mission from God), and superior to all the previous high priests and their sacrifices. The introductory section will go on to emphasize the fulfillment of a foundational, creational theme of the whole story: Jesus has been enthroned in heaven (God's realm) in order to exercise his rightful rule over the earth (our realm). Crucially, the point is that this rule is exercised precisely as a fellow member of our human family:

It is not to angels that he has subjected the world to come, about which we are speaking. But there is a place where someone has testified:

"What is mankind that you are mindful of them,
a son of man that you care for him?
You made them a little lower than the angels;
you crowned them with glory and honor
and put everything under their feet."

In putting everything under them, God left nothing that is not subject to them. Yet at present we do not see everything subject to them. But we do see Jesus, who was made lower than the angels for a little while, now crowned with glory and honor because he suffered death, so that by the grace of God he might taste death for everyone.

In bringing many sons and daughters to glory, it was fitting that God, for whom and through whom everything exists, should make the pioneer of their salvation perfect through what he suffered. Both the one who makes people holy and those who are made holy are of the same family. So Jesus is not ashamed to call them brothers and sisters.

Psalm 8, quoted here in Hebrews, is about God's intended place for humans within his creation-temple. In this respect, the world to come will be as the world God first made—it too will be given to humans to look after. But now, Hebrews argues, we have a new Adam, the truly human one in whose path we follow. Jesus comes into the story as the one who authentically images God ("the exact representation of his being") and who then proceeds to take up the human vocation to reign in God's world. That he does so by giving up his own life for the sake of the world should tell us all we need to learn about what God intends for this vocation and the nature of both real leadership and true power.

Hebrews gives us insight into the heart of God's story, including the narrative given in the opening biblical scene of creation. God's intentions for creation find their fulfillment in the Son who took on flesh and blood—full humanity—in order to defeat God's great enemy, who terrorizes God's people as they are enslaved by the power of death. This is an especially clear example of what the New Testament does with the story that came before. The first story properly shapes where we expect the whole thing to go. The Jesus story fulfills that expectation while simultaneously surprising us with how all those threads are tied so elegantly together in Christ. And, as Hebrews makes particularly clear, the revelation of Jesus means we have to read and understand all those earlier stories as precursors to the Son who brings us something better, a story about a new city that will last. This point is so strong that Kevin Vanhoozer says that the entirety of Scripture "is the visible/audible representation of the lordship of Jesus Christ, a vital ingredient in his communicative self-presentation."[12]

The contention of the Bible is that before the foundations of the world the big story was centered on the Messiah. Before the oral tradition and the first papyrus scrolls or the ancient calfskin codex and the gorgeous illuminated manuscripts, before the printing press and the digital bits of the ebook, ever and always the narrative has been Christ infused. Our world drama has always been expecting him, needing him, longing for him and now it finds its true life in him. If we fail to read the Bible as this Christ story, we fail the Bible completely.

nine

PERFORMING THE STORIENTED BIBLE

The unity of a human life is the unity of a narrative quest. Quests sometime fail, are frustrated, abandoned, or dissipated into distractions; and human lives may in all these ways also fail. But the only criteria for success or failure in a human life as a whole are the criteria for success or failure in a narrated or to-be-narrated quest.

ALASDAIR MACINTYRE

The first answer to the question *What are we supposed to do with the Bible?* is to read it well. For this to happen, it's essential that we go *there*—into the world of the Bible. Reading well encompasses much, but it ends with grasping that the Bible is speaking the language we were made for: story. The second answer, however, has to do with coming *back again*—into our own lives in this present world. The point of the Bible must never be only about then. For the book to have the significance Christians claim for it, it must also be about now.

As we have already seen in earlier chapters, many modern strategies for dealing with the Bible fall down badly at precisely this point. Upon finding a book with too much strangeness for our contemporary tastes, many have assumed that we have no choice but to cherry-pick verses that seem good to us. This wreaks havoc on the authority of the Bible. How can the Bible possibly lead and direct our lives if we are the ones who predetermine which parts of it speak to us? Fragmentary patterns of reading entail a fragmented sense of authority.

AUTHORITY TO TRANSFORM LIVES

In a section titled "Theology, Narrative and Authority" Wright outlines what a narrative-based conception of the Bible's authority might look like.[1] Brief though it is, the promise of his proposal in these few pages is considerable, even revolutionary, as a fresh way to conceive of the role of the Bible in our lives. The proposal begins with a question: How might something like *a story* carry anything like authority? It's part of Wright's insight to ask this question with such a frank and accurate recognition of what the Bible actually is. Discussions of the Bible's authority have usually been premised on an understanding of the Bible as anything but narrative. But what we have in the Bible, says Wright, is a Christ-centered story that is as yet unconcluded. We live in this unfinished space. In telling us the story so far, especially in the sin-and-death-shattering work of Jesus, the Bible sets the stage for what should happen next. What the Bible does not do, though there are many who wish it did, is script our parts in any kind of detail. It's not as though we can simply go to the Bible and look up our lines for the day. So how does the Bible speak to, inform, direct, guide—in short, have any authority in—our lives today?

Building off of his five-act structure for understanding the story of the Bible, Wright sets forth his vision:

> This "authority" of the first four acts would not consist—could not consist!— in an implicit command that the actors should repeat the earlier parts of the play over and over again. It would consist in the fact of an as yet unfinished drama, containing its own impetus and forward movement, which demanded to be concluded in an appropriate manner. It would require of the actors a free and responsible entering in to the story as it stood, in order first to understand how the threads could appropriately be drawn together and then to put that understanding into effect by speaking and acting with both innovation and consistency.

"By speaking and acting with both innovation and consistency." In other words, we have a call for biblical improvisation. This is rich and largely unexplored territory for the church. We've been struggling with what exactly to do with the Bible for some time. Modern challenges have led some to dig-in-your-heels fundamentalism. The open possibilities of postmodernism have led others into lose-your-moorings experimentalism. What hasn't happened nearly enough is clear and coherent thinking about what the Bible actually is and exploration of honest and healthy ways to bring it to bear on contemporary life.

The recovery of narrative is a vital step in this direction. But drama does narrative one step better. Where narrative tells, drama does. A drama is a form of narrative, but it's a form of narrative that doesn't really become what it's meant to be until it is performed. A drama isn't a drama until it is enacted. Embodied. Seen. Lived. Drama activates story. And what this model for understanding the role of the Bible provides is a way of naturally inviting people to do what the Bible is so concerned that they do: find their lives transformed by entering a new story. This transformation will not happen because they've added a few beliefs to what they already believed or started obeying a few moral commands they previously ignored, but rather because they've discovered a whole new country and have now stepped into it. This is the strange new world of the Bible, a world in which the renewal of all things in Christ has already begun. The Bible is a doorway onto this new stage where we have the opportunity to live new-creation roles for the first time in our lives. The goal of the Bible is to change lives. And nothing serves this goal like a lived-out story.

Imagining Our Lives as Works of Biblical Art

The earlier acts in the drama inform us that we've been given a multitude of gifts to help us keep the redemption story going in our world. Exploring the implications of this is a work worthy of the sustained attention of the Christian community, surely worth much more than it has received. I don't have room here to show how all this plays out in detail, but in barest outline, here are some of the key aspects of the Bible-as-drama model and how they might potentially shape our own activation of the story of the Bible.[2]

God is the playwright, the author of the overall story. Because of this, we know going in that world history—our history—is not a random series of actions and speeches, signifying nothing. The story has a plot. This narrative, as Alasdair MacIntyre reminds us, has a beautiful way of embracing both unpredictability and teleology: we don't know what will happen next, but we believe our lives are headed toward some goal.[3] Further, God has supplied the story with a proper stage, the heavens and earth, which are intended to be a unified space for God and his creatures to interact in. Remarkably, we see that the author is also a player in the drama who accommodates to his creatures to an astounding extent. The heavens and the earth are the theater of God's glory, as John Calvin taught us. But what God had built as an integrated stage has, due to our rebellion, become disintegrated. God's realm and our realm were separated. A key part of the restoration project in the biblical drama is the reintegration of the stage.

Related to the actors in the drama there are two key points to be made. Again and again we see in the Bible that God is the initiator of the major movements of the drama. He chooses the players on whom he will focus his attention for larger purposes. He establishes covenants. He plays the roles of hero, savior, protagonist. As I have already emphasized, the whole story turns on how God is in Christ reconciling the world to himself. The traditional doctrines of God's sovereignty and providence can be expressed dramatically by noting that the Bible is first and foremost God's story. He is its author and the maker of its most decisive moves. Not even our strongest and most absolute resistance can derail his drama from reaching its divinely intended goal. It is not in our power to completely ruin the story.

But none of this should be taken to imply that the human role is unimportant. Within a page or two of the drama's opening God posits that his struggle with his enemy will be played out on the stage in and through the offspring of the woman. In fact, because he has given the world to humans, the key blow against the enemy will come from them. God in his freedom has determined that he will not simply take over the stage and do everything by himself. God leads, but he always invites us into the action. We are not merely passive observers of the drama. Traditionally this would be expressed within the doctrine of theological anthropology as statements about human significance, freedom and action. Dramatically it comes down to the fact that we are real players in the story, that our actions matter and that God honestly responds to them.

Next, if we watch how improvisation works in the theater, we can learn how we might carry the Bible's story forward in appropriate ways.[4] Much of the language of improvisation can profitably be used for a robust understanding of the Christian life. Our entrance into various human situations is helped by a firm grasp of how the Bible can guide our navigation of things like status negotiations, the acceptance and rejection of gifts in creative ways, questioning givens, and even reincorporating people and elements of the story that were previously discarded or overlooked. The ongoing action in any improvisation is initiated by offers, that is, any speech, action or even facial expression by an actor that functions as an invitation to others to respond. Other actors can accept (by continuing on in the direction suggested by the offer) or block (rejecting the offer, either mildly or strongly, and stopping that story-direction) and typically make a counter-offer.

Taking this model and applying it to the ongoing drama in the Bible brings fascinating and insightful results. God wants the story to go in a direction that leads to right relations being established throughout creation, resulting in life and well-being. Humans are constantly either accepting or blocking God's offers based on our own desires for the direction of the story. God in turn responds to our actions, working to keep the overall story on track.

It's here that another improvisation technique comes into play that sheds light on God's most significant actions in the drama. What does God do when he receives an offer or an attempted block by human players that is less than what he had hoped for? Early in the Bible's story, God often considers or implements blocks. The Noah story is a strong block in which the author, extremely displeased over the direction humans have taken the story, comes very close to shutting down the entire drama by flooding the stage. YHWH's negotiations with Moses over a faithless Israel in the wilderness (after hearing reports of giants in the land they were to take) also reveal threats of strong blocks: "How long will they refuse to believe in me, in spite of all the signs I have performed among them? I will strike them down with a plague and destroy them, but I will make you into a nation greater and stronger than they." Thankfully, Moses talks him down from this extreme response. Blocks are severe and express the view that there's virtually no hope left for the story in its current direction.

A breakthrough occurs, however, when God takes a different approach: overaccepting. This move responds to an offer that is contrary to God's overall intentions not by blocking but by taking the deficient action and creatively reincorporating it into the larger, redemptive story. Over-accepting is the result of God's gracious and skillful use of all the elements within the drama to bring even poor performances by his human partners back into line with his larger, life-giving goals. Overaccepting is accepting in light of the bigger drama. This is improvisational ability of the highest order. This is God watching David's especially poor performance of acquiring another wife through adultery and murder, and then responding by loving their son and making him the king of Israel and an ancestor to the Messiah. This is not unlike God's incorporation of whores, outsiders and victims into the royal line that ushered the long-promised One into the world—as Matthew went out of his way to point out at the beginning of his Gospel. This is the Lord telling Jeremiah that he will rework and reshape the flawed pottery that is Israel rather than simply throwing it away. This is the Father turning what is the worst possible action in the entire drama, the rejection and death of his own Son, into the very thing that brings the salvation of the world.

It would be no small part of our own developing skill at faithful and godly biblical improvisation if we were to learn how to overaccept as God does. Our immediate response is usually to block anything we don't like, to try and shut it down completely. But we are not in a position to see the specifics of the longer term and we certainly don't own the drama, so blocking, while sometimes necessary, is more often a response showing a lack of belief in God's greater ability to redeem the story of our lives and of those around us. It takes patience and a deep faith in God's bigger narrative to seek ways to creatively follow God's lead by overaccepting the myriad bad offers and poor performances we regularly encounter (and contribute to). If God's story in the Bible shows us anything, it shows us that setbacks, losses, pain and even significant wrongdoing can be turned into a crucial part of the greater story. This is not an apologetic for all the evil in the world, for God is surely battling against it. But the script of this drama *does* reveal a God who is constantly working with us rather than simply destroying us in his disgust.

CREATIVE FIDELITY

Now what can we do with the Bible in the service of finding good, true and faithful ways to speak and act and imagine in God's world? How does the authority of the Bible actually function in our lives if it's not a reference handbook for looking up the answers? The big answer here is to become so immersed in the script of the earlier acts that we come to know this story in our bones. We have virtually no chance of playing our parts well if we don't really know how the story goes. We must soak up the drama or, as I said earlier, feast on it by eating it up whole. Skimming the surface of what's gone before in no way prepares us for fine performances of the gospel today. We must read deep, long and slow. If we say we have no time or interest in this, then we are admitting up front that we don't expect to be serious gospel players. Perhaps we will be spectators to the good performances of others, but we will not be contributing to the advance of God's story in our world. Worse, if we don't know the story in this profound way, we likely will hinder it: We are all players already. We are already on the stage living our lives. The only question is what kind of players we will be.

An ongoing, deep immersion in the Bible will reveal two fundamental things to us: (1) there really are different acts in the drama, so things change, and (2) it really is a single story, so the acts are related to each other and there are abiding patterns that persist over time. A key skill in reading the Bible well is to discern the elements of both continuity and discontinuity. Some things change, so it is always important to know where we are in the story. We need a nuanced rather than a flat reading of the Bible. Certain practices and behaviors are appropriate only for particular moments in the drama. Israel was looking for another king on the model of David, but the Son of David came bringing a new way to fight against evil. This is why it is not appropriate to quote willy-nilly from anywhere in the Bible and assume it can be straightforwardly applied to players who live in the later scenes in Act 5 of the drama.

Some things do stay the same across the acts, so it's important to learn the Bible's abiding themes. God's intentions are expressed in motifs that persist in the drama: God's election of one in the service of the many, God's choosing to use the unlikely, the overlooked, and the second-born, the ongoing adoption of an incarnational model of ministry, the self-sacrificial nature of true leadership, the overcoming of normal sociological barriers to create an intended unity, the use of the materials of creation, the planting of small seeds of renewal and allowing them to grow and expand, and the recovery of beauty, diversity and health in the world. Our improvisation of the drama today will look for ways to implement these core redemptive patterns in our specific scene.

Finally, according to our script, the playwright has provided us with some critical aids to help us perform well:

- We have the core given of the canonical script itself—the Bible—which reveals the playwright's overall intentions and the major contours of what we can expect from this story.

- We are built to be receptive to the playwright, having been made in his image even as we are being remade in the image of his Son.

- We have the personal help of the playwright who sends his own Spirit to live within us.

- We have weekly opportunities to reenact the drama together in historic worship.

- We have local, spiritual directors (pastor-teachers) to guide and lead us.

- We are not alone on the stage performing monologues but have a community of gospel players to support, encourage and correct us.

- We have the assurance of forgiveness and restoration from the playwright when we stumble in our lines or misplay our parts.

It comes down to this: improvisation of the biblical script in our own time is not a matter of being clever, original or making it up as we go. It is certainly not a free-for-all. It's not randomly saying or doing whatever pops into our minds. Improvisation is always rooted in what has gone before, extending the same storyline into new times and new places. The authority of the-story-so-far compels us to good and appropriate performances of the gospel now. We are looking for, as Kevin Vanhoozer calls it, "creative fidelity" to the biblical script and we are working to avoid the "sad spectacle" of biblical failure.[5] The path to biblical obedience is found in the dramatic imagination. So how do we evaluate whether or not we are following the lead of the script and producing a worthy improvisation? We must ask whether our performance is fitting—whether it coheres well with what has gone before. (*Fittingness* as a normative concept is a feature of the world of aesthetics.[6]) Are we bringing the judging and restoring trajectories of the gospel into our lives and our world? Are we bringing apt presentations of the ongoing work of Christ into his creation? Are we offering, accepting, blocking and redemptively overaccepting according to the good way shown us in the Bible?[7]

So improvisation has this going for it as well: it recognizes that God takes us seriously as significant players in his drama. God calls on human beings to use all of his aids and to bring all of themselves, particularly their obedient imaginations, into playing their part in the story. Drama allows the followers of Jesus to see their lives ultimately as works of art, giving beauty back to beauty's giver. We are God's handiwork, and we are invited to create beautiful lives to adorn his creation-temple. This is what it means to engage and live the Bible. And this is the good and proper work of a Bible that's been saved—an authoritative story doing what it's supposed to be doing in the lives of God's people through the work of the Spirit. The Bible transforms us by opening the door into God's theater and giving us the chance to walk into its new world as new people, and then to *do something*.

CONCLUSION

The saddest part of the current captivity of the Bible is the loss of this way of seeing and living our sacred book. I've been advocating the recovery of the Elegant, Feasting, and Historical Bibles in order that we might recover the Storiented Bible, a narrative that we now live into as a drama. This significantly improves upon our diminished modernistic models of the Bible. It does not reduce the Bible to propositions, commands and principles, or inspiring snippets of hope. It takes up propositions, commands, and words of hope to play their part in the bigger, grander thing—the true story of God and the world. This is how we will save the Bible. We will help people take all the necessary steps to read it well, that they might begin to live it well.

The chiastic counterparts to our earlier chapters will work out the critical implications of our renewed appreciation for the Storiented Bible. Having taken onboard a healthier and more honest view of what the Bible is and what we're supposed to do with it, we will find other new understandings and practices flowing from this restored Bible. If we properly honor it, perhaps the Elegant Bible will have further gifts of beauty for us. We will see the Feasting Bible setting the table for many guests. The Historical Bible has already led us to our centerpiece, the Storiented Bible. It is propelling the drama of the Scriptures into the world through the lives of God's people. But this raises an important question: Does it matter *where* the story is about?

ten

OUR OTHERWORLDLY BIBLE

The soul said, "What binds me has been slain,
and what surrounds me has been overcome, and my
desire has been ended, and ignorance has died."

THE GOSPEL OF MARY

All I know is I'm not home yet
This is not where I belong
Take this world and give me Jesus
This is not where I belong

BUILDING 429, "WHERE I BELONG"

Evil. That's what it comes down to. There is evil in the world, and it is the job of religion to tell us what is to be done about it. The most common approach—the overwhelming favorite of religions and spiritualties throughout history and around the globe—is to say that the problem is the world itself. Matter. The earth. Bodies. Stuff. Evil seems so intimately bound to this materiality—surely the bond is unbreakable.

Isn't it in the very nature of things to break down, degrade, go wrong? There is something inherent in the *thisness* of the world—materiality itself—that pulls us down, that diverts or distorts or destroys. The body tempts and distracts and then it gets tired, grows old and fails. When our bodies are lying there, dying or dead, is that us lying there? Or are we something deeper and purer that longs to be freed from all this limitation and pain? As for the world, what is it but an oversized body? It too tempts and pulls us down, grows old and fails. And so this world can't be our true home. The fact that we find ourselves longing so much when things go wrong reveals it. We are longing for something—something other, something different. Some*place* other. Our hope lies elsewhere. No more of this. Not here. There.

So the answer to evil becomes clear: leave it behind. Either through mystical insight or actual escape, the way to overcome evil is to overcome the world itself. We'll see that this world is an illusion once we clearly apprehend the One, the deep unity that is ultimately all in all. Either that, or we'll anticipate some final victory in the coming cosmic fire. The great end-times vision sees the end of the earth and all its woes followed by the revelation of a higher, better, different plane of existence. One way or another, if evil is to be defeated, the world has got to go. Or so it is commonly believed.

A major question must arise for those who seek to be guided in life and hope by the Christian Scriptures. Where does the Bible stand on the problem of evil? Is evil so strongly wed to the world that it cannot be separated out? Does the Bible present a kind of two-stage story—where the first part focuses on earthly matters, and the second part on the heavenly realm?[1] Or does the Bible approach the story of evil and its defeat from another direction entirely? Have we significantly misread the narrative found in our sacred writings, and would such a misreading make us miss what the Bible is really trying to do?

RESURRECTION AND THE ELYSIAN FIELDS

One of the earlier writings of the New Testament (AD mid-50s) is the apostle Paul's first letter to the church at Corinth. He insists in this letter that the message the Corinthians originally heard and responded to was already functioning as a settled tradition within the young Christian movement:

> Now, brothers and sisters, I want to remind you of the gospel I preached to you, which you received and on which you have taken your stand. By this gospel you are saved, if you hold firmly to the word I preached to you. Otherwise, you have believed in vain.

For what I received I passed on to you as of first importance: that Christ died for our sins according to the Scriptures, that he was buried, that he was raised on the third day according to the Scriptures, and that he appeared to Cephas, and then to the Twelve. After that, he appeared to more than five hundred of the brothers and sisters at the same time, most of whom are still living, though some have fallen asleep. Then he appeared to James, then to all the apostles, and last of all he appeared to me also, as to one abnormally born.

Paul states that the gospel is a set of specific claims about the nature of God's victory accomplished through the Messiah's work. All of this, he said, is of "first importance."

This foundational teaching about the resurrection is the content of the word *gospel* for Paul. It reveals both the means and the result of God's battle against the great enemies of his creation, sin and death. God's Son has confronted those twin powers on the cross and has now triumphed. The Messiah died, yet he lives! Paul had rejected the story as a scandal until he was confronted with the resurrected Messiah himself. This received tradition he then shared with the nations of the world.

Zealous Paul, who had been immersed in the Jewish story and taken up the role of enforcer of what he understood as its appropriate limits, discovered a surprising outcome within that story. The trajectory of the story ("according to the Scriptures") was always God confronting the rebellion that rose up within the world. But it was essential, and clear from the nature of God's interventions in the story, that he wished to do so in a way that preserved his good work in creation. Escape from creation was never the plan. Confronting and defeating evil within creation was. The precise means by which God did this—through his chosen Messiah—was unforeseen by those eagerly looking for God's salvation. The gospel accounts reveal that even those closest to Jesus did not decipher its real shape. Not until it was validated by his resurrection from the dead was the Messiah's triumph seen as a triumph. The fully embodied and creational life of the slain king was restored and renewed, clearly seen by his followers as he stood upon the earth once again.

So the gospel announcement about the defeat of sin and death through a king raised from the dead went out to the people of the world. This was a deeply biblical message, based on key points about the goodness of creation, the intentions of the one true God who is the Creator of all things, and his choice of Israel as his means of rescuing the world. The world on the receiving end of the message, however, already had its own understanding of certain core questions: What does it mean to be human? What is the nature of life on earth? What is death? What, if anything, comes after death? Not that there was uniformity of opinion on all this, but all the available options excluded anything like the Jewish story as fulfilled through the work of Messiah Jesus. Already in Paul's letter to the church at Corinth we can see the difficulty a Hellenistic pagan would have had with the received tradition of the Jesus story. Paul is compelled to ask: "But if it is preached that Christ has been raised from the dead, how can some of you say that there is no resurrection of the dead?"

But the typical pagan would reply to Paul, "How can you say there *is* a resurrection of the dead?" This was one of the strangest ideas of this new sect of Christ-followers. Resurrection? The Hellenistic mind had been shaped in other directions entirely.[2] It began perhaps with Homer, whose great stories revealed a post-death shade-like existence, not unlike the shadows of Sheol in the Bible. But soon enough Plato intervened with a bigger, bolder proposal. Human beings, he said, are essentially souls that have been badly trapped in bodies. Plato reversed Homer. Rather than this life being the real thing and the next life the pale imitation, Plato characterized bodily, earthly existence as the weak distortion while real existence would come in the afterlife when the soul is set free. Plato's mighty dialogues came to rule the ancient classical world to a large extent and later to exert long-term influence on Western thought and imagination.

The effect of Plato's vivid and compelling story of human existence was a deeply and widely embraced understanding that the soul is innately immortal. Thus the "real" or "essential" person could be found in that being who escapes earthbound life at death and returns to its true homeland in the heavens. The original state of the soul was with the stars and so it belongs with the stars. Therefore the best life on earth was simply training and preparation for the soul's return to the realm above. Earthly existence was little more than an ordeal to be suffered and a sorry distraction from the soul's true purpose. In Phaedo, Plato's Socrates explains the path of the mind's purification to his dialogue partner

Simmias, telling him how death is nothing more than the completion of this cleansing process:

> Now this purification . . . consists of isolating the soul as completely as possible from the body; of practising the concentration of the soul until it becomes a matter of habit for the soul to be self-contained and independent of the body; and of making it accustomed to existence in isolation, both in this world as far as possible, and in the world to come. In other words this purification is a matter of liberating the soul from the body as it were from a prison.[3]

As this perspective soaked into the Hellenistic mind, poets and dramatists bolstered its strength and extended its reach. More details of the afterlife were added, various names were given, such as the Isles of the Blessed or Elysium (the Elysian Fields), and various specific locations proposed: in the underworld, beyond the ocean in the West or above the sky in the heavens.

However, a negative space was needed for those who failed to meet the conditions for a positive ending. In book six of the Aeneid, the Roman poet Virgil presented an extended scene in which the Trojan Aeneas traveled to the underworld and was presented with the two great options in the afterlife.[4] Virtuous souls enjoyed the comfort and rest of the Blessed Groves, while the unworthy faced the terrifying Rhadamanthus, who pried confessions of crookedness from wayward folk and then inflicted pain and suffering. At one point Aeneas and his guide encountered a path that came to be split in two: the branch on the left lead downward into dark Tartarus while the one on the right rose into bright Elysium.[5] The passage is striking in its similarity to later medieval visions. Unsurprisingly, Virgil would be honored in the Middle Ages as a Christian prophet.

The specific conditions for one's destination could be adapted to new cultural situations. Whereas Greek philosophers saw rewards based on the virtues of clear thinking and right perception of ideas, the Roman heirs of this viewpoint claimed a righteous life was centered on loyalty to the state and performing one's civic duties. Details varied, but this was the dominant perspective throughout the classical world.

Considering Paul's congregation in Corinth, it's no wonder some were perplexed with the proposed central and foundational teaching about the resurrection of the dead. What would be the point? Why would anyone even want to be resurrected? Restored physical life would be merely reimprisonment, a kind of punishment. As religious historian Alan Segal says of the resurrection message: "It is most puzzling and disquieting to the Hellenistic world."[6] And so now we can understand one of the great challenges the Christian movement faced as it spread throughout the Hellenistic world around the Mediterranean Sea.

FINDING A CHRISTIAN ELYSIUM

When the young faith expanded from Judea into the Roman Empire and began to climb the social hierarchy, it ran straight into the established views of the afterlife. This was a guaranteed conflict—the two perspectives were fundamentally at odds. Paul in the Corinthian correspondence was contending for the received tradition and its claim that sin's hold on the world, expressed most clearly in the reign of death, was now broken. God's creation could be liberated. Succeeding generations of Christian leaders, however, would falter on this point. They weren't always so sure that the standard pagan views could not be accommodated. Death could be perceived as friend more than foe.

Besides the powerful force of societal pressure to conform Christianity to already existing beliefs, Segal proposes two key explanations for why the tide slowly turned and the church not only found a place for Hellenistic views of the afterlife, but eventually moved them to the center of the Christian story.[7] First, early Christian teaching made a key point of the return of Christ as the rightful judge of the world, thus giving a certain urgency to the call for repentance. We can see this clearly in the evangelistic sermons in the book of Acts and again in the New Testament letters that Christian leaders wrote to their congregations. But the more time passed without this return, the pressure increased for Christianity to offer an alternative, more pressing reason for accepting the faith. Facing one's judgment immediately upon death and being consigned to either heaven or hell would fit this bill.

Second, Segal explains that once the Platonic view of the immortality of the soul is accepted, a system of rewards and punishments must accommodate it. The soul does not die when the body does, and so its ultimate destination must be revealed at once. Further, since the soul lives forever, this fate must likewise be eternal. And so the doctrines of heaven and hell became more precise and more crucial. Whether for the reasons that Segal cites, for others or all of the above, the change in emphasis from the apostolic period compared to later centuries is clear enough.[8]

Once the move was made on the question of future destinies, it was natural for the Christian story to begin reflecting the ancient pagan hope. Of course, there was variety among Christian leaders regarding how much or little of the Hellenistic picture they adopted. But there is no question that a significant shift occurred: the core content of Christianity's narrative of the future came to be supplied by the well-known and philosophically respected Hellenistic vision. There certainly seemed to be real points of contact with the biblical data if you were looking for them, and the names could easily enough be changed to reflect Christian language. Thus without too much difficulty Elysium and Tartarus could and would morph into heaven and hell.

But we should not underestimate how this changed the tenor of the faith. As we've already seen, core questions are at stake here: What does it mean to be human? What is the nature of life on earth? What kind of victory does the gospel announce? What is the relationship between creation and salvation in the Bible? What is death? What, if anything, comes after death? The immortality of the soul, a longed-for existence away from the prison of the body and into the realm of light, the diminishment of physical life on the earth in favor of a true home in heaven, and moving Christianity's emphasis to the immediacy of reward or punishment at the moment of death—all this resulted from a Christianized Platonism that took up residence and settled in to the house of faith. Pagan givens about the afterlife were accommodated, but not without a price. A clear teaching and emphasis on the resurrection, a steady focus on the Messiah's future presence with us and the establishment of his kingdom throughout the world, a deep appreciation for the gift of creation life, and the realization of the reconciliation of all things in Christ—all this was demoted, sublimated or even outright denied.

Paul had written that these things were of primary importance in the Christian narrative. I made the case earlier that when the books of the Bible are read together they create a story that's historical. That is, the story is both grounded in history and is about the nature and direction of that very history. So is the history of life on earth to be merely escaped, abandoned and replaced at last with something else? Or is it to be transformed from within history itself? Where is the realm in which salvation takes place? Changing what the story says about our destiny is more than quibbling about a few details tacked on at the end. It alters the fundamental nature of the biblical drama, and it revises our understanding of how we live our roles within the story. It changes why and how we read the Bible.

THE SCRIPTURES RECLINING IN ELYSIAN FIELDS

Christianity ended up trying to align the two views by marrying them into a single, unified perspective. But the tension was never overcome. The two views live uneasily together—they're not really compatible. Still, tension or not, it became somewhat obligatory to locate the new schema within the pages of the Bible. Looking full into the face of paganism, we turned our eyes to an innovative reading of the biblical narrative. The fully grounded historical Bible of creational monotheism grew strangely dim as a new understanding of our sacred books emerged: B.I.B.L.E. = Basic Instruction Before Leaving Earth.

Having moved beyond Judea and into the broader world in the post–New Testament era, the narrative likewise was distanced from the received Jewish story about a creation regained. It turned out it was possible to read the Bible as a description of God's intention to do something otherworldly all along.

The new telling went something like this: In the beginning God created human beings in the world, temporarily housing living souls in corruptible fleshly bodies. As things went badly, God began dropping hints about how he would intervene to make things right. True, these hints were embedded in very down-to-earth stories of Israelites, their neighbors, their kings and how they all were doing in the world. But the deeper point was always substantially about something quite different. Atonement for sins is coming, but here's something to point you to it now (a scarlet thread hanging from a window, animals being sacrificed). A great king is coming, but here's a rough picture of what he'll be like (a powerful king David, a wise king Solomon), along with some specific factual prophecies. A religion of grace and forgiveness is coming, so here is a large set of laws that you can never obey to teach you that you cannot earn your salvation. Too many in Israel, however, mistook the incidental setting of these hints for the point of the story itself. Therefore when the great king showed up, they rejected him because their hearts were wrongly set on their earthly prospects, something the new king was not interested in.

When the long-awaited time arrived and the Bible told us the story of the king in the Gospels, we could see that he spoke of a heavenly kingdom. Like the earlier parts of the Bible, he told earthly stories of sowers and pearls and wheat fields, but they all had a heavenly meaning. The time of your reward for following the way of God's righteousness will be in this otherworldly realm. So store up your treasure there, not here on earth where there is moth, rust and thievery. His kingdom is not of this world, so don't look for it there. The kingdom is within you. Make him king of your heart, and one day, when you die, you will be released from your temporary posting to this world and find your true place in that spiritual kingdom. And before the king died, he told his followers that he'd go to his Father's house and prepare mansions of glory for them there. The Gospels close with the king returning to heaven and ruling there next to his Father.

From there on, the rest of the New Testament confirms the picture: the good news of the possibility of salvation and escape from this world through Jesus Christ goes out to all people. The choice before everyone is heaven or hell. Because Jesus died on the cross for their sins, they have the option of believing in him and being rewarded with the gift of heaven one day. The book of Acts shows this message going out across the world while the theology of Paul's letters tells us the right path to finding this salvation. The earth will wear out like a garment, until it finally disappears forever in a great fire. The book of Revelation gives us a unique glimpse of the promised future: the horrors of eternal torment and the glories that await us in heaven. Heaven is a beautiful and majestic city with streets of gold, gates of pearls, and crucially, no more death or mourning or crying or pain. There we will be home, home at last.

There's just enough Bible quoting here to make the entire picture plausible to many. Once we've been freed from the constraints of the full message of the text and decided instead to look for something else, we've largely invented our own view of the specific shape of the afterlife.[9] Colleen Mc-Dannell and Bernhard Lang summarize the history of the idea of heaven this way: "Typically, Christians believe in two lives. One spans the time between birth and death and the second reaches out beyond death. This second existence has a beginning but no end. It is characterized by unsurpassable happiness in a place commonly termed 'paradise' or 'heaven.'"[10] This is also a good description of the ancient, pagan view of things.

The picture in the Bible is more accurately seen as a three-stage journey: life, death and then restored bodily life at the return of Christ.[11] But the "two lives" view has been taught for so long across so many Christian traditions, reinforced by so much hymnody and gospel singing and then verified by intriguing personal accounts of short-term visits to heaven that it can be difficult to even find exceptions to this view of things. Those both inside and outside the faith regularly assume that this is the whole point of the Christian enterprise, and its association with orthodox Christianity is so strong it becomes difficult to question. But question we must if we are to be people of the book. At the end of the day, the place we discover the contours of our story must be within the biblical text. Our task is to respectfully hear and be informed by our traditions, the readings that have been handed down to us, and our already existing Christian communities. Yet we know from that very history that errors can be made and persist over time. We must continually test our views by running them hard against the text, reading as well and as honestly as we are able. Attempting this, what might we find wrong with a would-be biblical vision of a sanctified Elysium?

REJECTING THE REJECTION OF THE WORLD

Reading the Bible as the story of salvation based on an escape from this world to heaven has been disastrous. This is for two main reasons: First, this reading mishandles the text by interpreting key passages based on false assumptions brought to the text and by doing so redirects us from the crucial message of restoration and renewal that is actually in the Bible. Second, this reading blinds us to the richly textured instruction on earthly life the Bible does offer. There are many resources in the Bible that can help us be carefully attentive to the world in ways that serve the advancement of God's saving rule. An exclusive focus on the afterlife misshapes our understanding of Christian discipleship in this world and causes us to misstate the goal of Christianity in our evangelism.

It's well beyond the scope of this book to go into detail through all the passages brought forward in support of a heavenly hope as the central offer of salvation we have in the Bible. But perhaps by touching on a few key issues as examples we can see the overall landscape more clearly. Below I list four crucial places where the Otherworldly Bible fails us:

1. Israel's story prior to the coming of the Messiah takes up about three-fourths of the Bible's entire length. Any claim to a viable reading of the Bible must account for the role of Israel in the overall story. But an Elysium Bible lacks precisely this narrative unity. It refuses to take the Israel story seriously. The Israel story is consistently and insistently about the questions of God's sovereignty on earth: Whose place is this? What's life here supposed to be like? If YHWH has created this place and initiated this story, why have things gone so terribly wrong and what is he doing about correcting them? From start to finish and from top to bottom, the Israel story is about life here on earth and God's intentions for it. We can only get a different story for the Bible by a large-scale campaign to write the First Testament out of our understanding, simultaneously manufacturing a different purpose and ending.[12]

2. All four Gospels open with significant references to the story of Israel and then proceed to connect that story to the coming of Jesus. Any claim to a viable reading of the New Testament and the stories of Jesus in particular must account for the relationship between the Messiah and his ancestors. Why was Israel chosen in the first place? What is Israel supposed to be doing in the world? What is the meaning of the word *salvation* for Israel? What is Israel's hope? What does Jesus have to do with any of this? Did he come to bring Israel's role, hope and salvation, to their climactic moment? Or only to announce the beginning of a completely different story with a different direction and goal entirely? The Gospels don't show Jesus presenting a case for people "going to heaven when they die." He is much more interested in his own immediate historical situation than in sharing timeless truths about humanity and the afterlife. Jesus uses the phrase "the kingdom of God" and its inauguration as the way to summarize his work.[13] He welcomes people into the kingdom, warns those who resist it, demonstrates its healing power, and effects its decisive moment when he confronts the prince of this world and the power of sin and death on the cross. Jesus says all of this is about God's will being done on earth as it already is in God's realm, heaven. An Elysium narrative account of the story of Jesus can't find support in the text

of the Gospels in any substantial way, and can't account well for what we do find there.

3. In his book *A Brief History of Heaven*, Alister McGrath writes that the perspective of Paul's letters, as with all the New Testament, points to a hope "beyond history" or "beyond this world" to a substantially different reality in another place.[14] According to McGrath we can see this clearly in places like Paul's letter to the church at Philippi, where Paul reminds the Christians that they are "citizens of heaven." McGrath elaborates:

> By speaking of the Christian community in this way, he naturally encourages his readers to think along certain lines. Those strands of thought would certainly include the following. The Christian church is an outpost of heaven in a foreign land. It speaks the language of that homeland, and is governed by its laws—despite the fact that the world around it speaks a different language, and obeys a different set of laws. Its institutions are based on those of its homeland. And, one day, its citizens will return to that homeland, to take up all the privileges and rights which that citizenship confers.

McGrath then concludes on the appropriate development of this theme in subsequent Christian writers: "The world is not our homeland; it is the place to which we have been exiled. During the long period of exile from heavenly realms, believers keep alive the hope of returning to the homeland."[15] The outright adoption of Platonic language here is remarkable; there are marked similarities to Socrates's speeches in Phaedo. Similarly remarkable is the direct association of life on earth with exile. We should recall that biblically, and already in the Eden story, exile is associated with death. We see the same pattern in Deuteronomy where life is the gift of God, which finds its specific blessings in the flourishing of the land of promise. To be in exile is to be in the judgment of God and outside his land and his gift of life. To identify exile with earthly life *per se* is to set the biblical picture on its head.

Yes, among the sermons in the book of Hebrews we find language of ancient saints who were "foreigners and strangers on earth" and "longing for a better country—a heavenly one." But this is—consistently throughout all the New Testament voices—a contrast between earth and heaven *now*, a contrast to be overcome when the heavenly reality, God's promised future, is revealed and brought to us. This promised future is always heaven and earth reunited. *Time* will bring the estranged *places* back together.

It's worth pursuing this key distinction a bit more. Many have mistaken *here* and *there* (especially *down here* and *up there*) as the most important way to identify the contrasts associated with the overcoming of evil and the triumph of good. But the Bible's key contrast is of *now* and *then* (this present evil age and the hope of the age to come). There is indeed an aspect of this future reality being kept in heaven and not yet present on earth, but this is the temporary stage of the overlapping of the two ages. The final image in the Bible is not about here versus there, but about the reunification of God's sphere and our sphere (a new heavens and a new earth) as a single created reality filled with the glory of God. So a more consistently biblical way of thinking of "citizens of heaven" or "foreigners on earth" language is to see our Christian identity intimately tied to the presence of our king, who is now in heaven but soon to be back on earth at his return. We are outposts of the kingdom of God in the territory he has reclaimed as his own.

Significantly, in the letter to the Philippians that McGrath cites, immediately after the heavenly citizenship comment Paul goes on to write, "And we eagerly await a Savior *from* there, the Lord Jesus Christ, who, by the power that enables him to bring everything under his control, will transform our lowly bodies so that they will be like his glorious body." This reveals that Paul is thinking precisely of a present division that will be overcome at the Messiah's return. Then he will assert his claim to all that is his ("to bring everything under his control") and to restore his people to renewed bodily life ("transform our lowly bodies so that they will be like his glorious body"). This is anything but Plato's escape from the corrupt world below to a purely spiritual realm above.

4. Finally, we come to the book of Revelation, the place where the specifics of heaven are said to be made most clear. It turns out the Elysium Bible fails on the crucial first step—one of the first obligations a reader of any book has is to figure out what kind of writing the book is, and to identify the conventions of that kind of writing. Revelation is a clear example of apocalyptic literature, which in the world of ancient Judaism came with such well-known conventions as the use of vivid symbols, a visitor to or from heaven disclosing spiritual realities behind present earthly events, and the visitor then taking the recipient of the vision on a heavenly journey to review the recent history and look into the future. But rather than honoring our covenant with

John and reading Revelation accordingly, it's been common to read (at least parts of) Revelation as literal descriptions of spiritual realities. Of course, this can't be done consistently with the book or patent absurdities result: Is Jesus literally a lamb with seven horns and seven eyes? But with the description of the New Jerusalem toward the end of the book, there is a long-standing tradition of latching on to the symbols as straightforward facts about what heaven looks like. Reading well will send us in a different direction, however: seeking the spiritual meaning of all the symbols. Not to mention that the New Jerusalem is said to come "down out of heaven from God" and to be part of a "new heaven and a new earth."

The Elysium reading further exacerbates the mistake of literalism by confusing the description of God's great and final victory at the Messiah's triumphant return with what believers can expect to experience immediately upon death. John writes, "He will wipe every tear from their eyes. There will be no more death or mourning or crying or pain." But the final phrase of that passage says, "For the old order of things has passed away." This is a reference to *time*. John is not describing what heaven is like now, but what will happen at the arrival of the age to come. Interestingly, earlier in the book, when John describes the experience of some of those in heaven (a group of martyrs), they are calling out loudly to God, "How long until you judge the inhabitants of the earth and avenge our blood?" Apparently they're still more concerned with what's happening on earth and with God's coming kingdom than with their individual bliss. Once again, the Elysium Bible falls short of what we actually find in the Bible when we read closely and well.

As we have seen, the Otherworldly Bible has its historical roots in Christianity's engagement with paganism and its views about what it means to be human and what our final destiny is. But when we make the attempt to read the vision for Elysium back into the Bible, it fails. The Historical Bible cannot with integrity be overcome by the Escape-from-History Bible. To even try this is to misread the script at a deep level. An otherworldly hope is not only *not* in the text, but the typical expression of this distorted hope is also sub-biblical in profound ways.

It should startle and disturb us to find the biblical hope for cosmic redemption and the implementation of God's justice reduced to an overly individualistic vision for personal happiness and family reunions. The literary ancients (and later the Reformers) dreamed of engaging conversations with great classical philosophers and poets in the afterlife. Today our longings tend to be more domestic. Either way, the substantial vision of the Scriptures for God's creatures to follow his good path for living within his world has been left far behind. One need only attend the typical Christian funeral or memorial service to realize how little interest there is in the thrust of the Bible's message for world transformation and renewed creational life. We think we're headed somewhere else. Of course, no one wants to deny grieving people of the comforts of very personal hopes—the issue here is of the context and direction of these personal hopes. The very fact that we could posit an "afterlife" as a worthy description of the goal of biblical salvation is significant evidence that we are not attuned to the story the Bible tells. The language itself should set off an alarm in our minds. God's greatest victory through the work of Jesus Christ results in a mere *after*life? And what of life—full, creational, embodied life as God intended? What of abundant, fulfilled and flourishing life—for all things?

It's long past the time for a search and replace operation regarding our widespread use of dualistic, Platonic language as a description of the Christian hope. When our teachers tell us "Life on earth is a temporary assignment" and "Your identity is in eternity, and your homeland is heaven," we must resolutely demur.[16] The Earthly Bible would teach us otherwise. If we will listen, there's much to learn about the grain and texture of the good life intended for us in this good world, both in this age and the one to come.

eleven

GROUNDED IN THE EARTHLY BIBLE

For the first fact you must grasp is this: the renewal of creation has been wrought by the Self-same Word who made it in the beginning. There is thus no inconsistency between creation and salvation; for the one father has employed the same agent for both works.

ATHANASIUS

The shallow reading of the Otherworldly Bible fails to adequately communicate the kind of story the Bible tells. A recovery of the Earthly Bible will reorient us to a truer tale of creation, fall and new creation. This account of the world, the rebellion that has come into it and the long struggle to win it back is something different entirely. It's here in a narrative about us and our world that we learn who we are and what we were made for. It's here in the Earthly Bible that we learn how evil corrupts and twists things within an inherently good place. It's here in a couldn't-be-more-this-worldly set of writings that we are called to join the battle for the good, the true and the beautiful.

THE KIND OF STORY THE BIBLE IS

Martin Heidegger said, "The world is the house where mortals dwell." Crucially, according to the Bible's opening song of creation, the world is also the house where God intends to dwell. He built it as his temple and took up his residence and rest within it on the seventh and final day.[1] Rather than bringing our anachronistic origins questions to this text, if we will attend to its own agenda, we'll learn the determining trajectory for entire biblical narrative. This purpose is set out when we see God making his home right in the midst of his newborn creation, establishing boundaries and setting forth the good path that will lead to life for his creatures. The flourishing and development of the new world result from a partnership between God and his image-bearers.

When this intention is disrupted, the result is not an abandonment of the original purpose. The result is the beginning of a journey of recovery. The creation-temple could not simply be given over to evil—brokenness and despair, death and decay—because it is the newly-built dwelling place of the Most High. It is not enough for God to "rescue" some of his creatures out of the world to some other place while the temple itself goes down in flames. Where would they go? They are *adam* from *adamah*. The man is made from the ground, and the human fate is irrevocably bound to it. The story is one of restoration and life and not defeat and retreat to some other realm.

So God's plan unfolds in the direction of reclaiming the earth. As we have already stated, the Bible is a progressive revelation, that is, a genuine story that moves and changes as opposed to a static revelation that is the same from start to finish. Neither the final shape of things nor the means of getting there are revealed in toto at the beginning of the story. But as each step of redemption is unveiled, the fundamental assumption that salvation must be worked out on the ground remains.

Thus we see that Israel's overall place in the story is as a kind of do-over for the human race after the failure of the first humans in God's garden. N. T. Wright describes Israel's self-understanding in the first century:

> Granted the presence of evil in the world, what is the creator going to do about it? The answer given by a wide range of Jewish writers from the redactor of Genesis to the late rabbis is clear: he has called Israel to be his people. "I will make Adam first," says Israel's god in the midrash on Genesis, "and if he goes astray I will send Abraham to sort it all out." The creator calls a people through whom, somehow, he will act decisively within his creation, to eliminate evil from it and to restore order, justice and peace.[2]

Obedience, righteousness, blessing—these things only have meaning in the narrative as they are embodied, lived out and experienced by God's people. When the instruction of Torah is given to the people it is detailed in ways that reflect the creation story. For example, in his delightful and thought-provoking book *The Hungry Soul*, Leon Kass reflects on how Israel's food restrictions "pay homage to the articulated order of the world and the dignity of life and living form. . . . The dietary laws of Leviticus commemorate the Creation and the Creator and beckon us toward holiness."[3] The status of an animal as clean or unclean is directly related to how it reflects (or fails to reflect) the boundaries and intentions God revealed for creatures in the founding stories of Genesis. This is how the story proceeds. Each step, each advance of God's growing intervention, reveals yet another creation-related reclamation.

The conditions and consequences of the blessings and curses in the Deuteronomic treaty of the Great King are all about rain and crops, barns and kneading troughs, livestock and lending. The institution and evaluation of Israel's leaders—judges, priests, kings—have to do with the use of power and influence in the advancement of God's purposes for land and people. Everyone, servant and leader alike, is judged by their respect for God's justice. The role of the prophets within the canon is to report on Israel's success or failure as invited co-managers of the chaos that has invaded the creation. Sadly, it seems Israel is more often like the whirlwind than a force for peace and flourishing in the land. So the prophets are forced to announce the consequences: having defiled the land rather than function as a light for the nations, Israel must be exiled from the new garden of the Lord even as Adam and Eve were from the first. But even this cannot frustrate God's determined insistence to see his first purpose through to the end. Israel has been judged and found wanting, but exile will lead to return. The prophetic vision turns to a kind of double do-over. The renewed humanity (Israel), which had embraced the rebellion, will now be renewed.

What is the shape of this long-expected promise? What will this renewal accomplish? Will it be, finally, a major change of course? A reversal of the kind of story we've seen so far? Will the new king reveal a completely new hope, or perhaps a change of venue? A story no longer about earth, but about heaven? From both sides—promise and fulfillment—we see a continuation of the story so far. The prophesies are of healed bodies and a healed land, and of a king who embraces justice and peace, bringing a government the likes of which has never been seen before. Here the scales are fair and the bags filled with grain rather than sweepings. Bloated bovine women no longer cow the poor, swords are melted down, and public interest in small-scale farming and new wine go up. The stain of wrongdoing will be dealt with and removed. The Lord himself will instruct the people in his good ways on the path of life. The creation-temple will be rebuilt. Israel's hope was firmly set on the kind of things the drama had been about all along—life in the world, God's way.

When the story announces the arrival of the king, the references are all back to these promises. The Word that was there at the beginning has come here to dwell with us once again. The humble are lifted up and the hungry are fed. The rule of the prince of darkness over land and people is challenged. The Lord has kept his word to David's house so the do-over people can get back on track and to their task of bringing salvation to the ends of the earth. When the new king fights his decisive battle against evil and triumphs—not by escaping to another place but in a reversal of death that puts him firmly back on the ground—he issues fresh instructions to his followers. He has not a word to say about spreading the announcement of a new passport to Elysium, but he does claim authority over all of heaven and earth. He reaffirms his abiding presence with his people. Thus empowered, his disciples are told to reclaim the nations and instruct the peoples in obedience to the ways of the world's newly revealed Lord.

When we come to the final acts of the drama, it should be no surprise that the ending is in keeping with all we've read about up to this point. As Rikk Watts notes, the finale is like the opening, but more so. Eschatology recapitulates protology, and there will be a fittingness to the initial contours of the story when we see it come to its conclusion.[4] On the other hand, the Bible shows no strong interest in an afterlife. It is there, of course, but it functions merely as a necessary stage on the way to the ending that matters: the return of the king, his reckoning of the world, and the full institution of the healing and restoring reign of God over all things. It is a new creation story, not a post-creation story. There will indeed be a homecoming, but not one with souls longing to return to ethereal realms above. Rather, God will come back to his now rebuilt temple and make his home with us, here.

From start to finish, the story teaches us that salvation is fundamentally restoration. Al Wolters has noted that the key biblical words for God's saving action share this orientation. Redemption is buying back or restoring freedom. Reconciliation is the restoration of good relationship or friendship. Renewal is simply to restore something to a state of being like new, without the degenerative effects that time typically imposes. Regeneration is the restoration of life itself. And even the word salvation refers to the return to a state of health or wholeness after suffering an illness or loss.[5] This is why the Bible's own description of the destination of the story is never "heaven," but rather *resurrection, the renewal of all things, the time for God to restore everything*, the *liberation of creation*, a *new heavens and a new earth*, or *the life of the age to come*. This is the kind of story the Bible is. Historically, we lost this, not by attending closely to the text, but by being distracted and wooed by an altogether different narrative from somewhere else. We over-accommodated a Hellenistic worldview and our own first story was lost somewhere back in a Judean mist.

So if this is indeed what the content of the drama is (and not merely the ending but every part along the way), what are the implications for our reading of the Bible? What will the recovery of the Earthly Bible change?

READING THE BIBLE FOR LIFE

If we were to deeply accommodate our reading and living of the Bible to this creation-restoring narrative, the result would be a greater attentiveness to the texture and shape of the story in its granular detail. If the goal is no longer escape from the world but engagement with it in the interest of God's reclamation project, then we have reason to listen more carefully to what the text tells us about things like the nature of the created, the false ways of the rebellion and the path to life renewed. We will be more intimate in our Bible reading in order that we might be more attentive in our life in the world.

What I would call textured reading is based on all the Bibles we have recovered so far. We read whole books in their literary and historical contexts. We read them slowly, because when we read too quickly we can't read closely. We seek to receive and understand the books on their own terms. Then we gain an interest in how the books come together to form the bigger story that God is telling in the Bible. All of this has to do with first reading the

Bible to understand what it meant then and there. Once that's done, we have a fair chance of doing right by here and now. How does the Bible speak life to us in this time and place? Here we must learn the skill of discerning both the continuity and the discontinuity of the Bible's story with our story.

There is no formula or chart that will help us in this. Such a reading for apt dramatic performance of the story in our own scene and on our own stage is an art. We have to work it out together in community and with all the aids the author has given us. And this is how it should be. We are humans, significant creatures gifted in multiple ways. To be directly given the correct answers to all our questions in a mechanical way would diminish what God created us to be. The Bible's goal is to guide us into a stellar performance before the watching eyes of the world. As we've seen in chapter nine, the authority of the Bible is a narrative authority rather than a reference-book authority. A close and attentive reading of the story so far will teach us how the world works, what the perennial temptations are and what God's redemptive surprises consistently look like.

It's obvious that our world is vastly different from the Bible's various times and cultures, so of course discontinuities can be found. The exact shape of many cultural practices and entities changes through history—marriage arrangements, gender roles, means of warfare, economic practices, social structures, types of government, and on and on. But paradoxically, it's in finely textured reading—reading that pays attention to the small descriptive features of a passage—that we will discover the great continuities of the biblical drama with ours. The deep elements of the story don't change, and it's the details that most clearly reveal the depths of human nature, how sin works insidiously within us, how we can honor God and begin to be agents of healing and well-being. It's in a renewed commitment to this kind of earthy Bible reading that we will find light for our path.

What we have in the Bible, says Wendell Berry, "is a story and a discourse about the connection of a people to a place."[6] Since by God's design we too are emplaced people, it's in attending carefully to how those who came before played their parts that we will embrace and live in our places well.[7] Those ancient stories and songs and sayings will have more to say to us once we are properly focused on discovering God's path for this life in this place.

Perhaps if we're not thinking those stories, songs and sayings are prepara-
tions for a fundamentally different kind of life we will experience somewhere else, they will gain new stature in our eyes. For example, Robert Alter
has unveiled for us the artfulness of the biblical narrative form.[8] Because we
too eagerly jump to the world-be moral of the story, the small kernel of
timeless truth or even just the advancement of the Bible's overall plot, we are
typically not attentive to the word play, repetition, reversals and the careful
attention to settings and place names that carry deeper lessons, but do so
more subtly than we are used to. To illustrate this, Alter carefully unpacks
how the Joseph stories in the book of Genesis are tied together by repeated
reference to the words "to recognize" and "to know." It's in knowing and not
knowing, in being deceived and in having a lot to learn that the Joseph
stories turn again and again.[9] In the Joseph stories we can be instructed in
the nature of human foibles, our own temptations to thinking we know it all
and how we are often deceived by the outward appearance of things. In short,
we learn more about what it means to be human in a place like this. We learn
the value of combining a humble appraisal of our discernment of things with
a long-term faith in God's bigger purposes that will be revealed in good time.

If we embrace the Earthly Bible, such advantages will show themselves
again and again across the biblical landscape. In the ancient Torah we will
find untapped resources for discerning God's intentions for land use, economics, good governance, care for the poor and many other aspects of God's
longed for justice in human relations. This is not a matter of looking up
isolated verses (while ignoring others) and seeking direct application from
an ancient scene to a contemporary one. It's a matter of reading well how
Israel's instructions functioned in that time and place to advance human
well-being and shalom and to move the story of restoration forward, and
then considering the lessons for us today.[10]

Ancient wisdom literature will open up multiple case studies of how all
kinds of human endeavors (hard work, sleeping in, bragging), relation-
ships (husband and wives, fathers and sons, rulers and subjects), temptations (cheating, adultery, lying), and attitudes (humility, pride, eagerness,
patience) can be navigated, embraced or shunned for a greater chance at
success in the art of living. Israel's ancient songs will open up the world of
hearts crying out to God about conditions on earth, both in protest and

celebration. Ancient thundering prophets will reveal how seriously God takes what's happening on earth, what he expects from his people and the shape of his future intentions. First-century gospels will take us to the decisive turn in the entire story, how God moved once and for all to reclaim his creation and bring his kingdom to earth. The Son of God went so far as to become *adam* from *adamah*, a man from the ground, to engage the battle for God's good world. The New Testament letters provide us with examples of how others earlier in the story sought to live out the newly inaugurated Jesus-life in their own settings. We learn what our own pitfalls, struggles and personal triumphs are likely to be as we attempt to embody the Spirit-empowered new-creation life in the midst of an age that is passing away.

In all of this we can begin to learn the fundamental realities of human life on earth. What are the regular and persistent categories of failure that mark the ongoing human story? How can good speech and right actions contribute to the creation of shalom in God's temple? What's the right response to injustice? How should we live if we have bad leaders? Why pray? What is God doing to set things right in the world? How should we deal with conflict in the community of God's people? What is the role of lament? How does power operate for good or ill? What did the life and ministry of Jesus accomplish? Why does self-sacrificing servanthood matter? Where is our first allegiance due? Does it matter what we do with our bodies? What is the role of worship in our lives? Who is God? How do we know him? These are the questions of life on earth. These are the questions the Bible addresses and the issues it informs.

When all those finely-textured Bible readings come together they form a biblical metanarrative, which, as Richard Bauckham reminds us, moves determinedly from this present evil age to the renewal of life in the age to come, from one place to all places, and from one people to all peoples on earth in a "trajectory of blessing."[11] There is continuity between this life and our resurrection life in the world to come. After writing at length about the resurrection in 1 Corinthians, Paul's conclusion highlights this: "Therefore, my dear brothers and sisters, stand firm. Let nothing move you. Always give yourselves fully to the work of the Lord, because you know that your labor in the Lord is not in vain." This work of the Lord should be as broad in scope as the redemptive work of Jesus the Messiah that establishes and motivates it in the first place. Jesus has made peace through his blood shed on the cross, reconciling to God all that is in heaven and on earth. Our work is not in vain because God will regenerate us *and* our world. Good work will carry over. Though thick darkness can still seem to cover all things and to blunt our efforts and blind the world, we arise and shine because the light of renewal has already come into the world, and the light will complete its work. This is our story, this our drama, this our destination.

We are compelled therefore to seize upon a holy sensuousness. We will brook no narrow pietism that limits God's reign to our hearts and interior lives. Our passion for his reign is as wide as the world. Having been immersed in the particularities of the Scriptures, we turn our attention to all the particularities of life on earth. This is our Father's world, his temple, his home.

This is why the religion of worldly renunciation is so devastatingly wrong. This is why we are interested in all things. We want to know how they work, what their effects are in the world, what they do to us and to other creatures. We want to know the inner workings of God's temple. We want to know about weather, digital technology, soil, food, urban planning, physics, literature, politics, music, forestry, factories, wealth creation, management theories, sexual relations, brain chemistry and psychopharmacology, immigration, transportation, fashion, posture, friendship, theater, power plant engineering, how to survive in the woods, the ecology of oceans, accounting, sales and marketing, what babies know, microbrews, social media, cloning, space exploration, human history, the use and abuse of power, and the difference between Cool Whip and whipped cream, to name but a very, very few.

The good news of the Earthly Bible is that if we have turned away from our commitment to wrongdoing and our addiction to ourselves, then we are now a part of what John Dominic Crossan calls "collaborative eschatology."[12] God has invited us to join with him in the coming of the kingdom, the revelation of the new way to be human. We shun the temptation of living merely distracted lives in shallow entertainment, or to ignoring this world in our longing for another place. Rather, we are rapt with attention to all God has made and all God is doing. We read the Bible to learn this life.

OPENING OUR EYES TO A NEW KIND OF WORLD

In August 1990 I set out alone to climb two peaks in the Sawatch Range of central Colorado, Mts. Belford and Oxford, each over 14,000 feet above sea level. While these are relatively tame peaks by Colorado standards, any mountains at that height should be shown proper respect. The approach comes from the northwest of Mt. Belford, which is therefore climbed first. This allows someone to cross the saddle over to Oxford and complete two coveted fourteeners in one day. As usual for a summer day in the mountains, the morning was clear, bright and calm. The regular plan is to start early and try to get off the peaks before the afternoon storms would come in.

However, by the time I was coming down Belford and heading east over to Oxford, thick clouds were already rolling overhead and beginning to settle down on the highest points. I was feeling strong and doing well at that point, so I pressed on. When I got to the top of Oxford, it began to lightly snow. I headed back down quickly. I needed to re-ascend Belford in order to get to the access trail off its northwestern slopes. But coming down Oxford I rushed too much and got a bit reckless. My foot slipped off an icy rock and I badly twisted my knee. I was not completely immobilized, but from here on I was walking slowly and gingerly. As I finally hit the bottom of the saddle and started to head back up Belford, I found that upward movement brought terrible pain to my now-swollen knee. I tried again, but it became clear to me that I would not be climbing any more mountains on this day. I could slowly descend, but I could not climb.

Not wanting to panic, I sat down in the now-driving snowstorm to consider my options. I looked longingly back up at Mt. Belford to the west, knowing that way was shut off. I turned and looked down at the valley straight to the north. It looked passable, although there was no trail there. But I wasn't lost, I was merely trapped. I knew this drainage would eventually take me back to the road I'd come on, though I'd be to the east of where I'd parked. Seeing no other viable option, I started to hobble down the rocks toward the tree line below.

My knee held up and eventually I got off the rocks and onto softer ground at the lower elevations. But I saw a problem ahead. The line of vegetation spread out in front of me like a solid wall. A person can walk quickly through a forest when there is a trail to follow; bushwhacking is another matter entirely. With my handicap, I knew I was in no condition to fight through trees and bushes. I stood there for a long time, searching the edge of the trees for an opening: anything that might make the looming disaster somehow less, well, disastrous. I seriously considered setting up some kind of camp and spending the night, though the freshly fallen snow made that rather unappealing.

As I was standing there somewhat paralyzed, an unexpected and utterly remarkable thing happened. A large buck stepped out of the woods right at its edge. He stood there in the opening for several moments looking around and then quietly walked right back into the forest. It was one of those rare moments in the world when you see a big animal up close—wild and gorgeous. Such a thing commands your attention; such times are a gift from the Creator. But another gift was also given in that moment. I found what I so desperately needed: a path. There, right where the buck had stood, was the very faint line of a game trail, previously invisible. I kept my eyes fixed on that slender spot and began to move toward it. When I got to the slice in the wall of trees, I stopped before venturing in (and eventually finding my way home). I considered this: What kind of place is the world? I admit I hadn't even bothered to pray for help, foolishly focused instead on my own limited abilities and makeshift plans. And yet help had arrived, unlooked for. I was forever marked by what happened that day. From that time forward I have never doubted that the world we live in is an enchanted place. There is so much more to our dwelling place than our superficial, distracted glances would indicate. And from then on I knew it. I had found the woods where mystery lives, where goodness comes out of nowhere to aid the injured wayfarer.[13]

We live in a place that is within a story. What kind of place? What kind of story? C. S. Lewis invites us to consider the crucial truth about where we live: "Let us suppose that this everyday world were, at some point, invaded by the marvelous. Let us, in fact, suppose a violation of the frontier."[14] Invaded by what marvel, we ask? Invaded, indeed, by whom? Biblical commentator G. B. Caird wrote that the New Testament never actually uses the word *eschaton* (neuter), the end or final event. The holy writings do, however, know "the *eschatos* (masculine), a person who is both the beginning and the end."[15] Behold, the Earthly Bible says, the *eschatos* makes all things new. This is his world. We don't have to leave it, forsake it or even dim our eyes from it, for he has saved it all. If we want to know the Bible and do justice to it, we have to know this.

So saving the Bible opens our eyes to the saving of the world. We should find that when we take in the whole Bible on its own terms as the narrative of God's mighty work, the story is one of a glorious restoration. All we are and all God intended for his creation-temple will be found in the land of things made new. It was the Historical Bible that prepared the way for our understanding of this reclamation project described in the Scriptures. What, then, might be further implied by a Feasting Bible? Should our festival of eating books whole be done alone?

- twelve -

MY PRIVATE BIBLE

Ten thousand Reformers like so many moles
Have plowed all the Bible and cut it [in] holes
And each has his church at the end of his trace
Built up as he thinks of the subjects of grace

RICHARD McNEMAR

The second generation of Judeans who had returned from exile in Babylon were struggling to regain a secure place in the world and a sense of their identity as the people of God. Their capital city, Jerusalem, had been razed and the temple-home of their God had been looted and then destroyed. During their exile people from other places had settled in much of their land. The Judeans didn't have their own king and many of them were intermarrying with foreigners. There was little sense of any continuing vocation as a people. They were weak, confused, unsettled.

But Ezra the priest and Nehemiah the governor joined together to lead the people into a covenant renewal ceremony. Crumbled walls could be rebuilt. Stories could be retold. Purpose could be rediscovered. Then the community gathered together.

> On the first day of the seventh month Ezra the priest brought the Law before
> the assembly, which was made up of men and women and all who were able
> to understand. He read it aloud from daybreak till noon as he faced the

square before the Water Gate in the presence of the men, women and others who could understand. And all the people listened attentively to the Book of the Law.

Ezra the teacher of the Law stood on a high wooden platform built for the occasion. Beside him on his right stood Mattithiah, Shema, Anaiah, Uriah, Hilkiah and Maaseiah; and on his left were Pedaiah, Mishael, Malkijah, Hashum, Hashbad-danah, Zechariah and Meshullam.

Ezra opened the book. All the people could see him because he was standing above them; and as he opened it, the people all stood up. Ezra praised the LORD, the great God; and all the people lifted their hands and responded, "Amen! Amen!" Then they bowed down and worshiped the LORD with their faces to the ground.

The Levites—Jeshua, Bani, Sherebiah, Jamin, Akkub, Shabbethai, Hodiah, Maaseiah, Kelita, Azariah, Jozabad, Hanan and Pelaiah—instructed the people in the Law while the people were standing there. They read from the Book of the Law of God, making it clear and giving the meaning so that the people understood what was being read. (From the temple history of Chronicles–Ezra–Nehemiah)

It's an amazing picture from our Scriptures of a key moment in the overall drama. A monumental crisis had come, shaking the self-understanding of the community and nation, and here is the story of Jacob's tribe attempting to reengage their founding narrative. Who are we? they asked. Is our God still interested in us? For what purpose? Is the story of Abraham's descendants going anywhere—anywhere that matters?

One element of this story that's particularly striking is the communal nature of the event. All the people came together "as one" to join in this ceremony. Men, women and all who could understand were there. They stood as a group to hear the Law read. They wept together as they realized how far they'd fallen away from God's calling for them. And then they ate and drank together with great joy, sharing freely with those who had nothing prepared. The picture is of a corporate entity regaining its standing and renewing its commitment to be a unique force for God in the world. Together.

Once again we find within the pages of the Bible a crucial element that has been largely lost in our experience today. We just don't do things communally like this. We don't act as one, repent as one, commit as one, rejoice as one. We do these things (if we do them at all) as individuals. In fact, so deep is our Western individualism that it doesn't even occur to us that our experience with the Bible, and our role as significant players in the redemptive drama, should or could be centered on anything other than our own personal experience and actions. How did we manage to lose such a fundamental feature of the Scriptures? How did we turn a text that is for and about communities into a private book about me and God?

FROM SOLA SCRIPTURA TO SOLA ME

It can be a little disconcerting to our contemporary consciousness to consider that for the vast majority of Christian history people did not even have the option of studying the Scriptures in private. The Bible was a communal book because most people only encountered it in corporate settings. They might have been troubled by the roar of a shepherd prophet in the city center or heard the sacred writings publicly read (whether in worship gatherings of God's people or taught out in the open by traveling mendicant friars), or seen it performed in medieval street plays—but the Bible was always experienced in community. Folks couldn't have pursued the discipline of a personal "daily quiet time" with the Bible even if some time-traveling Navigator had told them they should. It's remarkable to realize how late in time the elements came together to even allow the existence of what is considered a standard element of the Christian life. My Private Bible is most definitely a modern phenomena. To this historical journey we briefly turn.

Colin Morris claims that as early as the twelfth century something close to the modern independent-thinking and assertive individual began to emerge in Europe.[1] It was the beginning of what would be a centuries-long transformation in the West away from the preeminence of community, clan and traditional forms of authority, and toward the self-reliant, independent individual so central to the modern age. This was a result of things such as increased trade and the subsequent sharing of ideas, the growth of cities, a new psychology that elevated self-awareness and self-knowledge, a weakening of the ties to traditional locations of power, and even a heightened emphasis on romantic love. In addition, within the Christian faith itself we can see a move away from the objective, corporate nature of Christ's saving work to emphasize the benefits for each individual, subjectively received and celebrated. Along with this came the development of a more fervent personal religious devotion. This "discovery of the individual," as Morris calls it, was the essential first step that led to what would become our characteristically modern way of engaging the Bible. "Me" and "mine" came to be firmly established as the center of modernist experience and expectation.

Later, other critical pieces began to fall into place. Bible historian and cataloger of medieval manuscripts Laura Light has written that the center of the European commercial book trade in the thirteenth century was found in a culturally vibrant and economically flourishing Paris.[2] It would be two more centuries before Johannes Gutenberg's printing press would begin assembly-line-style mass production of books. But Light reports that in late-medieval Paris "Bibles were copied in significant numbers, making them much more widely available to individuals than they had been earlier."[3] The surprising proliferation of these small, efficiently hand-copied and similarly featured sacred books earned them the designation *Paris Bibles*. A prerequisite for the me-and-the-Bible-alone paradigm was a technology that could produce enough copies for everyone to have one. That technology was at first simply more hands copying more Bibles. This happened because booksellers found a growing demand for Bibles among university students and teachers, leaders in the church, aristocracy and members of the royal court, and even the newly formed class of merchants and businessmen. The increasing appetite in the commercial trade for handy, affordable Scriptures was a crucial factor on the road to an individualized Bible experience.

All of this increased exponentially once mechanical, moveable type came along. In the 1450s Gutenberg quickly began producing Bibles, and in succeeding decades it became increasingly possible for Christian lay people to obtain copies of Holy Writ for themselves. This in turn was a major contributing influence on the shape of the revolution within the church that would become known as the Reformation. This reform movement (turned schism) claimed that its renewing spirit was born in the pages of the Bible. Of all the *solas* that characterized the Protestants (faith, grace, Christ, etc.), the Reformers would claim *sola scriptura* as the formal source of the others. Here, apart from any so-called sacred tradition, was found the only reliable source of spiritual truth. It was here that the protesters found the teachings that had been submerged under centuries of accumulated baggage and distortion.

The image of the bold reformer standing alone with the Word of God and defying something as weighty and history-laden as the Roman Catholic Church would be seared into the minds of generations of Protestants. Combined with a teaching like the priesthood of all believers, the effect was bound to be profound—and also to go further than that first generation of Reformers would have ever imagined. It can be argued that the leaders of the Reformation had never intended and would soundly disapprove of the idea of each and every person being their own interpreter of the Bible. But this cat was most definitely out of the bag and would prove impossible for Protestants to control. The theological splitting of hairs commenced, but it was any remaining semblance of church unity that was ultimately split.

People now had their own Bibles in the vernacular and were free to read and interpret however they wished. The once-solid foundation and giveness of centuries of hierarchical church authority had crumbled and was replaced by the commonsense readings of everyman. Further, the invention of a chapter and verse Bible made it easier than ever to latch onto quirky out-of-context teachings. With each numbered verse individually paragraphed, standing out like a beacon of divine revelation, there were now over thirty-thousand truthlets available to be mined and mixed into an inestimable number of new combinations. Such a Bible, placed into the hands of so many people, was capable of producing a dazzling array of interpretative and theological innovations. Who could contain such a thing? Not the church.

The combined effect of these factors should not be underestimated. New ways of handling the Bible would be invented (we've already noted Jaroslav Pelikan's observation about "the heaping up of proof-texts"). New expectations would be placed on the Bible. New understandings of the nature and form of biblical truth would emerge. New structures of church authority along with new patterns for challenging that authority would be developed. Among certain Protestant groups the phrases "Bible-based" and "Bible-believing" would become the preferred way of claiming the religious high ground. Many groups would place the word *independent* right into the name of their denomination. All of this because of the convergence of five streams: the rise of the modernist conception of the individual, the proliferation of printed Bibles, the emphases of the Protestant Reformation, the visual fragmentation of the text of the Bible, and finally, a new consumer-oriented delivery system for a commodified Bible. All of this would be more than enough to account for the birth of My Private Bible. But there's more.

All of these factors came together in one place more than any other, a place founded on the idea of individual liberty along with a self-conscious and deliberate turning away from tradition, history and authority. The unique cultural setting that is the United States of America would come to have a significant effect on both the form the Bible would take and the standard way of reading the text as speaking particularly to individuals. America's founding political philosophy would spill over into all areas of life, including religion.

Just as we would not be ruled by kings, we would not allow church authorities (especially priests and bishops) to tell us what to believe or how to worship. It was no accident that the "Bible alone" and "no creed but the Bible" movements would take hold here. Or that it was on this particular soil that Protestantism would splinter into thousands of denominations. America's populism, separatism, profound distrust of older ways of doing and believing, and bedrock trust in the good sense of the common man would lift private reading and private interpretation of the Bible to new heights. The democratization of America's Christianity was decisive for the establishment of an overly-individualized use of the Bible.[4]

Although the commodification of the Bible is not always brought up in discussions about the Bible in America, it's worth saying a bit more about it. In her book *The Bible and the People*, Lori Anne Ferrell has a lively chapter on the Bible as a commercial product in nineteenth century America.[5] It's a fascinating and little explored subject—how and why a collection of sacred writings that was explicitly in the care and keeping of the church came to be largely handed over to businesses that by their nature have a very different purpose. But for now our concern is with the specific question of how the increasingly commercial distribution of the Bible came to change what we thought the Bible was for.

Ferrell writes that Americans "were no longer the readers envisaged by ambitious Protestant theologians and translators but *consumers*."[6] She goes on to describe how one Bible-publishing firm, the J. G. Ford Company, instructed their traveling salesmen to "UNDERSTAND THE NATURE OF THE BUSINESS. . . . You must depend on your ability to describe the work so as to first excite an *interest* in it, and *then* a *desire* for it."[7] A commercialized society of course targets individual consumers. When the Bible becomes a commodity in such a setting it is inevitable that the Bible will be made to be sold and presented as something with special benefits for these individual customers. This perception was reinforced by the individual study aids added to the text, as well as the sales and marketing language that described these Bibles. Targeting Bibles to consumers has only strengthened in our day as publishers find that Bibles can consistently be their bestselling, most profitable book. The trick now is to find a way to sell people yet another Bible when the average American home already has four, and the average Christian household ten.[8] The answer has been to trumpet how this new Bible is *just for you*, helping you understand and apply the Bible to your personal life in a whole new way.

Stanley Hauerwas asserts that "the problem now is not how *sola scriptura* was used by the Reformers but how it is used by us."[9] The legacy handed down to American Christians denies that our own interpretations of the Bible should be interfered with by any outside authority, whether ecclesiastical or historical. We were led to develop an oversized confidence in the ability of common people using common sense to read a clear and plain text (the perspicuity of Scripture), with the help of the Holy Spirit, to arrive at spiritual truth.

It seems clear enough that individualism is one of the core assumptions that lie behind Bible reading in America. It's not something we argue for. I simply read the Bible alone and presume that it is supposed to speak first and foremost to me (and to do so directly) and that I already possess everything I need to understand it rightly. Harold Bloom, at the close of his book on the American religion (which he claims is preeminently about personal, enthusiastic and gnostic experience), writes that "large unconscious assumptions have far more to do with belief than do overt doctrinal teachings, at least among our vast Protestant population."[10] And as the authors of a more recent book on the distortions Western readers bring to the text of the Bible claim, our cultural assumptions are like the lenses through which we see Scripture.[11] We rarely stop to examine the lenses themselves, but it's now time to do so. The distortions of My Private Bible are yet another set of chains from which the Bible must be loosed.

What Reading Alone Looks Like

The young woman had been listening intently all week as counselors and fellow campers shared their personal experiences as followers of Jesus. She found all of it intriguing and, truth be told, very attractive. The Jesus she heard about seemed real, and he definitely had made a difference in how these people lived. She'd felt disoriented in her own life for quite some time. If these people were anything, they were focused and seemed to know where they were going in life. So on the last night of camp, when an invitation was extended for those who "didn't already know Jesus" to come forward and "receive him," she went for it. At that moment she felt confident and pretty eager, though not especially emotional. One of the counselors took her aside and spoke with her about what this moment really meant, and then talked her through a prayer.

A little later she was given a New Testament along with a set of questions to ask about whatever passage she was reading. These questions included Who? What? Where? When? Why? and then What do I learn about God? and What do I learn about me? The counselor told her that the main thing is to find something practical, something she could hang on to from the Bible and think about throughout the day. She was encouraged to set aside a certain time every day when she would read this New Testament and pray to God. If she would do this, she was assured, God would always teach her new things and she would grow closer to Jesus.

This little vignette, typical of evangelical practice in many of its features, reveals how individualism is simply one of the givens of our common pattern of biblical interaction. But the new Christian set on such a course has little chance of discovering the true nature of the Scriptures. She's been sent on an explicit mission to seek out what the text says directly to her every day in a very practical way. The context or parameters of her Bible reading have been determined from the outset to be focused on an inward and personal spiritual journey. She now has the expectation that this is what the Bible will do for her. But in addition to being untrue to the Bible in fundamental ways, the evidence now is that this model has failed to capture and hold the attention of those who aspire to Bible reading.[12]

For a variety of historical reasons, Bible reading in particular (and Christianity in general) has become an internal affair. The influences that led to a strongly individualized Bible have combined with the significant pietist impulse in evangelicalism to drive us inward. Reading the Bible has become less about reality outside of me and what God might be doing there, and more and more about my personal spiritual life, mostly viewed in isolation. There are two significant implications of this when it comes to our encounter with the Bible.

First, this way of reading the Bible leads us to mistake the intended audience of the Bible's messages. Having turned our attention inward, we now believe the Bible addresses us immediately. This can be seen clearly in the demand for Bible devotionals that morph Bible verses into God's private encouraging words just for me. In the introduction to her bestselling book *Jesus Calling*, Sarah Young explains the process by which historical writings grounded in particular realities of ancient religious communities can be made to sound like they were written only for me:

> I knew that God communicated with me through the Bible, but I yearned for more. Increasingly, I wanted to hear what God had to say to me personally on a given day. I decided to listen to God with pen in hand, writing down whatever I believed He was saying. I felt awkward the first time I tried this, but I received a message. It was short, biblical, and appropriate. It addressed topics that were current in my life: trust, fear, and closeness to God. . . . I have included Scripture references after each daily reading. As I listened to God, Bible verses or fragments of verses often came to mind. I have interwoven these into my messages.[13]

What is fascinating when we read the *Jesus Calling* devotionals is how these "fragments" from the Bible can be called into service for any number of personal errands. The overriding theme of the book is to constantly put the believer into firm contact with, as Jesus himself apparently calls them, "My Presence" and "My Peace." Thus any verse from any passage, regardless of its original context, is made to serve this purpose:

> Come to Me with all your weaknesses: physical, emotional, and spiritual. Rest in the comfort of My Presence, remembering that *nothing is impossible with Me*. Pry your mind away from your problems so you can focus your attention on Me. Recall that I am *able to do immeasurably more than all you ask or imagine*. Instead of trying to direct Me to do this and that, seek to attune yourself to what I am *already* doing.

When anxiety attempts to wedge its way into your thoughts, remind yourself that *I am your Shepherd.* The bottom line is that I am taking care of you; therefore, you needn't be afraid of anything. Rather than trying to maintain control over your life, abandon yourself to My will. Though this may feel frightening—even dangerous, the safest place to be is in My will. (Luke 1:37; Ephesians 3:20-21; Psalm 23:1-4)[14]

In similar fashion, Colin Urquhart's foreword to *Your Personal Bible* explains his goal this way:

I have been concerned to learn how to enable others to grasp the wonderful truths of Scripture in such a way that they will hear God speaking to them personally and directly. . . . Sometimes I write out passages of Scripture as they appear in the pages of the Bible. At other times I personalise the Scriptures so that God speaks the words directly to me. Or I write down in the first person singular, what the Word says to me about me.[15]

Urquhart then goes on to rewrite Bible verses on such inherently corporate topics as our election in Christ, our inheritance as God's people, the Good Shepherd (a common ancient Near Eastern image for a nation's king) and the new creation. If indeed the Bible is "to me about me," then those awkward plurals must be transformed:

"In love he predestined me"

"For I was like a sheep going astray, but now I have returned to the Shepherd and overseer of my soul"

"As in Adam I die, so in Christ I am made alive"

"Christ's love compels me, because I am convinced that one died for me, therefore I died. And he died for me that I should no longer live for myself but for him who died for me and was raised again. . . . All this from God, who reconciled me to himself through Christ and gave me the ministry of reconciliation"[16]

But, of course, these passages are actually about "we" and "all" and "us."

While these might seem like extreme examples, the general pattern is common enough. Tyndale's *Life Application Bible*, Zondervan's *VerseLight Bible* series (*Find Hope, Find Faith, Find Love* and *Find Prayer*, with select verses highlighted in blue so you can easily find the words you need), and in the digital realm, YouVersion's and Bible Gateway's most popular features are all verse-centric. In an atmosphere where consumer choice is the bottom line, the pressure is overwhelming on Bible providers to shape the Bible to these market-driven expectations. The core proposal is that these and similar tools will help you quickly find the small pieces of the Bible that seem to speak directly and meaningfully to you individually without having to bother with who these words were first written to and what they might have meant then. By keeping the treasured words few in number, they can be made to speak personally and immediately. If more words were included, references to Samaria and Corinth would start popping up and quickly confuse things, requiring more steps to figure out how and if the words can be made to apply to me.

The liberties taken here and their implications are rather staggering. In our zeal to get a Bible that is "Me first and Mine second" we're willing to deny the obvious character of the Scriptures as a collection of sacred writings to other people in particular times, places and situations and pretend instead that it was meant all along to be God's special words just for me. Plainly, this is not a high view of Scripture being put into practice, in spite of the claims of the practitioners. The Bible is what it is, and it was not inspired to be a field to be mined for my precious gem collection.

The weaknesses of My Private Bible are manifold. This approach fails to read the Bible historically and thus doesn't contextualize its messages in terms of original culture and setting or in terms of the progression of the biblical drama. By reading individualistically, I neglect the overriding concern of the Bible throughout its many pages to form the lives of a new community. In the story the Scriptures tell, the way for individuals to put the Bible into practice is by taking up their proper role in a gathering of God's people that is committed to God's mission of bringing life in Christ to the world. Helping individuals gain a strong sense of "My Presence" and "My Peace" all by itself is not at the center of the Bible's concerns. The Bible has a much bigger agenda and this agenda is forfeited when we merely scan for comforting verses and hopeful fragments.

The second major downfall of the interiorization of the Bible is that we've cut ourselves off from the valuable resources of a wider interpretive community. When my primary practice is to sit and read the Bible alone, the only filter I get is the one formed by my current circumstances, my personal history and my prior influences. I will be blinded to certain aspects of the text because I'm bringing only myself to the text. My own tendencies, my own interests, my own agenda will dominate. As Eugene Peterson puts it, "Sects are composed of men and women who reinforce their basic selfism by banding together with others who are pursuing similar brands of selfism, liking the same foods, believing the same idols, playing the same games, despising the same outsiders."[17] The way to break out of this is to begin finding intentional ways to experience the Bible with others, particularly those who are situated differently than we are.

In his article "Sola Scriptura and Novus Ordo Seclorum," historian Nathan Hatch describes how populist religious leaders in the early years of the American Republic turned increasingly to what he calls "the individualization of conscience."[18] Proceeding with a strong commitment to the clarity of Scripture and the common sense of every individual, the goal was to find a singular and unmediated experience of the Bible. Previous creeds and confessions of the church or any kind of standard or approved theological statements from ecclesiastical bodies were intentionally eschewed. Me and the Bible, alone—this was the best way. Well-known Baptist preacher Elhanan Winchester depicted the process this way: "I shut myself up chiefly in my chamber, read the Scriptures, and prayed to God to lead me into all truth, and not suffer me to embrace any error; and I think with an upright mind. I laid myself open to believe whatsoever the Lord had revealed."[19] Famous evangelist Charles G. Finney would claim, "I found myself utterly unable to accept doctrine on the ground of authority," and then added, "I had nowhere to go but directly to the Bible, and to the philosophy or workings of my own mind. I gradually formed a view of my own . . . which appeared to me to be unequivocally taught in the Bible."[20]

The idea that God intends for us to re-create the faith from scratch when we sit down with the Bible alone was firmly established as a worthy goal in our Americanized version of Christianity. We've inherited this perspective and it takes an active perception and then rejection of it to recover a healthier practice. Consider for a moment what such a perpetually new faith (or more accurately, faiths) created by individuals would turn out to be. The proliferation of religious sects in this environment can be no surprise to us. Because once Winchester or Finney started teaching their own interpretations, what were others to do? Accept them on authority, or ignore or reject them in their own independent quest for biblical truth?

Ongoing isolation from others in my Bible engagement simply allows my own idiosyncrasies free rein. I don't come to the text in a neutral position or as a blank slate open to all that it has to offer. I bring all of myself to the text and naturally slant it this way and that based on any number of things in my own life story. This in itself is not to be lamented (it's the only way I can possibly read; I can't escape myself), but it is to be balanced and circumscribed as I open myself to what others have found there. God's Spirit has been working through all of his people through all of his ages.

Is the Bible meant to lead to the enrichment and transformation of individuals? Of course, and read well, it can do so. But if I read it as a straightforward and immediate word from God to me, I can't help but regularly misread and misapply it. (Not to mention that I will be compelled to ignore large portions that obviously don't fit this expectation.) The Scriptures are a set of writings that were overwhelmingly produced by the community of God's people to address the life of that community. But within this bigger purpose and setting, they invite each of us to experience and participate in this community in a very personal way. These writings were not addressed directly to us, but that does not mean they are not for us. We merely have to get there the right way.

So could a rediscovered communal engagement with the Bible help us? Is there a way to change our Scripture-reading lens? Could My Private Bible with its Me First agenda be replaced by something different? Something bigger and better? What if the young woman at the Christian camp was given her New Testament along with an invitation to an experience of the Bible in community? What if that's what she had been part of all week at camp—substantial readings (or hearings) from the Bible in as much of their rich contexts as possible, discussed and digested together, and all of it in an atmosphere of prayer and commitment to the God at the heart of the story? And what if this young woman was discipled into not only a personal daily quiet time, but a regular practice of Bible exploration and immersion with others? What if this experience was not so much Bible study as in-depth and at-length Bible feasting and absorption?

- thirteen -

SHARING OUR
SYNAGOGUE BIBLE

I am not myself by myself.

EUGENE PETERSON,
CHRIST PLAYS IN TEN THOUSAND PLACES

In the oral culture of the biblical world, God's messengers typically interacted with groups of people in natural settings. Biblical scholars John Walton and Brent Sandy have recently reminded us that while we tend to project back onto the Bible our modern understanding of "authors" and "books," ancient communication was overwhelmingly oriented to hearing, including the passing on of key oral traditions that were shaped over time.[1] So many of the great biblical interactions around God's messages took place in settings like shared watering places, city gates, temple courtyards and other community gathering places. Mostly, the word was heard, and it was heard together with other people. The two main speakers of the New Testament, Jesus and Paul, clearly favored a particular gathering place—the synagogue. It's difficult to reconstruct exactly what early synagogue services were like since most of the historical data comes from a later period. But within the stories of the New Testament we get some of the best early evidence of the nature of Jewish worship and instruction in these local assemblies.

All four gospels present Jesus as frequenting Sabbath services as he traveled and using the synagogues as significant locations for his ministry of healing and teaching. Luke, Matthew and Mark all emphasize that Jesus "went throughout Galilee, teaching in their synagogues," or that he "went through all the towns and villages, teaching in their synagogues, proclaiming the good news of the kingdom and healing every disease and sickness." In John's telling of the trial of Jesus before Annas, Jesus proclaims, "I have spoken openly to the world. I always taught in synagogues or at the temple, where all the Jews come together."

But it's Luke who gives us the clearest picture of what a synagogue experience was like, both at the time of Jesus in Israel and then later for Paul in the Diaspora. First is the account of Jesus beginning his public ministry immediately following his time of temptation in the wilderness:

> Jesus returned to Galilee in the power of the Spirit, and news about him spread through the whole countryside. He was teaching in their synagogues, and everyone praised him.
>
> He went to Nazareth, where he had been brought up, and on the Sabbath day he went into the synagogue, as was his custom. He stood up to read, and the scroll of the prophet Isaiah was handed to him. Unrolling it, he found the place where it is written:
>
> > "The Spirit of the Lord is on me,
> > because he has anointed me
> > to proclaim good news to the poor.
> > He has sent me to proclaim freedom for the prisoners
> > and recovery of sight for the blind,
> > to set the oppressed free,
> > to proclaim the year of the Lord's favor."
>
> Then he rolled up the scroll, gave it back to the attendant and sat down. The eyes of everyone in the synagogue were fastened on him. He began by saying to them, "Today this scripture is fulfilled in your hearing."

Luke's second volume tells us of Paul's story, and it's worth noting that some of its key features are similar to the description of Jesus in Nazareth's synagogue. After Paul had experienced the revelation of the risen Jesus near Damascus, within days he was openly preaching in the local synagogues that Jesus is the Messiah. Actually, even before his encounter with Jesus, Paul regularly frequented synagogues. In his persecution of the Jesus followers earlier in the story, Paul (then Saul) had asked for letters from the high priest in Jerusalem to the synagogues in Damascus giving him permission to arrest those who belonged to the Way. And in his legal trials, where Paul recounts his personal journey, he claims he went from synagogue to synagogue chasing the Lord's people. Interestingly, this tells us that the earliest Christians were accustomed to using synagogue gatherings as venues for proclaiming the revolutionary new story of Jesus.

Given all this, we should not be surprised when Luke describes Paul's practice in Thessalonica: "As was his custom, Paul went into the synagogue, and on three Sabbath days he reasoned with them from the Scriptures, explaining and proving that the Messiah had to suffer and rise from the dead." Jesus, his first Jewish followers, and then Paul all made a point of going to the place where the Scriptures were regularly read in community and where people were used to interacting over them together. Here, then, is how Luke describes Paul's experience in the synagogue in Pisidian Antioch (in central Asia Minor, now Turkey):

> From Paphos, Paul and his companions sailed to Perga in Pamphylia, where John left them to return to Jerusalem. From Perga they went on to Pisidian Antioch. On the Sabbath they entered the synagogue and sat down. After the reading from the Law and the Prophets, the leaders of the synagogue sent word to them, saying, "Brothers, if you have a word of exhortation for the people, please speak."
>
> Standing up, Paul motioned with his hand and said: "Fellow Israelites and you Gentiles who worship God, listen to me!" . . . [Paul then gives a review of Israel's history, which culminates in the story of Jesus.]
>
> As Paul and Barnabas were leaving the synagogue, the people invited them to speak further about these things on the next Sabbath. When the congregation was dismissed, many of the Jews and devout converts to Judaism followed Paul and Barnabas, who talked with them and urged them to continue in the grace of God.
>
> On the next Sabbath almost the whole city gathered to hear the word of the Lord.

Taking Luke's accounts together, we can identify some important features that will inform our discussion about reading the Bible in community:

- There was an ongoing communal immersion in the Scriptures. By the first century the Jewish people had established a regular weekly rhythm of gathering together in local settings to hear (at least) the Torah and the

Prophets being read. (It's likely that a triennial reading cycle was in place with selected passages.)[2] In addition, we know that public Scripture readings were a regular part of festival celebrations.

- "As was his custom" describes the actions of both Jesus and Paul: it was their usual practice to go to the synagogue and participate in the service of Scripture reading, prayer and instruction. Both men were fully involved in the Jewish way of life and community participation.

- After the official readings were completed (note the mention of an "attendant" whose job was to care for the scrolls) there was time for a sermon or instruction. This appears to be a rather open event. For instance, Paul and his friends were traveling guests and yet they are invited to bring "a word of exhortation" to the gathered people. Clearly this was extemporaneous in delivery rather than planned remarks made by predesignated speakers. With both Jesus in Nazareth and Paul in Antioch of Pisidia there is an element of interaction with those gathered. This accords with reports in the other gospels of Jesus performing many acts of healing in synagogues and then engaging in dialogue with his followers and other observers. In both cases that Luke reports, the ongoing dialogue spilled out of the synagogue itself and into the streets. And in Paul's case the discussion went on into the next gathering a week later. Luke concludes that because of this community-based, in-depth engagement with the Bible and the message about Jesus, "the word of the Lord spread through the whole region."

- It's also fascinating to note that in these particular cases, Jesus' and Paul's comments fall in the category of what we are calling storiented. Jesus claimed that Israel's longed-for moment of prophetic fulfillment and the end of exile had arrived, and he placed himself and his work within a narrative sequence. We don't know what the two Scripture readings were in Paul's case, but he uses the opportunity to deliver a retelling of Israel's history that begins with Israel's election for God's missional purposes. He covers the Exodus, the time of the judges and then the kings, leading to David, whose son Jesus has fulfilled all God's plans. Paul brings in other readings from the Psalms and the prophets to support his presentation. It's a richly Scriptural, narrative-based invitation for his hearers to take up their own places within God's ongoing intention to "bring salvation to the ends of the earth."

The synagogue can provide a model for us as we recover a more community-based interaction over the Bible. I'm not proposing a rigid reproduction of ancient practices, but the outline of a way forward and a realization of what's missing from the individualistic pattern that most of us follow in our Bible reading. In the centuries before the coming of the Messiah the synagogue had developed into much more than a common building—as a community center it had become an institution within Second Temple Judaism, taking up the role that was previously served by such gathering places as the city gate. The ancient city gate had been a natural place to buy and sell, issue official pronouncements, have the village elders hear and adjudicate a case, or simply share news and gossip.

The synagogue came to serve as a key focal point for community activities. Besides the religious services and regular instruction that took place there, it was also the place where communal meals were shared, local justice was administered, charitable activities were housed and educational work would come to be centered.[3] But reading and discussion of the Scriptures would occupy the central function of the synagogue along with prayer. In the first century the Torah was viewed as the holiest object within Israel outside of the Temple itself. While variety existed in how individual synagogues were designed, the architecture and building plan was centered on the care, reading and interaction over the Scriptures, especially the Torah.

In many ways, Israel kept its story alive in the synagogue, both in the province of Judaea and throughout the Diaspora. In its education of the young, steady proclamation of the ancient texts, and openness to dialogue and debate on the meaning of those texts, the synagogue was the weekly heartbeat of God's people. And it's important to know that this institution was able to accommodate a fair amount of diversity in terms of how people were reading and understanding those texts. First-century Judaism had a significant variety of interpretations regarding where Israel's story was going. Essenes and Pharisees, powerful ruling elites, and rough-and-tumble zealots were all vying for control of the drama. And even the Israelites who were simply living their lives out in villages, who were members of no particular party, would have had their own emphases and perspectives on the current situation and the meaning of the texts. The synagogue was the place where much of this could be hashed out (though not all the parties were participants there). This is why the synagogue was the obvious choice for presenting the Jesus story as the appropriate climax of the entire Jewish narrative. The earliest Christians presented a heavily Scripture-laden interpretation of that narrative to their fellow Jews. And we can see from the biblical windows into the synagogue experience that these presentations were followed by much give and take, often heated, by the participants in the service.

What does the synagogue have to teach us? There are three aspects of ancient synagogue life that can positively speak to the nature of our community engagement with the Bible: having regular immersive experiences in the Bible matters, leaders matter, and openness to others matters.

First, it's time for the church to reprioritize the public reading of the Scriptures. Just as we regularly communicate (subtly or not so subtly) that people should maintain a faithful private engagement with the Bible, we should build into our Christian communities the expectation of regular communal gatherings around the sacred writings. We should meet together and read, out loud and at length, as a constant practice. Along with this we can learn from Judaism's practice of including significant Scripture readings at major festivals and celebrations.

Listening is a different sort of communication experience than private, silent reading, which involves more processing (seeing the marks on a page, mentally converting those marks to words and then processing those words as connected language). Listening is more primary in human experience and goes more directly and easily into our minds. Further, the books of the Bible came into being as oral literature, and many of the features of these books were fashioned to be effective as an aural experience for the audience. As readers, we have to adapt to these features and thus probably miss many of them; as listeners we can experience and appreciate them more directly, particularly if we redevelop the art of listening well by practicing it more.

Second, the church needs spiritual leaders who combine the skill of proclamation with that of promoting a genuine community participation in reading and understanding the Scriptures. There's the interesting dynamic of the synagogue leader who appears to have been asked to play the role of both teacher and group facilitator. Philo describes the practice of his synagogue in Alexandria: "Then the senior among them, who also has the fullest knowledge of the doctrines which they profess, comes forward and with visage and voice both quiet and composed gives a well-reasoned and wise discourse."[4] Recovering the communal aspect of our life with the Bible does not mean that leadership, experience and knowledge become irrelevant. In fact, those gifts and skills become even more important in such a setting. There is ever a need for well-trained and authoritative teaching within our communities by those who know the great tradition of the Christian faith and can guide and shape our conversations so they remain centered on the right things. The good news about Jesus is the core of our story and the revelation about him must condition our reading of every part of the Bible. It is our spiritual leaders who preeminently carry the responsibility to make sure this happens.[5]

Our spiritual leaders must also be geared toward true community engagement, not an expert monologue existing in a vacuum. The leader's reading and presentation of the Bible is perhaps the first reading in the community, but it should not be the last. It should be the opening of a conversation. Along with real leadership there must be genuine opportunities for group dialogue and mutual listening. And as we'll see, this conversation is not only to be with our own small group or local congregation (we are ever drawn toward tribalism—limiting our interactions to people just like us—and must actively work against it). The conversation of God's people around the Bible already has a long history, and we have global partners. "Community" must encompass all of this.

So third, we should take up the synagogue practice of vigorous interaction over the text. When a group comes together and is immersed in the Bible as a community, we should expect there will be varying perspectives. As it is commonly quipped, wherever there are two Jews discussing together there are at least three opinions. In a polarized world like ours (not unlike the first century), this can be extremely challenging. But the skill of learning how to appropriately share a viewpoint and also allow and respect the free expression of others' viewpoints is essential if we are to have a good life together with the Bible. We must unlearn the habit of harsh antagonism toward those who read differently.

Community is a nice word, but since it involves other people, it will necessarily take an ongoing commitment to living reasonably and peaceably with our differences. We can disagree without having to be disagreeable. Too often, especially in a Protestant environment, we assume that the right response to every disagreement is to pull up our stakes and move where we can stay among those who think just like we do.

In his book *The Bible Made Impossible*, sociologist Christian Smith reminds us that every group has a strong impulse to heighten its own importance and credibility (the "in-group") while depreciating others (the "out-group").[6] It is precisely this tendency that Christians must strive to overcome, and that the New Testament claims is overcome in the new communities of Jesus-followers by the power of the Holy Spirit. If this is not the case where we live, we must ask honestly if we are living authentically as a community of the Spirit who binds God's people together. According to the New Testament, since the previous outwardly-visible boundary markers of the chosen community are now gone (food laws, sabbath observance, etc.), the one crucial sign that replaces them is the visible unity of the Messiah's people across all the sociological lines that used to divide them.[7] This unity that is bigger than our disagreements must be seen as fundamental to the Christian story and to our witness to the world.

If we commit to sharing our Synagogue Bible as a crucial part of our life together as God's people in the world, we will once again discover that our reading of the Bible changes significantly. My Private Bible directs me away from many of the gifts the Scriptures are offering: if I am on my own closed-off quest for personal enlightenment and my own unique practical application, I will fail to resonate with the *community formation emphasis* the Bible has throughout. If we learn to read and live the Bible together in a deeper way, each of us will paradoxically find our own identity and true purpose as full members in Christ's body.

WHAT READING TOGETHER LOOKS LIKE

The Bible was written by communities, for communities, about communities. Even those writings that we typically think of as the most individual and personalized, like Paul's letters, are more community based than we realize. Often in his opening headings, Paul includes the names of others who are with him: 1 Corinthians is from Paul "and our brother Sosthenes," 2 Corinthians is from Paul and "Timothy our brother," while the two letters to the church in Thessalonica are both from "Paul, Silas and Timothy."

Romans, while mentioning only Paul in the opening address, ends with an extended community relations section. Paul sends official greetings to twenty-eight people by name and for good measure adds references to "all the churches of the Gentiles," numerous churches that meet in homes, households associated with particular individuals, and, in case he's missed anyone, "other brothers and sisters" and "all the Lord's people who are with them." So, pretty much everybody. The letter then closes with greetings from Timothy, Lucius, Jason and Sosipater, along with Tertius (who notes that he's the one who actually wrote down the letter), Gaius, Erastus and Quartus. With audiences like this for his letters, it's no wonder that most of the addresses to "you" in the New Testament are plural, even though we regularly read them as singular.

What's true for Paul and his letters is even more so for the rest of the Bible. Most of the material in the Bible was developed over long periods of time, beginning with oral composers whose works became shared traditions that were passed on by the community and then were written down by scribal collectors. Much more than a collection of books by authors, the Bible is a tradition-shaped and community-developed gathering of material that eventually took the form of vital and authoritative writings.[8] The Scriptures are as much generated by the communal people of God as they are addressed to them.

If this is how the Bible came into being, and if the focus of these writings is on the gathered people of God and the nature of their life together, then it would seem to follow that the primary way to experience and implement those writings would also be communal. My Private Bible is thus deeply inadequate as the path to quality Bible engagement.

Coming together intentionally as a community around the Bible means changing some of our patterns. First, as in the ancient synagogue pattern, our regular rhythm should be one of group immersion in the text. We have tended to follow the modern estimation that only by dissection can a thing be known. What if, rather than always "studying" the smaller pieces of the Bible in our home groups or jumping around the text in our topical studies, we were to simply spend more time reading or listening to the Bible at length? What if we were to develop a full-fledged "reading culture" in our churches, not unlike that of ancient Jewish and early Christian assemblies "wherein texts were typically performed and shared communally"?[9] The shortcoming in our day is not analysis—we are lacking a sense of the bigger work, the longer patterns and the unique voices present throughout the Bible. Of course, there is a time to look closely, to discuss and learn together, but communal feasting on long sections and whole books would feed us in a new way. Perhaps we need less "use" of the Bible and more simple absorption of it in its natural and full forms.

My friend Ann Plantinga Kapteyn works with Wycliffe Bible Translators in Cameroon in central Africa. She reports:

> Here people are very communal, and they also don't know how to read their mother tongue very well (even if they read French or English to some degree). Because of that, we have found it is very effective to do recordings of each Bible translation we do. This might be a recording of the whole Bible or maybe just one book. Then listening groups are set up. People listen to a passage for about thirty minutes, and then they discuss what they have heard, with input from a pastor. The audio Bible organization Faith Comes by Hearing pays for the recordings and trains the leaders. This method is very popular in Cameroon because most of the cultures here are very oral and aren't too fond of reading. The last I heard there were between one or two thousand such groups.[10]

This is a case in which majority world cultures are closer to the kind of experiences that first formed the Bible. Those of us in the West have something to learn from them about this way of engaging the Bible together.

After coming together intentionally as a community, we can begin to change how we think about living the Bible well. Typically in a Bible study setting, after the preliminary work of reading and understanding the Bible on its own terms (one hopes), the focus changes to what we call personal application. This is considered the essential work, the real point of the whole experience. What does this Bible passage mean for me and my life? But at this point I must ask what it would look like if we gave equal care to search for communal ways of carrying the biblical narrative forward. What does this Bible passage mean for our life together? As a body of believers, are we living this story? In other words, what if we read the Bible as if the formation of a new community was always the first goal in mind?

Similar work must be done in our preaching of the Bible. The encouragement and correction that our pastors and teachers find in the Bible and share with their congregations should be unpacked in ways that address the entire community. The over-individualization and interiorization of Christianity is too often reinforced by preaching that also assumes the big takeaway is always the purely individual application. But corporate questions must also be asked: Are we a distinctly biblical community? Do we think of ourselves as the body of Christ first, and as individual Christians second? Does our shared life embody this drama of the Bible in a way that others can clearly see the difference it makes?

First Testament scholar John Goldingay notes that the order of things in the ancient world is the opposite of our modern pattern. We think of corporate entities as collections of individuals, so even in community settings "the individual 'I' remains the starting point."[11] He notes that in traditional societies the primary reality is the bigger, communal body (family, clan, tribe), and the individual finds their place within these groups. The biblical narrative takes this inherently corporate view of things and then reshapes it around Jesus, making our participation in him our primary identity. Only together are we the body of Christ. This view of things is extremely countercultural in our Western world. But the more we can shed our excessive individualism, the deeper we can go into the storiented biblical worldview. In the Scriptures, the new community is the thing, and every "I" only finds its meaning and place within that community.

The ongoing story in the Bible prioritizes the social throughout. God covenanted with ancient Israel, inviting them to be a light to the world by embodying his wisdom in areas such as economics, the land, the treatment of the poor, politics, the legal system and family life. Chris Wright comments,

> God created a people and entered into relationship with them. By this means Old Testament ethics could never be a matter of timeless and universal abstract principles, but rather were hammered out within the historical and cultural particularity of this people, this community, this society, this 'house of Israel.' . . . God's answer to the international blight of sin was a new community of international blessing.[12]

As the new community built on the foundation of the apostles and the prophets, with Messiah Jesus himself as the chief cornerstone, the new covenant people of God are to continue in this social pattern. We are the assembly—the public society—of Jesus. New Testament letters characteristically open with bold statements about the status of the fledgling first-century Jesus communities. They are a new humanity, God's own building and the temple in which he lives (Ephesians). These small communities are part of God's reconciliation and renewal of everything in creation, breaking down the old divisions between Gentile and Jew, barbarian, Scythian, slave and free (Colossians). Scattered gatherings of believers are to see themselves truly described through renewed-Israel language: a chosen people, a royal priesthood, a holy nation, indeed, God's special possession (1 Peter). As these letters go on to unfold the particulars of what this Jesus-life looks like on the ground, their tangible outworking is directly based on the communal understanding of who they are in the Messiah. The followers of Jesus are a new *polis*, a people whose citizenship is now in God's realm. Their life together shows this to the watching world. This is the pattern we have so often forgotten in our Bible reading, understanding and living. We almost always ask our Bible application questions as if the implications are just for individuals acting independently.

It's crucial that we gain a real appreciation for how reading, listening and learning the Bible from multiple perspectives can be a gain, not a threat. For too long we've labored heavily under the view that there's only one right thing to say about any Bible passage. The implication so often is that there is one single truth to be found and our job is to determine it. But regularly experiencing the Bible in community will shatter this expectation. It is imperative that we embrace a multiperspective approach without slipping into pure subjectivity or a postmodern relativism.

Take note that the Bible itself exhibits this diversity. We find in the collection fascinating examples of biblical teaching and events presented from more than one angle. Why are there two presentations of Israel's history? Why within one of those histories is the giving of the Mosaic law presented twice, with variations? Why are there three disparate presentations of Israel's wisdom, from the solid certainties of Proverbs to the serious questionings of Ecclesiastes and Job? Why was it necessary to present the life and ministry of Jesus from four unique perspectives? Paul was not always on exactly the same page as the other early Christian leaders Peter and James, yet our canon includes writings by all of them.

The Bible is polyvocal in ways that enrich and deepen truth. There are those who play this card too hard and claim that it ends up presenting contradicting points of view. But we cannot allow this to prevent us from appreciating the tremendous value of the multiple perspectives in the Bible. And so it should be with our community Bible engagement. Hearing from others who are differently situated will aid us in our desire to hear all that the Scriptures have to teach. God's people have been gathered from every nation, all tribes, the full range of socioeconomic groups, and they've lived across a long historical arc. Unlike the populist religious leaders of nineteenth-century America who actively tried to banish all previous thought and reflection on the Bible, we must welcome the participation of others in our Bible conversations.

We can only live out the continuing drama of the Bible in community. God's Spirit moves among us all. It takes more than the echoes of our own thoughts to do justice to this text. Therefore, it's our responsibility to actively seek out the voices we don't normally hear when we engage the Bible—from the early church fathers to day laborers on the other side of the globe.

CONCLUSION

My Private Bible is an imprisoned Bible, restricted from doing its God-given, community-building work. I am too small a person to read the Bible only by myself. I don't see, hear, experience or know enough to read the Bible *sola me*. Saving the Bible in our day necessitates the rediscovery of truly communal engagement. The Bible assumes that the only way to be properly human is to find one's identity in a community, and the Bible has one on offer. We are invited into the synagogue, the place where the sacred writings are safely housed. This synagogue is a miniature world, the assembly of God's people, the congregation of his new creation. The folks gathered here have been given the gift of the life of the coming age. They are the first tenants of the city that is to be. They, collectively, are God's new temple, the place where he dwells. This is because they share in the life of the firstborn of all creation, the firstborn of a new humanity. The holy text addresses them as a complete body and expects them to respond to it as a complete body. The only way the people of God can fulfill this calling and live up to their status is to pursue the vision together. Selfism will not do. Has Christ been divided?

- fourteen -

OUR UGLY BIBLE

But you wanted proof instead of mystery,
justification rather than beauty.

Makoto Fujimura,
Letter to North American Churches

The Song of the Firstborn from Paul's letter to the Colossians is regularly described in scholarly treatments and Bible commentaries as having a definite lyrical quality. And it's true.

> He is the image of God, the invisible one,
> The firstborn of all creation
> For in him all things were created,
> In the heavens and here on earth.
> Things we can see and things we cannot—
> Thrones and lordships and rulers and powers—
> All things were created both through him and for him.
>
> And he is ahead, prior to all else
> And in him all things hold together;
> And he himself is supreme, the head
> Over the body, the church.
>
> He is the start of it all,
> Firstborn from realms of the dead;
> So in all things he might be the chief.

For in him all Fullness was glad to dwell
And through him to reconcile all to himself.
Making peace through the blood of his cross,
Through him—yes, things on the earth,
And also the things in the heavens.[1]

In content, expression and structure these are majestic and awe-inspiring words. But the poetic aspects of this hymn to Christ have apparently not been enough to move many translators to actually set the text in a form that would help readers see this quality. N. T. Wright's rendering here (from *The Kingdom New Testament*) stands out in this regard. The way Wright has set the text naturally brings out the parallelisms of the poem as well as its inherent chiastic structure.[2]

Part of the problem, no doubt, is that we expect sections like this in epistolary literature to be didactic, linear, and instructional. We aren't disposed to look for lyrical material in apostolic letters. But this is also a sign of a bigger tendency: most Bible readers today aren't disposed to look for lyrical qualities anywhere, even in lyrics.

Wright notes that poems arise in the biblical tradition by growing out of the biblical worldview. The Jewish people produced poetic laments in the face of tragedies (things that should never happen if God is the creator and he's chosen Israel) and poetic celebrations in response to triumphs (victories and vindications wrought by the creator God who has chosen Israel). Bare statements of the facts are not enough when these things happen. Greater strength of expression is called for, something that will feed and call forth the fitting affective response. Beauty of form does this, revealing in aesthetic expression the innate power of compelling ideas.

This hymn to the Messiah in Paul's opening section of Colossians is the natural fruit of this "rich tradition of Jewish psalmody."[3] Just as Israel had always seen God the redeemer of Israel as also the creator of the world (see the books of Genesis, the Psalms, Isaiah, etc.), so the Song of the Firstborn sets forth the same parallels in an appropriately poetic celebration. Now in a climactic way, Jesus has embodied these twin divine roles so that as the center of the chiasm proclaims, "he is ahead . . . he is supreme." The maker has become the mediator, and a renewed world is to be peopled with a renewed humanity. The firstborn has done this, and song is the only apt reply.

Now, going further, it's important to point out that the passage is about the creation and reconciliation of all things in Jesus the Messiah. The redemption and appropriation of the arts is certainly one of the outworkings of this vision. So this stunning theological poem embodies part of the vision it sets forth. To limit our apprehension of these words to only our poor printed versions (which misleadingly set this carefully created language as regular prose) is to refuse the meaning of the words themselves. The whole creation is reconciled to the Lord. Our world belongs to God! It's all his, including the beauty.

The Song of the Firstborn should call forth a full range of human responses: intellectual, emotional, volitional and, yes, artistic. We should apprehend and embrace the theological teaching, willingly join in with the community that celebrates and embodies this reconciling vision, and appropriately decorate, celebrate, and proclaim this message through artistic means. Our Bibles should be formatted to help readers recognize literary forms like this. The majesty and power of the song should be treated royally in exquisite physical expressions of our sacred book that evoke the fitting responses of awe and reverence. The words themselves should be skillfully and dramatically read aloud in our churches. For that matter, they should be set to music, that blessed gift that most powerfully combines what's in our hearts and in our minds. Renewed-in-the-Messiah communities should encourage the artists in their midst to reflect on and then express this world-transforming message in fresh ways.

Such a treatment would begin to do justice to what the Bible has given us in the Song of the Firstborn, but we don't even attempt a fraction of this. We've settled for an information Bible, a principled Bible that sticks to the plain facts. Although there was a time when the assembly of God's people actively pursued fitting artistic responses to the Bible, the modernist turn has been away from the aesthetic in religious matters. Having been persuaded by the cultural project centered on microanalysis and knowledge gathering, we've neglected other ways the holy words should move us.

BIBLES ARE THINGS, AND THINGS MATTER

Any given Bible (even an electronic or audio edition) is a physical artifact in this world. What kind of artifact is it? And how does it reveal the beautiful expression found within the Bible itself? Our Bibles weren't always this pedestrian. While we've become so used to the modern reference version of the Bible that we routinely think of it as simply "the Bible," there is actually a fascinating history to the development of the Bible as a physical artifact. And unless we're gnostics, we believe that the physical presentation of the Bible matters. The embodied form of an object works its magic on all kinds of levels, and if we choose to ignore the importance of the form of a thing we ourselves will be unwittingly formed by it.

Referring to the earliest Christian manuscripts, Harry Gamble wrote,

> The physical object is also a social artifact. Its content was composed, its vehicle selected, and the words transcribed in a particular way. The book was made accessible to an audience or readership, and the text was subsequently reproduced to enable its further transmission and reading in varying circumstances. All aspects of the production, distribution, and use of texts presuppose social functions and forces—functions and forces that are given representation, or inscribed, in the design of the text as a concrete, physical object.[4]

Gamble's point applies equally to the physical forms of the Bible in any era. We've already referenced the history of the chapter and verse intrusions in the thirteenth and sixteenth centuries respectively, but what were Bibles like before that? There's a connection between physical form and the ways in which the Bible was used in earlier ages. The various forms the Bible has taken deeply affect (and reflect) equally varying Bible practices. The Bible as an artifact is a sign of what we think the Bible is, and what we think we're supposed to do with it.

As the Messiah-centered apostolic Judaism of the first Jesus-followers spread its kingdom-colonies around the Roman Mediterranean, it soon started what would become a long-term cultural transformation. Books—that is, literary writings—in those days were always in the form of a scroll. Leaf books (codices) were known, but were reserved for mundane uses (household lists, business accounts, etc.). But Christians developed an early and quite decisive preference for the codex form of the book. This is interesting in two particular ways. First, as noted, this stood out sharply from the cultural pattern of the day. But second, this preference did not apply indiscriminately to all Christian writings, but only to those texts that were regularly read and used in worship settings, that is, to texts that were eventually acknowledged as Christian scripture.

The explanation for this codex preference seems to be neither convenience nor economy but rather an early, decisive and precedent-setting development in the publishing of authoritative Christian writings. Scholars posit that an early collection of Paul's letters would fit this bill. A "seven-churches" (but ten letters) edition of Paul's writings would have been seen as reinforcing the fact that Paul addressed the church universal.[5] Thus the particularity of the letters themselves (having some problems at Corinth, Paul?) was overcome by the physical presentation of the whole set. It turns out the codex was perfectly suited for this—a scroll couldn't fit all the letters. The need was to show that Paul's epistles are crucial for the church at large. The unified codex form of the collection thus became part of the message.

As I mentioned in the chapter on Our Complicated Bible, other features of early Bible texts point to a concern for ease of public reading. Compared to typical classical literary texts, Christian texts had generous margins, larger letters and fewer letters per line. In place of the usual *scriptio continua* (no spaces between words and no punctuation), there was allowance made for breathing and paragraph marks, cues for marking the beginnings of new words, and page numbering.

These ancient Scripture texts were not merely neutral or invisible conduits of spiritual information: they were designed specifically and simply to enable better use of the Scriptures in the growing Christian movement. These "Bibles" were published not as private copies, nor as products for the commercial trade, but as in-house, active-use documents for small communities of believers. It is fascinating to note that while these Bible publishing practices (codex form; marks or space to give reading help) were not undertaken with the intent of influencing culture, over time all of them were taken into standardized publishing practices for all books, many of which we still follow today.

As the form of the Bible continued to develop, we saw the introduction of a whole new phenomenon: artistic enhancement of the Bible text. In his *Ecclesiastical History* Eusebius reports that Constantine the Great ordered that copies of the Scriptures be written in gold and silver on purple vellum and distributed throughout the empire to reflect the honored status of the new official religion. Four centuries later when a scriptorium artisan named Godescalc presented his Gospel lectionary to Charlemagne, a new way of making Bibles came into its own. These were books designed to extravagantly showcase a text that told the truth. The physical aesthetics of the old codex were taken to a whole new level. Godescalc included a poem at the end of the book describing his work:

> Golden words are painted on purple pages,
> The Thunderer's shining kingdoms of the starry heavens,
> Revealed in rose-red blood, disclose the joys of heaven,
> And the eloquence of God glittering with fitting brilliance.[6]

Metallic lettering and dyed pages were just the beginning. Symbolic images were applied and sometimes great picture cycles—early Bible comic strips—illustrated the biblical story. Decorated initials, geometric shapes and hidden numbers were woven into intricate designs. Unique new scripts were developed and reserved only for Scripture. The Lindisfarne Gospels implemented elaborate cross-shaped "carpet pages" to introduce the actual Scripture text. These were a sort of literary prayer mat, a chance for readers to stop and reverently prepare themselves before entering into the holy ground of the text, revealing influences from the Middle East on several levels. All of this was bound within elaborate covers of carved ivory or leather studded with jewels. It was impossible to simply read these books. One was forced to stop and meditate on the forms, their meaning and their relationship to the text. The combination of all this reveals an impressive attention to detail and a firm commitment to incorporating visual beauty into the Bible.

Few had the chance to actually read these books, but many were able to see them. Their embodied glory was deemed "fitting" for a divine book. Some were great missionary editions, sent by popes and bishops to kings and rulers of other lands to demonstrate the revelation of God's word in a worthy manner. They also filled the need for imposing Scripture volumes in prestigious churches and they were displayed prominently in worship. The democratization of printed scriptures would have to wait; most lay people gained their knowledge of the Bible through such communal events as open recitations, sermons, publicly available art (especially in churches), and the sharing of stories and songs at festivals and gatherings. But by investing in and commissioning such bold physical presentations of the Bible, the church was making a statement about the place and the honor of God's inscripturated revelation.

Why even have such beautiful, iconic, illuminated Bibles? For Godescalc the answer centered on Christ's two natures: the Word lived among us, and we have seen his glory. The Lord became human flesh. Why shouldn't the gospel book of Christ reflect that glory? Even in his earthly life Christ's true radiance shone through at times (as at the transfiguration). Physical books are viewed with bodily eyes, but spiritually this leads to a contemplation of the invisible divinity. If nature and grace are brought together in Christ, then in the Scriptures truth and beauty should also embrace.

But the mighty often fall. The age of great and beauty-filled Bibles came to a close and the age of blurring and whirring Bible presses began. The transition happened quickly, driven mostly by advancing print technology, but also by the newly recognized marketability of the Bible. It was in the early modern period that the transfer of the Bible's stewardship passed from the institutional church to independent merchants. The Bible passed from the scriptorium to the printer and bookseller, and this proved to be decisive for the shape of the Bible as a book. The first mechanically printed Bibles were a kind of bridge between hand-copied, illuminated Bibles and the later mass-produced editions. Gutenberg's Bibles, for example, had type meant to imitate handwritten letters and left room for illuminated initials in the text and marginal decorations and images done in color. But the overall trend was clearly in a new, plainer, text-only direction.

With the Reformation came the victory of word over image. Hans Belting, a professor of art history and media theory, notes the nature of this triumph:

> The Reformation taught the dominion of the word, which suppressed all the other religious signs. Christianity had always been a revelation through the word but now the word took on an unprecedented monopoly and aura.... As the tool of rational argument, the word was the refuge of the thinking subject, who no longer trusted the surface appearance of the visual world but wanted to grasp truth only in abstract concepts.[7]

So it was that Luther, while allowing images especially of biblical stories to be made, required that "mottoes" (bible quotations) be included.

Calvin, more strictly upholding the Reformation principle, was against images of any kind. Belting summarizes how Calvin viewed the matter: "Only the word allows us to see 'God in the manner of a mirror.'"[8] The Bibles of the Reformation were not unlike its churches: rather stark and heavy in their visual appearance. With the degradation of a sacramental view in Protestantism, the quality of Christianity's communicative physicality took a direct hit.

Living as we do in the late modern period, we are historically most closely tied to this view that Bibles are about conveying information. The covers may be fashion statements these days, but the thing itself embodies the perspective that straight-up ideas are what matter. Our Bibles are largely mass-produced, commodified collections of reference-like material, typeset, printed and packaged with a preset economic formula in mind. And the formula has not been particularly honoring to the presentation of the sacred words. In our minds we hold the text in high esteem, but in reality we haven't cared much how it's dressed.

And as for the bits of digital code that can also be configured to resemble the Scriptural words, it must honestly be said that in terms of design, digital text is a decidedly backwards step compared to what print can accomplish. Electronic Bibles are certainly handy for quick reference, but they are distressingly lacking in any aesthetic quality. If beauty and form matter, if presentation and pleasing, inviting design matter, then so far digital Bibles matter less than we've been told. Immediate, utilitarian access to information is not enough. But since it appears that the digital realm will be with us for some time, it would seem appropriate for the Bible geeks so constantly obsessed with the code to take the time to meet some book and type designers. Together, they might develop a sense of craftsmanship about the appearance of their finished digital products. Computers are smart, so why not employ them to deliver smart design? This means paying close attention to every aspect of the text on the screen, the use of space, the use of color—all the digitally-produced-but-still-physical attributes that our eyes take in.

We're used to the things that are our Bibles and have likely never thought much about the fact that Bibles could be very different things. But Bible things have gone through some dramatic changes over time. Other ages have developed different forms for the Scriptures—we have options. We are responsible, collectively, for what these things are. We could start by paying more attention to form. I use "form" here to refer to the interior design of the text in pleasing and faithful presentations of the varied literature of the Bible, the appropriate use of illustration and decoration to frame and illumine the text, and the overall shape, quality, and physical presence of our Bibles.

In short, we could make better choices that enhance our sensory experience of the Bible. We have neglected this. Creational monotheists of all people should believe that such experience matters. There is one true God and he is the Creator. He intended for the material world to be the appropriate setting of our experiences and for us to thoughtfully attend to those experiences. Ugliness in our physical environment is dehumanizing. When we make homely, ill-shaped things we degrade our experiences in God's glory-filled creation. Part of our cultural mandate is to embrace, create and extend beauty in our world. Even in the things that are our Bibles. Perhaps especially there.

Our Bible is the place where we learn about God's high wishes for his world and his creatures. It's there we're told of God's victory over all that would mar his creation. The Bible is the announcement of the good news that results in the arrival of a new creation. It's a beautiful story. Of all the places where an unattractive appearance and an ill-fitting form are unwelcome, it should be here. We could reincorporate beauty into our Bibles, bringing beauty back together with the true and the good to reestablish the old trinity.

MISSING THE MIND OF THE MAKER

In 1689 Enlightenment philosopher John Locke published *An Essay Concerning Human Understanding*. His goal was to establish a firm foundation for human knowledge by making the case for empiricism. In the *Essay* Locke fires a hard salvo against the use of poetic and other figurative language:

> Language is often abused by figurative speech. . . . If we would speak of things as they are, we must allow that all the art of rhetoric, besides order and clearness; all the artificial and figurative application of words eloquence hath invented, are for nothing else but to insinuate wrong ideas, move the passions, and thereby mislead the judgment; and so indeed are perfect cheats; and

therefore, however laudable or allowable oratory may render them in harangues and popular addresses, they are certainly, in all discourses that pretend to inform or instruct, wholly to be avoided; and where truth and knowledge are concerned, cannot but be thought a great fault, either of the language or person that makes use of them.[9]

The Scriptures, however, seem to have taken a strong liking to these perfect cheats. So when the mindset of Locke is more widely embraced—especially in our view of what constitutes a valid expression of truth in the spiritual realm—we face a very real problem. As Jamie A. Grant explains it, "Modernity has tended to assume that anything significant should be explained 'factually,' by our using propositional ideas. The poetic (with its use of metaphor, imagery and emotive description) is often considered to be insubstantial by comparison."[10]

The loss is all ours. When we devalue the expression of truth in other than just-the-facts-ma'am propositional forms, we close ourselves off to much of the Bible. Modern tradition posits that the best knowledge and the truest words are not artistically expressed. In the modernistic thinking adopted by so many Bible students, artistic expression is viewed suspiciously as too emotional, imprecise and even mysterious. Such qualities are perceived as not holding up in the face of hard challenges to the Christian faith and factual questions about the reliability of the Bible.

We've been conditioned to look for timeless Bible principles, moral instruction, statements of doctrine, or for warm, encouraging devotional thoughts. And we expect them to be expressed as basic, straightforward propositions. This conditioning is a kind of captivity. It happens first through the physical presentation of the text we encounter. As we have noted, the early modern bibles obliterated the literary form and set each numbered verse in the Bible as a new paragraph. Natural thought-unit? Poetic stanza? Prophetic vision? Long-form narrative? Didn't matter. These literary forms disappeared as the arrival of every little number meant starting over. Contemporary Bible translations have been laboring to overcome this template.

More often now we see paragraphs that overrule the numbered chapter and even verse breaks in the interest of preserving the natural flow of the text. This is to be welcomed as a partial recovery of the natural passages of the Bible. But the presence of the digits continues to influence our reading of the text as a collection of small, distinct units to be taken in as propositions. The Bible's inherent literary forms and natural literary breaks are typically still not revealed in our visual display of the text. So if readers are to find them, they have to search against the grain of the presentation. Why should this be? If we were to embrace the Elegant Bible described in chapter two, it would open the way for readers to more readily see and appreciate the varied literature of the Bible.

It's a serious deprivation that we've not been taught to look for and appreciate the Bible's manifold use of literary characteristics, because they're employed precisely in service to its expression of truth. Art is not the enemy of the Bible's knowledge. The problem, rather, is our limited view of what constitutes knowledge. The Bible we actually have welcomes a wide variety of ancient literary forms as allies and partners in telling God's story, revealing God's instructions, sharing God's wisdom and singing God's songs. This kind of fully human Bible is not a problem but a gift to us—it uses our own native art forms to communicate.

Perhaps the reason the intrusive avalanche of numerals scattered throughout the Bible text doesn't bother more of us is tied to the fact that many of us are looking first and foremost for a reference tool. Utilitarian and idea-centered, we want to look something up fast rather than slow down and experience the Bible on its own (literary) terms. Failure to receive the gift and insisting the Bible be only what a modernist bias values has blinded us to the rich tapestry of biblical material. It's anachronistic to ask of the Bible only what our expectations allow. The Bible has its own agenda, and it freely and creatively uses a full range of literary devices to communicate with depth and power.

If we won't enter this ancient literary world, learning its ins and outs, we will come to know merely the shell of the Bible, and not its heart. Cold, factual readings bypass crucial elements of the Bible. If our hearts are hard, we will focus on our modernist apologetic mission and miss the joyful celebration that is the Bible's opening Song of Creation. If we don't have eyes to see, we will read into John's apocalypse only the vain literalistic imaginings of our own fearful minds, when John wanted us to see and feel what happens when the power-hungry kingdoms of this world clash with the way of the Lamb who was slain. If we don't have ears to hear we will be constantly seeking the moral of the story while remaining oblivious to the fine skill Israel's narrators used in crafting their revelatory tales in subtle ways. If we gain no interest in how exactly the Scriptures function as communication, we will not feel the rhetorical heat in Paul's letters to the Corinthians, the bite of Isaiah's sarcastic denunciations of idolatry, the irony in John's depictions of Jesus' controversy with the Pharisees. We won't know the agony of Lamentations' acrostics of devastation or Mark's rising dramatic tension over the question of Jesus' identity. In our eagerness to learn the facts of how sinners can find a gracious God, we won't notice that the opening of Paul's letter to the Galatians completely skips the standard prayer of thanksgiving, thus shaming his audience right from the start. This blindness, this deafness, these manifold omissions are all to our loss. The depth and vigor of the Bible's messages are all tied up with these literary features, so when we miss them, those messages are diluted and the Bible's power is drained.

CONCLUSION

Where do we see, hear or experience beauty in relation to our Bibles? Visual presentations of the sacred text are generally poor: an unimaginative cut-and-paste, default-font afterthought projected on a big screen at our church service, or those visually anemic digital ghost words we hold in our hands. Even our printed editions, which hold the most promise for delivering a visually compelling text, fail because the tangible aesthetics of great print design are rare in the Bible world, and greatly illuminated texts are now virtually nonexistent.[11] The oral presentations of the sacred text most of us hear are weak, uninspiring and flat public readings by people typically not trained for dynamic, skillful oral performance (and this loss in particular distances us from the standard experience of the Bible's original audiences).[12] The way we deliver the content of the sacred text is held captive to the modernistic bias toward short, staccato propositional statements of truth. Again and again the unique genres of the various books are overlooked when we teach and preach the Bible. Perhaps worst of all, we miss that more than anything, the Bible invites us to live our lives as works of art in their entirety. The Bible's overall story-turned-drama is begging for our artistic response, our beautiful participation in the project of setting all things right.

Aesthetic gifts are writ small and large throughout the Bible. They are the vehicles of its truths. The Ugly Bible is an attempt to take the Bible out of the world, to transfer it to the realm of ideas alone. When we pay no attention to the form of the Bible we are attempting to disincarnate the Bible. But God's word in the Scriptures, like the Word of God himself, is fully incarnate—delightfully embedded in this world. So when we find that the church fails to bring creativity and a winsome artistic sense to the experiences of God's people with the Bible, it's a failure to let the Bible be the Bible God gave us.

If the Bible is failing to capture the imagination of today's generations, perhaps it's because we have failed to honor the imaginative and aesthetic nature of the Bible itself. The final act of recovery for our Bible is to welcome it back to the place where artistry, style and grace hold court. That is, we need to recognize the beauty already employed within its pages, but also begin anew the artistic projects that will redeliver the Scriptures to us in fresh and pleasing ways.

- fifteen -

BEHOLDING THE ICONIC BIBLE

Some things can be too beautiful to be wrong.

ALBERT EINSTEIN

The Bible never refers to itself, at least in the sense of the complete collection of writings that we now possess. However, there are places where the Bible does refer to the "word of God" in a broader sense, and it's here that we learn the crucial quality of God's speech. According to the Bible the preeminent characteristic of the word of God is that *it does things* in the world. God's speech is God's action. His word is an active way of bringing his intention to fruition. The word of God accomplishes, commands, exposes, comforts, cuts, sets free, protects, judges, guides, reveals, promises, hammers, saves and even brings new things into existence. God's word is a force in the service of God's purposes.

The form of God's word we have available in the Bible retains this aspect of power and action. The Bible is the record of God's doings in other times and places, but also a means by which he continues to do new things today. The same Spirit who is at work now was at work then. The Spirit at work through the Scriptures takes up the richness of human language and employs it for his purposes. Human language is meant to be richly experienced. It's capable of being used in surprising and pleasing ways in order to accomplish its work. The Bible is a work of literary art. Its various authors and editors, collectors and scribes actively made use of a wide variety of literary forms common to their own day in order to communicate their messages. From simple puns to elaborate metastructures built across whole books (and even across whole sets of books), the Bible crafts words well in order to do God's work in our world.

In other words, God's word is a literary speech-act. And as theologian Kevin Vanhoozer notes, specific biblical genres do particular things well on behalf of God's overall script.[1] The surprising diversity of kinds of writing in the Bible should help us realize that certain kinds of things can only be said well with certain kinds of writing. Vanhoozer notes, for example, that only the literary form of apocalypse can adequately communicate the visionary nature of the content of a book like Revelation. Historical narrative would not do. Likewise for other biblical genres: they serve well the purposes of the kind of content they are delivering. And as I've noted, biblical communication is not just about sharing "messages." When God wants to do certain kinds of things, certain kinds of writing must be chosen to best perform the action.

The ancient letter was an effective way for apostles to be forcefully present to distant congregations (to guide and instruct them) when their physical presence was impossible. The extended poetic dialogue in the book of Job is appropriate to the nature of the profound wisdom question at stake. When ancient Israel wanted to express the struggles and triumphs of the ongoing journey of life with YHWH and then talk to God himself about them, mundane and literalistic reporting and description wouldn't serve the cause. But the metaphor, rhythm and parallelism of Hebrew poetry set to music would convey the appropriate emotion and power of the complaints and the celebrations.

Two Gospel writers give us explicit insight into why and how they crafted their telling of the story of Jesus. The form of writing they chose was suited to their unique purposes. John writes that Jesus performed many signs "but these are written that you may believe that Jesus is the Messiah, the Son of God, and that by believing you may have life in his name." Luke introduces his Gospel by saying, "I too decided to write an orderly account for you, most excellent Theophilus, so that you may know the certainty of the things you have been taught." Gospel writing, therefore, serves to confirm what can confidently be known about Jesus (Luke) and to personally invite the reader into the story (John). The form fits the purpose. For these and similar reasons across the canon, the Bible's writings took shape. Literary art was taken up to more effectively communicate and more powerfully enact the mission of the various books of the Bible.

Therefore, learning to read the Bible well entails becoming familiar with these different kinds of writing and their conventions. Translators must craft their works with serious effort to transfer as much of the literary art of the original as possible into their receptor languages. And as readers we must endeavor to absorb as much of this as we can. Literary appreciation of beauty through words is one thing. But the Scriptures will more effectively work in us when we are attuned to their forms and the way these forms operate. Biblical scholar Robert Alter has been sharing his gift of intimate and perceptive reading of the text for many years. It's no accident that his titles bear names like *The Art of Biblical Narrative* and *The Art of Biblical Poetry*.[2] For Alter, the artistry evident in ancient Hebrew texts reveals how these texts perform their theological task.

This is one reason why the literary turn associated with postmodernism has been good for the Bible. It's helped in the retrieval of long-neglected literary aspects of biblical texts, including genre criticism, speech acts, irony, sarcasm, word plays, intentional repetition, rhetoric and poetics. Such retrievals enhance our Bible engagement because these devices have been intentionally deployed by biblical authors. To recognize them not only helps us know what the words say, but also discern the subtlety of their subversion or feel their sheer force.

If we know the way typical Hebrew parallelism works, we can begin to watch for it in our reading. Does this second line intensify, concretize, amplify or talk back to the first line? We can learn that the edges of a passage at the beginning and end are a way of framing it (called bracketing or *inclusio*), giving critical clues to what's at stake there. Placing something squarely in the center gives it extra power, like the affirmation of hope right in the middle lines of the middle song in Lamentations. (Of course, isolating that statement of hope from its context and then verse-jacking it, as usually happens, can only diminish its force.) When we feast on an elegant, holistic presentation of the biblical text we can more easily discern story-crafting and rising tension in narratives, dramatic surprises, the flow of an apostolic argument and regular devices like chiasms. We can recover the art of reading the Bible well in natural units and exploring its widespread use of literary devices.

It was the late professor John H. Stek of Calvin Seminary who taught me to pay closer attention to line spacing and stanza breaks in the book of Psalms. "The Bible is more than words," he used to say, "so watch for what gets built by whole units." Gets built? There is such a thing as architecture in the Bible? Yes, according to Stek. He had many examples in his beloved Psalter, but one very striking case can be found in Psalm 44. Stek points to the work of N. R. Ridderbos who explored "architectonic structures that indicate deliberate design governing whole poems."[3] Ridderbos noted that Psalm 44 was in essence built like an ancient ziggurat (a stepped or terraced temple-tower of Mesopotamia). The opening hymn of ten lines extols God's faithful care for his people in the past, followed, however, by eight lines charging God with current neglect, then six lines to protest that Israel didn't deserve this punishment, and all of it leading steadily up to an earnest four-line petition asking God to "rise up and help us!" The psalmist walks up the song's temple steps to offer his final prayer. So if Psalm 44 is to be released to do its proper work in helping us ascend and plead with God ourselves, we would do well to pay attention not just to what it says, but how it says it.

How it says it. This is the key to our recovery of the Bible's inherent beauty. Content is content, and can always be stated baldly. But style elevates content, enhances it, delivers it more effectively and winsomely. The prophets don't merely denounce the idols, they mock and parody them. John doesn't merely point out Jesus' conflict with the Pharisees in the story about the healing of the man born blind, his account drips with irony and sarcasm: the blind have come to see, while those who claim to see have become blind. Achish king of Gath doesn't merely posit David's mental instability but couches his commentary in the form of a rhetorical question, thereby simultaneously disparaging the competence of his own court entourage: "Am I so short of madmen that you have to bring this fellow here to carry on like this in front of me?"

One of the original English stylists for the New International Version, Calvin D. Linton, makes a compelling case for gaining a developed literary appetite:

> Style is that which delights us every time we encounter it, without diminishment, even when the content is completely familiar to us. We do not refuse to listen over and over to music we love, simply because we know every note

of it, nor do we refuse to read and reread Shakespeare simply because we already know how the plot comes out. . . . Style (or form) never sates. The body can become replete, the brain weary, but the aesthetic capability never tires. The more it is used, the more it expands. Hence the importance of much reading, much study, much experiencing. Each expansion of familiarity with a work of beauty intensifies our expectations, which, being gratified, provide a requickened joy. The more we know, the more we enjoy what we know.[4]

Our modernist obsession with mere fact and with lists and lists of bald propositions has hidden the real Bible from us. It proposes that only such a strict view will protect the truth of the Bible. But the actual Bible delights in making liberal use of the manifold literary gifts available to it. It shares its truth richly and well, startling us and rebuking us, making us laugh and cry, cry and hope. The Bible speaks to us in our own language. That God would chose to use such a thing for his own purpose is not something to be feared or overcome, but welcomed. It means that the Bible is fully with us and for us.

The word of God takes on all kinds of human literary forms so its living voice can move the redemptive story forward with style. But William Wordsworth warns us:

Our meddling intellect
Misshapes the beauteous forms of things:
We murder to dissect.

It would be better if we tried not to kill these beauteous forms when we engage the sacred words.

A Strange Narrative Beauty

It's not inaccurate to say that the Bible is about beauty made, beauty lost and beauty regained. Of course, this struggle for beauty is precisely about the struggle for justice in the big, positive sense of setting things right in God's world. But this merely shows that beauty and justice are meant to be kissing cousins, just as justice and peace are (Psalm 85). The land where justice lives is a land of beauty, and a people who do right are a delight to God's eyes. It's the great narrative of the Bible that creates this vision for us. Beauty in the Bible starts from the ground up, first in the words themselves and in the creative use of those words. But biblical beauty doesn't stop there—it's equally revealed in the overall development and creative surprises found in the Bible's story. This is the second step in rebuilding our awareness of the role of beauty in the Scriptures.

Richard Bauckham's tiny but forceful book *Bible and Mission* opens the way for us to see a strangely beautiful tale in the biblical metanarrative that surprises and yet attracts us at every turn.[5] Again and again the story doesn't go the way we would expect. This road-less-taken approach is exactly where the power of the story is. Yes, the Bible is a metanarrative, but the reason it is not oppressive (postmodernism's usual charge against "totalizing narratives") can be found in the peculiar way the Bible goes from a place to all places ("ever-new horizons"), from one to the many ("an ever-new people"), and from this present, broken time to redeemed time ("the ever-new future").[6] All the particulars of our world retain their uniqueness because "the goal is not an abstract universal but the gathering of all particulars into the one kingdom of the one God."[7] And the reign of this one God brings the flourishing of the creation, not its homogenization.

When things go wrong in the big story of the Bible, God's response is not to take on universal concerns all at once, but to start choosing particular people to work with. Abraham alone is selected, but the point of his election is to return blessing to a cursed creation. Israel (Abraham's family) is but one family, but their calling is to be the vehicle for the revelation of God to reach all families on the earth. David is chosen to reign from Mount Zion in Jerusalem, but again, the vision is broader: David's son is promised an extended rule that brings God's kingdom to all of creation. The blessing of restoration, the light of the knowledge of God and the justice-bringing rule of God— these are what the first part of the story promises. Mission, as the Bible sees it, is about extending these gifts in all directions. Election is a strategy in the Bible, a temporary narrowing, always in service to the long-term goal of bringing the reconciliation and renewal of all things.

So far it all sounds potentially beautiful, but how is it strange? Bauckham goes on to explain: it's strange, he says, because of the particularity of Jesus. Jesus embodies all the singular elections that have preceded him in the story. He is a child of Abraham, a member of Israel, the Son of David. In Jesus the story narrows to a single person. Only in and through him do all these prior choosings find their fulfillment. He is the one who brings blessing to all people. He is the light of revelation to all nations. He is the Lord and ruler who brings God's reign to the earth. God's mission to reclaim his entire creation, as told in the biblical narrative, comes down to one person: Jesus. And Jesus is a strange choice.[8]

All along, God has been making unusual choices. Israel was the least of the nations, an unlikely candidate for a chief role in the story. Jacob (Israel) was a second-born and a deceiver. It took Rahab, a prostitute, to step forward and intervene on behalf of God's people in a crucial battle. King David was the last and least of his brothers, not even invited to the royal candidating party. And then it turns out that David's son, the one who will be king, would come from the line that David established by murdering another man and then taking that man's wife as his own. From start to finish it's always the same: from the unlearned disciples of Jesus and social misfits in Corinth, all the way to the least of the apostles (weak and pitiful Paul) and the suffering-yet-faithful believers of Revelation, God keeps choosing the least of these. They are the ones who will overcome. They are the ones who will find God's beautiful ending.

The story is beautiful because Jesus himself is unexpectedly beautiful. From his birth to his death he seemed to be on the wrong side. The king had come in disguise. He welcomed others from among the least to his dinner parties. He restored the down-and-outers and lifted them up. And in his climactic moment when everything was on the line, Jesus went out and *lost* the battle to the Romans. On behalf of all Israel. On behalf of all the world. But appearances deceive—in losing he actually won. He confronted evil on a Roman cross, died to it, absorbed it, and lo and behold, defeated it. He turned the tide and changed the story forever. The greatest one had to become the least, and then the least became the greatest in service to all. His name is lifted above every name. This is God's beautiful, surprising story.[9]

Let's be clear. This narrative is not the way we would have written the script. We as members of the present evil age would have given preference to the usual path to success, the one bestowed by power, status and good looks, always staying on the lookout for our own interests. But God subverted this and turned it all upside down. The one who humbled himself, who was obedient all the way to death itself, is the one whom God raised up. Furthermore, this pattern of embracing humility in service to others is not only the path for Jesus. We are to have the same mindset. This is the story the Bible invites us to continue into our own time and place. It's a story of the age to come, but that age has already been born in our world. We are called to live according to it. It's the only lasting future the world has.

Bauckham helps us find the proper conclusion to all this: "God's way to his universal kingdom is through a movement of identification with the least."[10] This is why postmoderns need not fear the biblical narrative. It's not a story of self-aggrandizement and power over others. It's a story of self-sacrificing servanthood and love for others. Love for the least of these at the heart of the story. This is the means by which the life that is truly life regains its place in our world. The only way to legitimately take up our own roles in this strange drama of backward, unexpected redemption is to embrace the path of the surprising hero of the story. If we will not fill up his sufferings and take up our own crosses, then it is not his story we are living.

I've already made the case that the primary recovery we must make is the rediscovery of the Storiented Bible. All the other recoveries are in service to this key one. Now I am simply urging that we recognize the deep and profound sense of beauty that attends this story. This is the beauty of all things being set right in an unexpected way by a king who neither looked nor acted like a king on the usual models.

We've been trying hard to make the case for the Christian faith on the basis of modernist-style apologetics and reasoning. Increasingly this approach isn't working, if it ever did. Meanwhile there's evidence that we are simultaneously losing the attention and interest of our own young people. What does Christianity have to offer them? Perhaps we could address both of these issues profitably by presenting a much clearer and stronger case for the strange narrative beauty of the Bible. The regular pattern of Bible reading in our communities should be shaped by a story emphasis. Do we encourage people to read the Bible this way? Do our Bible studies model this? Does our preaching make the big connections that the story exhibits? Does the surprising nature of God's actions in the narrative come out clearly when we teach and talk about the Bible? Connecting the books of the Bible into a coherent and compelling drama that people today can enter into and live out is essential. Then the Bible can play the role in our lives that God intended. Seeing this as a particularly beautiful story is how the hearts and minds of people will be won over to it. Let's learn once again to read the Bible with an eye for redemptive beauty, strangely won. This is the story we are all looking for, and we should be delighted God has given us one.

The Return of the Great Bible

In the summer of 2014 a remarkable thing happened. A book designer named Adam Lewis Greene from Santa Cruz, California, raised just short of 1.5 million dollars in thirty days (and one million of that in a single week) for a personal Bible project intended to bring craftsmanship and a simple beauty back to the Scriptures. Greene found 14,884 backers for his crowdsourcing campaign, each contribution amounting to the placement of an order for one or more copies of his final product. His initial goal was to raise thirty-seven thousand dollars in order to produce five hundred sets of the four-volume work.

The project was described this way: "The biblical literature designed and crafted for reading, separated into four elegant volumes, and free of all numbers, notes, etc." In the well-crafted introductory video for the project, Adam shared his vision for a new kind of Bible: "It should be elegant. It should be simple. It should be pure."[11] The result is *Bibliotheca* (Latin for "library"), a presentation of the books of the Bible in a form that attempts to do the contents justice. Greene designed his own custom typeface, set the type with a ragged right edge (so unnatural spacing wouldn't occur within each line horizontally, as when the text is justified), took out the additives (chapter and verse numbers, notes, cross-references, etc.), upgraded the usual ultrathin Bible paper, and pulled it all together with a nice lay-flat, sewn binding.

Greene summarizes his dream this way, "In my opinion a book is to be cherished. A book is a precious artifact that should last you a long time—that should span generations in your family. I want to give people the opportunity to read the biblical library with a fresh set of eyes, to experience it anew." The vision is compelling and embodies what I've described here as the Elegant Bible, which should lead to the opportunity for the Feasting Bible. What's especially fascinating about the *Bibliotheca* campaign is the speed with which it gained national and international attention and garnered the support of so many people, for what would by anyone's reckoning be called a specialty Bible for a very niche audience.

We can take this as a hopeful sign, first, that more people are ready for a new kind of Bible reading experience. Perhaps the nearly five-hundred-year dominance of the modern reference format of the Bible is showing signs of weakening. Perhaps more people are ready for a regular, steady experience with the Bible centered on reading holistically and well, "reading as literary works of art" as Greene puts it. But second, there is the issue of the craftsmanship and production of a high-quality, physical edition of the Bible. *Bibliotheca* gives an equal amount of attention to the physical attributes of the printed volumes (paper, binding, cloth and ribbon) as it does to the design features of the text itself. Higher-level supporters for the campaign won a handcrafted walnut slipcase for holding the four volumes. Such a Bible becomes something other than a mere carrier of the ideas found within. Such a Bible becomes a presence in its own right.

In 2006 the International Bible Society (now Biblica) published a special edition of the Psalms in a clean, additive-free literary style and with a simple, decorative design on each page. It was printed on a cream-colored, soft, smooth, no-show-through paper. In the "About This Book" section in the back, Lisa Beth Anderson wrote,

> At International Bible Society, we've been wondering how the physical parts of the Bibles we publish—maybe even the height, width, color and font—change the way we read those books. We started asking questions like How does a certain font make reading more enjoyable? Or How might the texture of the book change the way we understand its message? We're hoping that when we decide how a particular text opens and closes or feels, we're participating in the way it moves and breathes and shapes the lives of its readers. We're thinking that as we do so, it will shape us, too. The physical part of a book, after all, is part of the total experience—for better or for worse.
>
> For this book, we asked What if these psalms, which are long and narrow on a page, meant that the shape of the book, too, was long and narrow? What if we got rid of the little numbers that get in the way and instead encourage readers to read whole thoughts and ideas without so much distraction? Would that help readers understand the psalms' messages and imagery more fully?[12]

Anderson and Greene have both laid out the case for Bibles as good things and precious artifacts. The case is for Bibles to be presented in forms that honor and embody the beauty of the message they contain within. The case is for a *unified experience* of spiritual truth in our Bibles, in which the form truly does fit the content. Beautiful literature that comes together in a beautiful story deserves to be held in a beautiful book.

Philosopher of technology Albert Borgmann has written that "material culture constrains and details practice decisively."[13] The danger with the way we've technologized the Bible is that it has become less of a thing, more a mere device. Our Bible practices change when the form of our Bible changes. We already started down this path with the advent of the mass production and commodification of Bibles. Now with mobile digital devices we are in even greater danger of having our sacred words lose their weight entirely. Weightiness is a characteristic that helps remind us of the substance of a thing. The recovery of the Bible can be aided by a renewed appreciation for material culture. Borgmann emphasizes the importance of what he calls focal things, something "concrete and of commanding presence."[14]

It may be that our time of ephemeral ghost words on screens and the overmultiplication of assembly-line Bibles is perfectly ripe for the comeback of the Great Bible. The Great Bible has a concrete and commanding physical presence. Its very form and texture is a testimony to the weight of the words that lie within. The Great Bible embodies beauty and demonstrates to all observers that, as Godescalc said, the eloquence of God can be wed with a fitting brilliance of presentation. Such a Bible would honor the Scriptures, speak their value and proclaim their worth. We could find our lost artists, recommission the craftsmen and begin to produce such Great Bibles once again.

But surely this is impractical. We can't all have copies of *The Saint John's Bible* or Makoto Fujimura's illuminated *The Four Holy Gospels*, and even if we did we couldn't carry them to our Tuesday night Bible study. But such Great Bibles needn't be for everyone anyway. The objection itself reveals the depth of our commitment to individualism. The first great illuminated Bibles weren't for sale at the shops in medieval villages. These community-held Bibles were shared public demonstrations of the beauty of God's revelation. They were important symbols and conveyers of meaning. Some were sent to statesmen and kings as tangible witnesses of the vital importance of the Bible. They were shown in times of worship, visible embodiments of the glory of God's revelation. In some ways the rediscovery of the Iconic Bible, the Bible of great aesthetic value, is the outworking of our acceptance of the Earthly Bible and the Synagogue Bible. A Bible well made of the stuff of earth and shared by a local community of God's people would not do any harm to our sense of the status and place of such holy writings.

And so I close with a proposal that we reimagine the scriptorium for our time. The reappearance of a role within our church communities for crafting Bibles would be a clear sign that we were once again taking seriously the role of beauty in the presentation of the Bible's truth. It would also be a way for the church to reclaim its rightful place as the primary caretaker of the sacred books, a task it lost with the rise of secular copy-shops and then printers serving merchant booksellers. If we were no longer driven to feed the monster of a Bible industry, we would recover a deeper respect for the Bible in practice.

Research into how we actually live with the Bible reveals a troubling paradox: Americans overwhelmingly have good things to say about the Bible while simultaneously ignoring it.[15] The proliferation of factory-produced Bibles is not currently leading to widespread or deep engagement. Perhaps there is a stronger link than we appreciate between the learned, embodied wisdom that goes into handcrafted, well-made artifacts and the use we make of such things. Savoring the local microbrewed autumn stout is not the same thing as downing a few Bud Lights. There's been a revolution in the making of beer (and coffee) in this country—why not for Bibles too? What would it take for us to embrace the task of crafting community-scale illuminated Bibles for local churches?

We could produce Great Bibles once again for our churches to publically showcase the Scriptures as the writings we value above all others. We could produce Great Bibles as great gifts that would share our faith with grace and strength. We could produce Great Bibles as tangible signs and symbols of the momentous claim that our sacred writings are more than a record of ancient religious experiences or previous spiritual conversations—they are a living voice in service to God's continuing actions in the world to judge and to restore. Great Bibles could provide a concrete, corporate center for our Bible focus. In them we could find a place to see and touch and hear that living voice. They would show and not merely tell that God has not left us alone in the darkness.

CONCLUSION

The Word of God is in our midst. He came to live among us and is now made of the stuff of earth. So too with the words God has sent us. These words have come into our world, made of the communicative forms of this world, birthed in the real stories of this world. They too are fully human. We should read them well, paying close attention to the rich variety of literary forms they employ. We should revel in the beauty of this story above all stories. We should honor these words with more than our lips and demonstrate their worth more substantially than having a few good thoughts about them. Light has come into this darkened world. Showcasing the brilliance of that light is our appropriate response. Imaginations can be captured. Lives can be turned. Beauty has already saved the world, is saving it, and will finish the task. The ark of this beauty—this strange and wonderful narrative centered on Jesus— is the Bible. It must be attended to with an aesthetic sense that matches the strength of the beauty that lies within. Saving the Bible includes saving the beauty of the Bible.

- Conclusion -

RETURN

Anything will give up its secrets, if you love it enough.

GEORGE WASHINGTON CARVER

They all found their lives within the Bible, though none of them could read. But they knew the stories and they knew them well. This was because the woman was constantly telling the stories, mostly the ones about Jesus and King David and Daniel and his friends. But it was the Joseph stories that got them through the darkest turns of their own story. The boy's mother would ask him, "Why you want 'em told over'n over?"[1] It turns out the boy wanted them told and retold because he was finding his way *through* them. The family knew pain. Poverty. Racism. Injustice. Even a shotgun blast to the head of their great coon dog Sounder.

His mother had been to the meetin' house lots of times, and she had heard the stories being read from the big book. Often at night she would sit and rock in her chair and teach the children. The stories in those Scriptures were a lot like their own story. The boy's father had been unjustly charged and found guilty, and now the family didn't know where he was. The boy was considering a journey. He wanted to find his father, who was in some prison farm or stone quarry working off his time.

The boy hoped the Daniel story would end up being his father's story. His mother had told him about Shadrach, Meshach, and Abed-nego and how they had ended up in a giant, hot jailhouse furnace. But the Lord was with them, and the fire couldn't hurt 'em at all. That ol' jail keeper opened up that door and there was Shadrach, Meshach, and Abed-nego singing

> Cool water, cool water;
> The Lord's got green pastures and cool water.[2]

But the boy's mother was worried about him taking off like that to strange places, not even knowing where to look for his father. The boy, though, got his bearings from the stories he'd been soaking in for so long:

> "Why are you so feared for me to go?" he would ask, for now he was old enough to argue with his mother. "In Bible stories everybody's always goin' on a long journey. Abraham goes on a long journey. Jacob goes into a strange land where his uncle lives, and he don't know where he lives, but he finds him easy. Joseph goes on the longest journey of all and has more troubles, but the Lord watches over him. And in Bible-story journeys, ain't no journey hopeless. Everybody finds what they suppose to find."[3]

So the boy set out on the journey, and in fact, went out again and again. A lot of things happened—mostly hardship—but he couldn't find his father. The boy returned home after long months, alone and discouraged. He walked lonely roads and got yelled at and chased away by the prison guards. He got hurt and slept in the cold. But one day he found a schoolyard and stood outside it. The teacher finally noticed him and tended to his wounds while learning his story. And then he made a promise: I will teach you to read. The boy returned home, seeking permission from his mother to go to the man's school.

His mother saw the Lord's hand in the boy's journeys, so the boy went off to learn to read. He returned, not just with ability, but with books. Now he read often to his family. And then one day, after much time had passed, the boy's father came limping back down that road. He had found his way home, though the journey had been harrowing. Half his body was laid waste by a dynamite blast at the prison quarry, but he was home. And the boy remembered all the hours and days and years he had heard the stories:

> If she felt good and started long enough before bedtime, he would hear about Joseph the slave-boy, Joseph in prison, Joseph the dreamer, and Joseph the Big Man in Egypt. And when she had finished all about Joseph, she would say, "Ain't no earthly power can make a story end as pretty as Joseph's; 'twas the Lord."[4]

They had all found their lives within the Bible. They had embraced those stories, and those stories in return had welcomed them in. "The Lord do powerful things," his mother would say.[5]

ON PROPERLY LOVING THE BIBLE

The Bible is on its own journey in the world. The Lord has put it in our hands. It remains, of course, his Word. But we translate it, package it or digitize it, and we are the ones who sell it or give it away. Less and less we hear it, read it and take it down deep into our lives. But we can help the Bible in its journey. We can aid the Bible as it seeks its destination and strives to accomplish its mission in our world. It was sent here to transform our life together, to help heal our land.

As we embarked on the journey of this book, I wrote that our chiastic journey would seek salvation in a Bible that is presented as literature, eaten in natural forms, grounded in history, inviting in its narrative, restorative in its theme, engaged in community and honored in its aesthetic presentation. I've merely attempted to introduce what the contours of this Bible recovery might look like:

- Elegance
- Feasting
- History
- Story-turned-drama
- Creation
- Community
- Beauty

There is much more to explore in each of these areas. But the key markers of the trail are in place.

I believe that if we would embrace this sevenfold restoration project, our collected Scriptures could be substantially healed—their errand in our lives and in our world enhanced. The Bible comes to us as something fully embedded in human realities, using our language, our way of writing, our way of telling stories, and it's about the place where we live. But the Bible also comes to us as a force for divine action in the world. God has determined to use these words to make a difference. He is working through them to change things. The Bible has agency in service to the new world that has been born in the midst of our dark and broken age. It's in the full embrace of this intersection of human and divine, this inscripturated incarnation if you will, that we can be of service to the Bible. If we accept this Bible honestly and quit pretending it's something else, then the chains we've wrapped around the Bible will fall away. The Bible will be released to do its work.

As we regain our love for the Bible, we can come to know it once again too. This love, as we've been reminded, is not control. It's not forcing the Bible to be what we want it to be. This love is accepting the "known" as something other than ourselves. The Bible is bigger than our previous ideas, our regular prejudices, our self-loving distortions. The Bible really is a strange new world. And yet it invites us in. The Bible doesn't want to merely reflect us; it wants to remake us. What if we knew the Bible down deep, in our bones? What if moment by moment, day by day, we made sense of our lives by seeing them as active continuations of the narrative we find in the sacred words? What if we tied our journeys inseparably to the great journey we find in the Holy Scriptures? What if we found the beauty always intended for the stories of our lives by rediscovering the profound beauty of this great, preeminent story?

In Bible-story journeys, ain't no journey hopeless. The Lord does powerful things, and he surprises us again and again. May it be so for each of us in our own journeys, and may it be so for the Bible in its journey. We can do better by the Bible. We can begin to do it justice. We can come to love it once again, and by loving, to know it. Perhaps we can even save it.

ACKNOWLEDGMENTS

My thanks are due to many people:

To all those who taught me and formed me by this new life we have in the Messiah, Jesus. I've had a lot that was solidly biblical in my life from the start, from growing up in Third Christian Reformed Church to my years in the Denver Christian Schools (K-12), and on to Calvin College and Seminary. Professors John Stek and Andy Bandstra in particular opened my eyes to all kinds of wonders in the books of both the first and the new covenants. A word must also be said about the knowledgeable and engaging gentleman at the old Eerdmans outlet bookstore on E. Jefferson in downtown Grand Rapids, Michigan (whose name, sadly, I never learned). It was clear that he worked there not so much to sell books but to talk to people about the good ones. He introduced me to the work of N. T. Wright, in particular his then recently released *Jesus and the Victory of God*. Reading Wright was, as they say, a game-changer for me, and the debt I owe him is obvious on many pages here.

To my colleagues at International Bible Society (Biblica), who, along with Bible scholar Christopher R. Smith and Scripture compositor John Kohlenberger III, formed the Bible Design Group. That working community proved its worth by creating a most elegant Bible. The efforts of Lisa Beth Anderson, Paul Berry, John Dunham, Jim Rottenborn, Gene Rubingh and Micah Wierenga led to the birth of *The Books of the Bible*. It is now changing how people around the world are reading the Scriptures. There are already editions in Arabic, Chinese, Creole, English (American and Anglicized), French,

Hindi, Italian, Korean, Portuguese, Spanish and Tagalog. And new plans are in the works for editions in Bengali, Chhattisgarhi, German, Kannada, Malayalam, Russian, Tamil, Talugu and Ukrainian.

To Steve Rabey and Fr. Joel Pinson. We don't meet often enough, but when we do it's always at Jack Quinn's Irish Pub in downtown Colorado Springs and that makes up for a lot. Fr. Joel is the deeply soulful man who urged me on every chance he got. And in the early days as I tried to begin this project, when I was completely stuck, it was Steve who sat me down one night at Jack's and wrote out a sensible plan for writing a book. Steve is a true writer, and it was his prodding that got me started.

To Paul Caminiti, Ben Irwin and Scott Bolinder, Bible mavens all. Formerly of Zondervan Bible Publishers, they joined our team at Biblica and single-handedly transformed *The Books of the Bible* from an unknown, experimental Bible presentation into the centerpiece of a church-based Bible experience that has now reached more than three quarters of a million people and continues to spread globally.

To *Christianity Today*'s Andy Crouch and American Bible Society's Geof Morin, who invited me to American Bible Society's Scriptorium event in March 2009 at Ecclesia Church in Houston, Texas. Pastor Chris Seay and a small group of folks spent several days having one of the most engaging and insightful discussions about the Bible that I've been a part of. Much of my thinking came together at that event.

To my longtime Friday morning reading group, the Ents (we do things *very* slowly): Alex, Aaron, Bill, Elizabeth, Marsha, Lois, Dan, Israel, Joshua and others over the years. You were the first ones to read my manuscript! You managed to both improve it and encourage me at the same time. A part-time Ent, and my personal rabbi, Scott Hiemstra, is above me and beyond me in many ways. His flat-out passion for the Scriptures, and even more for the Holy One behind them, has inspired me beyond measure.

To Wilson Brissett, Fr. Matt Burnett, Jeff Culver, Patton Dodd, Jim Knutsen and BJ Strawser, who together form my own Metaphysical Club. These are the smartest, warmest, most irreverent-in-a-good-way men I know. They are not just about books and ideas (though they are that, and brilliantly), but about life. There is very little in the world better than close and honest friends who go deep and journey together.

To book publisher Volney James (with Authenic, and then Biblica books) who was the first one to show enthusiasm for these ideas to actually become a book. Volney honored me greatly by hosting a little contract-signing event one sunny afternoon at the previously mentioned Jack Quinn's.

To Patty and Greg Ralston, who offered their mountain cabin to me. Just off the western slopes of Pikes Peak, it's a place with no Internet and no TV. Surrounded by the quiet, calming, entrancing beauty of Colorado's Rocky Mountains, it proved to be the perfect place to sit and look out the window and occasionally get back to writing this book.

To the good folks at InterVarsity Press, especially Drew Blankman, who expertly guided this first-time author through all the steps of getting my manuscript from a rough collection of Biblish thoughts into a real book.

To Christopher R. Smith and his lovely, always encouraging, and never doubting wife, Priscilla. Priscilla always knew that this vision for mo' betta Bible engagement would find its way in this world. Her response to this project not getting noticed at first was to matter of factly state: "God knows our address." Her confidence gave all of us confidence. And Chris, more than anyone else, taught me what the Bible really is, and what we're supposed to do with it. He is a brilliant, gentle and ever-faithful man, and he is as hope-filled as Priscilla. We are players together in God's drama, Chris, and I am more grateful than I can express that this script brought us together.

And finally to Jain: you know more than anyone that I'm a couple steps off the path of normal, and often preoccupied with my own thoughts. But you simply love and support me anyway. I owe you more than I can say.

NOTES

Introduction: Embarking

[1] See Philip Goff, Arthur E. Farnsley II and Peter J. Thuesen, "The Bible in American Life," a national study by the Center for the Study of Religion and American Culture, March 2014, 2, www.raac.iupui.edu/files/2713/9413/8354/Bible_in_American_Life_Report_March_6_2014.pdf.

[2] Timothy Beal, *The Rise and Fall of the Bible* (New York: Houghton Mifflin Harcourt, 2011), 80-83, 179.

[3] For recent surveys on the Bible's downward trajectory in the United States, see Goff, Farnsley and Thuesen, "The Bible in American Life," and also "State of the Bible" released by American Bible Society and Barna Group in March 2014. Both reports are pretty clear on the significant downward trajectory of the Bible. For a more global perspective, see the World Evangelical Alliance's Bible Engagement Project. Their research reveals a worldwide problem, and thus they are convening a multiagency group to commit to a "Decade of Bible Engagement" globally.

[4] See Daniel Radosh, "The Good Book Business," *New Yorker*, December 18, 2006.

[5] Christopher R. Smith, *The Beauty Behind the Mask: Rediscovering the Books of the Bible* (Toronto: Clements Publishing, 2007). See the introduction, pp. 7-11, for an explanation of the metaphor.

[6] C. S. Lewis, *An Experiment in Criticism* (Cambridge: Cambridge University Press, 1961), 88-94.

[7] N. T. Wright, *The New Testament and the People of God* (Minneapolis: Fortress Press, 1992), 45.

[8] Ibid., 45.

[9] Wendell Berry, *Standing by Words* (Berkeley, CA: Counterpoint, 1983), 12.

Chapter One: Our Complicated Bible

[1] Christopher R. Smith personally related this story at First Baptist Church of Williamstown, Massachusetts, April 1994.

[2] An intriguing examination of these early textual interventions can be found in Larry Hurtado, *The Earliest Christian Artifacts* (Grand Rapids: Eerdmans, 2006).

[3] I follow scholar John Goldingay in preferring "First Testament" to "Old Testament," which carries the connotations of being antiquated and no longer relevant. See his

three-volume series *Old Testament Theology* (Downers Grove: InterVarsity Press, 2003–2009). See also the usage in the book of Hebrews, referring to the "first" covenant, and then the "new."

[4]David Norton, *A History of the Bible as Literature* (Cambridge: Cambridge University Press, 1993), 1:168.

[5]From the preface to John Locke's *A Paraphrase and Notes on the Epistles of St. Paul*, 1705–1707.

[6]The term *data smog* comes from David Shenk, *Data Smog* (San Francisco: Harper SanFrancisco, 1997).

[7]Eviatar Zerubavel, *Hidden Rhythms: Schedules and Calendars in Social Life* (Chicago: University of Chicago Press, 1967), p. xvi, quoted in Alfred W. Crosby, *The Measure of Reality: Quantification and Western Society, 1250–1600* (New York: Cambridge University Press, 1997), 230.

CHAPTER TWO: UNVEILING THE ELEGANT BIBLE

[1]Matthew May, *In Pursuit of Elegance* (New York: Broadway Books, 2009), 35-65.

[2]Ibid., 56.

[3]Ibid., 55.

[4]See, for example, Philip J. Lee, *Against the Protestant Gnostics* (Oxford: Oxford University Press, 1993).

[5]See Christopher R. Smith, *After Chapters and Verses* (Downers Grove: InterVarsity Press, 2010), 193-197.

[6]For more on the problems with chapters and verses, see ibid., 17-49.

[7]Ibid., 105.

[8]The following is based on Smith's article "Literary Evidence of a Fivefold Structure in the Gospel of Matthew," *New Testament Studies* 43 (1997): 540-51.

[9]See the "Invitation to Matthew" in *The Books of the Bible* (Colorado Springs: Biblica, 2012), 1698.

[10]Smith, *After Chapters*, 30.

[11]From "Electrical Units of Measurement," a lecture delivered at the Institution of Civil Engineers on May 3, 1883.

CHAPTER THREE: OUR SNACKING BIBLE

[1]David Norton, *A History of the Bible as Literature*, vol. 1 (Cambridge: Cambridge University Press, 1991), 168.

[2]Jaroslav Pelikan, *The Reformation of the Bible/The Bible of the Reformation* (New Haven: Yale University Press, 1996), 36.

[3]Charles Hodge, *Systematic Theology*, abridged ed. (Philadelphia: Presbyterian and Reformed, 1997), 27.

[4]Mark Noll, *The Scandal of the Evangelical Mind* (Grand Rapids: Eerdmans, 1994), 133-34.

⁵Ibid., 135.

⁶Ibid., 135.

⁷Lori Anne Ferrell, *The Bible and the People* (New Haven: Yale University Press, 2008), 27.

⁸Christian Smith, *The Bible Made Impossible* (Grand Rapids: Brazos Press, 2011), viii.

⁹Ibid., 5.

¹⁰Ibid., 8-10.

¹¹Adam Kirsch, review of *The Rise and Fall of the Bible*, by Timothy Beal, "The Baffling Book," *The New Republic* (online), Feb 24, 2011, www.newrepublic.com/book /review/rise-fall-bible-timothy-beal.

¹²From the title of Karl Barth's 1916 essay, "The Strange New World Within the Bible," in *The Word of God and the Word of Man* (Gloucester, MA: Peter Smith, 1957), 28-50.

¹³Smith, *Bible Made Impossible*, 128.

¹⁴Scot McKnight has explored the reduction of the gospel to these soterian steps in *The King Jesus Gospel* (Grand Rapids: Zondervan, 2011).

¹⁵The highly-descriptive and provocative term "verse jacking" was coined by my colleague John Dunham in "High Fructose Scripture," Leadership Journal (online), June 5, 2007, www.christianitytoday.com/le/2007/june-online-only/high-fructose -scripture.html.

¹⁶See Richard Schultz, *Out of Context* (Grand Rapids: Baker, 2012).

CHAPTER FOUR: SAVORING THE FEASTING BIBLE

¹Thomas S. Kuhn, *The Structure of Scientific Revolutions*, 3rd ed. (Chicago: University of Chicago Press, 1996), 5.

²Ibid., 23.

³Christian Smith, *The Bible Made Impossible* (Grand Rapids: Brazos Press, 2011); Rachel Held Evans, *A Year of Biblical Womanhood* (Nashville: Thomas Nelson, 2012); Richard Schultz, *Out of Context* (Grand Rapids: Baker, 2012); Peter Enns, *Inspiration and Incarnation* (Grand Rapids: Baker Academic, 2005).

⁴Kuhn, *Structure of Scientific Revolutions*, 6.

⁵Ibid., 43.

⁶Krister Stendahl, "The Apostle Paul and the Introspective Conscience of the West," in *Paul Among Jews and Gentiles* (Minneapolis: Fortress Press, 1976), 83.

⁷Ibid., 86, 94.

⁸N. T. Wright, *Justification* (Downers Grove: InterVarsity Press, 2009), 40.

⁹Ibid., 42.

¹⁰David Ulin, *The Lost Art of Reading* (Seattle: Sasquatch Books, 2010), 150-51.

¹¹I do recognize that some books are themselves collections of smaller compositions and are better engaged in ways that allow these individual units to have their full

impact—for example, song collections like Psalms or Lamentations, or certain wisdom books like Proverbs or James.

[12]The work of New Testament scholar Richard Hays is particularly helpful in showing us how the Bible itself does this. See *Echoes of Scripture in the Letters of Paul* (New Haven: Yale University Press, 1993) and *Reading Backwards* (Waco: Baylor University Press, 2014).

CHAPTER FIVE: OUR "THE GODS MUST BE CRAZY" BIBLE

[1]This is a summary of the story presented in the South African comedy film *The Gods Must Be Crazy*, 1980.

[2]N. T. Wright, *Jesus and the Victory of God* (Minneapolis: Fortress Press, 1996), 17.

[3]Mark Noll, *The Scandal of the Evangelical Mind* (Grand Rapids: Eerdmans, 1994), 133.

[4]Ibid., 139.

[5]Ibid.

[6]N. T. Wright, *The New Testament and the People of God* (Minneapolis: Fortress Press, 1992), 4.

[7]Eugene Peterson, *Eat This Book* (Grand Rapids: Eerdmans, 2006), 101.

[8]Krister Stendahl, "The Apostle Paul and the Introspective Conscience of the West," in *Paul Among Jews and Gentiles* (Minneapolis: Fortress Press, 1976), 78-96.

[9]N. T. Wright, *The Challenge of Jesus* (Downers Grove: InterVarsity Press, 1999), 27.

CHAPTER SIX: FINDING GOD IN THE HISTORICAL BIBLE

[1]In this book, when Scripture is quoted, the context will be noted and the book name referenced, but without chapter and verse numbers.

[2]Gregory Mobley, *The Return of the Chaos Monsters—And Other Backstories of the Bible* (Grand Rapids: Eerdmans, 2012), 70.

[3]B. B. Warfield, "The Divine and Human in the Bible," *Presbyterian Journal*, May 3, 1894, quoted in Mark Noll, *Jesus Christ and the Life of the Mind* (Grand Rapids: Eerdmans, 2011), 132.

[4]Peter Enns, *Inspiration and Incarnation* (Grand Rapids: Baker, 2005), 21, emphasis original.

[5]Geerhardus Vos, "The Idea of Biblical Theology," in *Redemptive History and Biblical Interpretation*, ed. Richard B. Gaffin Jr. (Philadelphia: Presbyterian & Reformed, 1980), 11.

[6]Ibid., 7.

[7]N. T. Wright, *The Challenge of Jesus* (Downers Grove: InterVarsity Press, 1999), 10, emphasis original.

[8]See, for example, Wright's chapter "History and the First Century" in *The New Testament and the People of God* (Minneapolis: Fortress Press, 1992), 81-120.

[9]Vos, "Idea of Biblical Theology," 12.

[10]Ibid., 23.

CHAPTER SEVEN: OUR DE-DRAMATIZED BIBLE

[1]Thomas Cahill, *The Gifts of the Jews* (New York: Anchor Books, 1998), 8.

[2]Ibid., 19.

[3]Hans Frei, *The Eclipse of Biblical Narrative* (New Haven: Yale University Press, 1974).

[4]See Stephen Greenblatt, *The Swerve: How the World Became Modern* (New York: Norton, 2011).

[5]Frei, *The Eclipse of the Biblical Narrative*, 38.

[6]Walter Brueggemann, *Theology of the Old Testament* (Minneapolis: Fortress Press, 1997), 206.

[7]Gregory Mobley, *The Return of the Chaos Monsters—And Other Backstories of the Bible* (Grand Rapids: Eerdmans, 2012).

[8]Ibid., xi-xii.

[9]Ibid., 6.

[10]Ibid., 7.

[11]N. T. Wright, *The New Testament and the People of God* (Minneapolis: Fortress Press, 1992), 138.

[12]Craig Bartholomew and Michael Goheen, *The Drama of Scripture* (Grand Rapids: Baker Academic, 2004), 12.

[13]Barbara Hardy, "Toward a Poetics of Fiction: An Approach through Narrative," *Novel* 2 (1968): 5.

CHAPTER EIGHT: REDISCOVERING THE STORIENTED BIBLE

[1]N. T. Wright, *The New Testament and the People of God* (Minneapolis: Fortress, 1992), 6. For an extended treatment of story as a key category for understanding the New Testament see ibid., 31-80.

[2]Karl Barth, "The Strange New World Within the Bible," in *The Word of God and the Word of Man* (Gloucester, MA: Peter Smith, 1957), 28-50; Walter Brueggemann, *An Introduction to the Old Testament* (Louisville: Westminster John Knox, 2003), xiii.

[3]It's worth noting that the rabbis used to debate the sequence; it would be a sign that our fixation on atomistic thinking was loosening and the recovery of a holistic approach was well underway if we were to take up the discussion once again.

[4]See G. K. Beale, *The Temple and the Church's Mission: A Biblical Theology of the Dwelling Place of God* (Downers Grove: InterVarsity Press, 2004); John Walton, *The Lost World of Genesis One* (Downers Grove: InterVarsity Press, 2009); Rikk E. Watts, "The New Exodus/New Creational Restoration of the Image of God: A Biblical-Theological Perspective on Salvation," pp. 15-41 in *What Does It Mean To Be Saved?*, ed. John G. Stackhouse Jr. (Grand Rapids: Baker Academic, 2002), and others.

[5]Following here the original grouping of Torah, Prophets and Writings rather than the later Septuagintal ordering common in Bibles today.

[6]Gregory Mobley, *The Return of the Chaos Monsters—And Other Backstories of the Bible* (Grand Rapids: Eerdmans, 2012), 67-96.

[7]There's a published alternative to the usual structure of the New Testament, one that attempts to do justice to the early concerns of the church and seeks to provide more help for readers than the traditional approach. *The Books of the Bible* (Biblica) is an Elegant Bible presentation that strengthens the ancient fourfold gospel concept without the usual smushing effect of grouping them all at the front of the New Testament. Instead, by combining each gospel with the other books that have natural affinities with it, the priority and foundational nature of the good news about Jesus is maintained. The whole New Testament takes on a cruciform shape as these four sets now give witness to the one gospel of Jesus the Messiah, each from a different direction. It also has the benefit of recombining Luke's two-volume work. The new arrangement more clearly highlights the unique contribution of each Gospel and avoids the harmonizing tendency that arises from grouping all four together. And again, I would contend that a willingness to reopen the question of book order would reflect and contribute to a renewed interested in reading the Bible holistically.

[8]See, for example, how in the Corinthian correspondence Paul refers to the Passover, the Law of Moses, the veil over the face of Moses, the story of Israel in the wilderness receiving water from the rock, and so on.

[9]Wright, *The New Testament and the People of God*, 143.

[10]Craig Bartholomew and Michael Goheen, *The Drama of Scripture* (Grand Rapids: Baker Academic, 2004), 25-26.

[11]N. T. Wright, "How Can the Bible Be Authoritative?" *Vox Evangelica* 21 (1991): 7-32; see also Wright, *The New Testament and the People of God*, 139-43.

[12]Kevin Vanhoozer, "The Apostolic Discourse and Its Development," in *Scripture's Doctrine and Theology's Bible*, ed. Markus Bockuehl and Alan Torrance (Grand Rapids: Baker Academic, 2008), 198.

CHAPTER NINE: PERFORMING THE STORIENTED BIBLE

[1]N. T. Wright, *The New Testament and the People of God* (Minneapolis: Fortress, 1992), 139-43.

[2]A few of the key sources for what follows are Todd E. Johnson and Dale Savidge, *Performing the Sacred* (Grand Rapids: Baker Academic, 2009); Kevin J. Vanhoozer, *The Drama of Doctrine* (Louisville: Westminster John Knox Press, 2005) and *Faith Speaking Understanding* (Louisville: Westminster John Knox Press, 2014); and Samuel Wells, *Improvisation: The Drama of Christian Ethics* (Grand Rapids: Brazos Press, 2004). Keith Johnstone's work on the intricacies of theatrical improvisation is rich in implications for our conception of the Christian life. See his *Impro*

(London: Methuen, 1981). Musical improvisation is a closely related and equally fruitful analogy: see Jeremy Begbie, *Theology, Music, and Time* (Cambride: Cambridge University Press, 2000) and Frances Young, *Virtuoso Theology* (Eugene: Wipf & Stock, 1993).

[3]Alasdair MacIntyre, *After Virtue* (Notre Dame: University of Notre Dame Press, 1981), 216.

[4]See especially Wells, *Improvisation*, on how Christian ethics in particular can use these elements, picking up on key terms used in Johnstone, *Impro*.

[5]Vanhoozer, *The Drama of Doctrine*, 344, 438.

[6]Vanhoozer and Wright both reference the work of philosopher Nicholas Wolterstorff: see Vanhoozer, *The Drama of Doctrine*, 257; Wright, *The New Testament and the People of God*, 141. The references are to Wolterstorff, *Art in Action: Toward a Christian Aesthetic* (Grand Rapids: Eerdmans, 1980).

[7]The New Testament itself models this approach to living out the story of the Bible. We have to remember that the players whose scenes are recorded in the Bible didn't have a script with their lines either, and they were called to do what we are: improvise based on their own location in the story and where it was headed. Consider how the book of Acts describes the deliberations of the early council in Jerusalem regarding the issue of Gentiles coming into the Jewish Messiah's assemblies of believers. Communicating their decision in a letter to the churches, they wrote: "It seemed good to the Holy Sprit and to us." Or consider John's description of the instructions Jesus gave to his disciples before his death. He didn't give them a detailed blueprint; he promised them that the Spirit would come and guide them into all truth. This also accords with what both Paul (to the Corinthians) and the author of Hebrews did when recalling earlier failures by actors in the drama as warnings to performers in their own time to better performances.

CHAPTER TEN: OUR OTHERWORLDLY BIBLE

[1]This is the view that the Bible at first focused on the state of affairs here below—kings and kingdoms and land and exile—but then later, in part two, God revealed that his true interest all along was on bringing his people into an altogether different realm. This is the picture that lies behind the familiar characterization that has the Jews incorrectly expecting an earthly king who would bring them an earthly salvation, while God had actually sent them a Savior to die for their sins and rescue them from the world to bring them to a better place above. Mistakenly focused as they were on this world, the contemporaries of Jesus just didn't understand that God had decided it would be best to bring them to another world.

[2]Overviews of the classical options for life after death in the Greek and Roman periods can be found in Alan Segal, *Life After Death: A History of the Afterlife in the Religions of the West* (New York: Doubleday, 2004), 204-47; and N. T. Wright, *The Resurrection of the Son of God* (Minneapolis: Fortress Press, 2003), 2-84.

[3]The dialogue is found in Phaedo, part of the collection in *Plato: The Trial and Execution of Socrates*, trans. Peter George (London: The Folio Society, 1972), 109.

[4]Virgil, The Aeneid, bk. 6, trans. Robert Fitzgerald (New York: Vintage Books, 1990).

[5]Ibid., lines 721-28, p. 178.

[6]Segal, *Life After Death*, 533.

[7]Ibid., 488-89.

[8]N. T. Wright lays out the two options and their histories in *Surprised by Hope* (San Francisco: HarperOne, 2008).

[9]See George Gallup Jr. and James Castelli, *The People's Religion* (New York: Macmillan, 1989), 47-48, for a list of the most common features of the popular conception of heaven.

[10]Colleen McDannell and Bernhard Lang, *Heaven: A History* (New York: Vintage, 1990), p. xiii.

[11]N. T. Wright has coined the phrase "life *after* life after death" to describe this. See his *Surprised by Hope*, chapter 10, pp. 147-63.

[12]For a detailed and sustained case for understanding the unity of the Bible in terms of God's sovereign mission of reclaiming the world, including the entire created order, see Christopher J. H. Wright, *The Mission of God: Unlocking the Bible's Grand Narrative* (Downers Grove: InterVarsity Press, 2006). On how Israel's story presents an ethic that still speaks today, see also Christopher J. H. Wright, *Old Testament Ethics for the People of God* (Downers Grove: InterVarsity Press, 2004).

[13]See N. T. Wright, *How God Became King: The Forgotten Story of the Gospels* (San Francisco: HarperOne, 2012), for the case that overall the Gospels are making the point that through the work of Jesus, God is effectively implementing a sovereign role over his people and his world.

[14]Alister McGrath, *A Brief History of Heaven* (Oxford: Blackwell, 2003), 9-10.

[15]Ibid., 177-78.

[16]See Rick Warren, *The Purpose Driven Life* (Grand Rapids: Zondervan, 2002), 47-48.

CHAPTER ELEVEN: GROUNDED IN THE EARTHLY BIBLE

[1]For more on this perspective, see the resources listed in chapter eight, note four.

[2]N. T. Wright, *The New Testament and the People of God* (Minneapolis: Fortress, 1992), 251-52. The midrash referenced is from Genesis Rabbah 14.6.

[3]Leon Kass, *The Hungry Soul: Eating and the Perfecting of Our Nature* (Chicago: University of Chicago Press, 1999), 198.

[4]Rikk E. Watts, "The New Exodus/New Creation Restoration of the Image of God," in *What Does It Mean to Be Saved?* ed. John G. Stackhouse Jr. (Grand Rapids: Baker Academic, 2002), 16.

[5]Albert Wolters, *Creation Regained* (Grand Rapids: Eerdmans, 1985), 57-58.

[6]Wendell Berry, forward to Ellen Davis, *Scripture, Culture, and Agriculture* (Cambridge: Cambridge University Press, 2009), xi.

[7]See Craig Bartholomew, *Where Mortals Dwell: A Christian View of Place Today* (Grand Rapids: Baker Academic, 2011) for an in-depth treatment of how the concept of place is crucial for the biblical drama.

[8]Robert Alter, *The Art of Biblical Narrative* (New York: Basic Books, 1981).

[9]Ibid., 155-77.

[10]See Christopher J. H. Wright's *Old Testament Ethics for the People of God* (Downers Grove: InterVarsity Press, 2004).

[11]Richard Bauckham, *Bible and Mission: Christian Witness in a Postmodern World* (Grand Rapids: Baker Academic, 2003), 27.

[12]John Dominic Crossan, in *The Resurrection of Jesus: John Dominic Crossan and N. T. Wright in Dialogue*, ed. Robert B. Stewart (Minneapolis: Fortress Press, 2006), 26-27.

[13]I am aware that such occurrences are rare in our world. Very often trouble looms, no help comes and disaster wreaks its havoc. In my opinion, this only shows that moments like the one I've just described have the status of being *signs*.

[14]C. S. Lewis, "The Novels of Charles Williams," in *On Stories* (San Diego: Harcourt, Inc., 1966), 22.

[15]G. B. Caird, *A Commentary on the Revelation of St. John the Divine* (New York: Harper & Row, 1966), 266.

CHAPTER TWELVE: MY PRIVATE BIBLE

[1]Colin Morris, *The Discovery of the Individual 1050–1200* (1972; repr., Toronto: University of Toronto Press, 1987).

[2]Laura Light, "The Bible and the Individual: The Thirteenth-Century Paris Bible," 228-46 in *The Practice of the Bible in the Middle Ages: Production, Reception, and Performance in Western Christianity*, ed. Susan Boynton and Diane J. Reilly (New York: Columbia University Press, 2011).

[3]Ibid., 228.

[4]Nathan O. Hatch, *The Democratization of American Christianity* (New Haven: Yale University Press, 1989). See also Lori Anne Ferrell, *The Bible and the People* (New Haven: Yale University Press, 2008); Nathan O. Hatch and Mark A. Noll, eds., *The Bible in America* (Oxford: Oxford University Press, 1982); George M. Marsden, *Fundamentalism and American Culture* (Oxford: Oxford University Press, 1980); and Mark A. Noll, *America's God* (Oxford: Oxford University Press, 2002).

[5]Lori Anne Ferrell, "Traveling Companion: The Bible in the Nineteenth Century," in *The Bible and the People*, 192-220.

[6]Ferrell, *The Bible and the People*, 224.

[7]Ibid., 209.

[8]Daniel Radosh, "The Good Book Business," *New Yorker*, December 18, 2006.

[9]Stanley Hauerwas, *Unleashing the Scripture: Freeing the Bible from Captivity to America* (Nashville: Abingdon Press, 1993), 27.

[10]Harold Bloom, *The American Religion* (New York: Simon & Schuster, 1992), 267.

[11]E. Randolph Richards & Brandon J. O'Brien, *Misreading Scripture with Western Eyes* (Downers Grove: InterVarsity Press, 2012). See especially chapter four on individualism and collectivism: "Captain of My Soul," 95-112.

[12]Alec Gallup and Wendy W. Simmons, "Six in Ten Americans Read the Bible at Least Occasionally," *Gallup News Service*, October 2000.

[13]Sarah Young, *Jesus Calling* (Nashville: Thomas Nelson, 2008), introduction.

[14]Ibid., reading for February 15.

[15]Colin Urquhart, *Your Personal Bible* (London: Hodder & Stoughton, 1994), xv-xvi.

[16]Ibid., 24, 54, 34, 116.

[17]Eugene Peterson, *Christ Plays in Ten Thousand Places* (Grand Rapids: Eerdmans, 2005), 242.

[18]Nathan Hatch, "Sola Scriptura and Novus Ordo Seclorum," in Hatch and Noll, *The Bible in America*, 59-78.

[19]Elhanan Winchester, *The Universal Restoration* (London, 1788), xvii-xviii, quoted in ibid., 68.

[20]Charles G. Finney, *Memoirs* (New York, 1876) 42-46; quoted in Hatch, "Sola Scriptura," 75.

CHAPTER THIRTEEN: SHARING OUR SYNAGOGUE BIBLE

[1]John H. Walton and D. Brent Sandy, *The Lost World of Scripture* (Downers Grove: InterVarsity Press, 2013).

[2]Lee I. Levine, *The Ancient Synagogue*, 2nd ed. (New Haven: Yale University Press, 2005), 151.

[3]See ibid., particularly chapter two, "Origins," and chapter five, "The Second Temple Synagogue—Its Role and Functions."

[4]Philo, *The Contemplative Life*, 28, quoted in ibid., 157.

[5]See Jim Belcher, *Deep Church* (Downers Grove: InterVarsity Press, 2009) 153-159, on "centered-set preaching"; and Christian Smith, *The Bible Made Impossible* (Grand Rapids: Brazos Press, 2011), 93-126, "The Christocentric Hermeneutical Key."

[6]Smith, *The Bible Made Impossible*, 136.

[7]N. T. Wright claims this revolutionary unity of the people of God is the major worldview symbol possessed by the church. See N. T. Wright, *Paul and the Faithfulness of God* (Minneapolis: Fortress Press, 2013), 387-404.

[8]Walton and Sandy, *The Lost World of Scripture*.

[9]Andrew B. McGowan, *Ancient Christian Worship* (Grand Rapids: Baker, 2014), 79.

[10]Ann Plantinga Kapteyn shared this with me on February 26, 2014.

[11]John Goldingay, *Old Testament Theology*, vol. 3, *Israel's Life* (Downers Grove: Inter-

Varsity Press, 2009), 18. Christopher J. H. Wright makes exactly the same point in *Old Testament Ethics for the People of God* (Downers Grove: InterVarsity Press, 2004), 364.

[12]Wright, *Old Testament Ethics*, 48-49.

CHAPTER FOURTEEN: OUR UGLY BIBLE

[1]N. T. Wright, taken from Colossians in *The Kingdom New Testament* (San Francisco: HarperOne, 2011), 409.

[2]N. T. Wright, "Poetry and Theology in Colossians 1.15-20," in *The Climax of the Covenant* (Minneapolis: Fortress Press, 1992), 103-4.

[3]Ibid., 108.

[4]Harry Gamble, *Books and Readers in the Early Church* (New Haven: Yale University Press, 1995), 43.

[5]The earliest extant manuscript we have of a collection of Paul's letters is $\mathfrak{P}^{46}$, dated about AD 200.

[6]Quoted in Herbert L. Kessler, "The Book as Icon," from *In the Beginning: Bibles Before the Year 1000*, ed. Michelle P. Brown (Washington, DC: Smithsonian Books, 2006), 77.

[7]Hans Belting, *Likeness and Presence: A History of the Image Before the Era of Art*, trans. Edmund Jephcott (Chicago: University of Chicago Press, 1994), 465.

[8]Ibid., 466.

[9]John Locke, quoted in Jamie A. Grant, "Poetics," in *Words and the Word*, ed. David G. Firth and Jamie A. Grant (Downers Grove: InterVarsity Press, 2008), 189n2.

[10]Grant, "Poetics," 189.

[11]For two exquisite examples of the rebirth of the illuminated Bible tradition see *The Saint John's Bible* (Collegeville: Liturgical Press, 2011) and *The Four Holy Gospels* (Wheaton: Crossway, 2011).

[12]See Max McLean and Warren Bird, *Unleashing the Word: Rediscovering the Public Reading of Scripture* (Grand Rapids: Zondervan, 2009).

CHAPTER FIFTEEN: BEHOLDING THE ICONIC BIBLE

[1]Kevin J. Vanhoozer, *The Drama of Doctrine* (Louisville: Westminster John Knox Press, 2005), 272-85.

[2]Robert Alter, *The Art of Biblical Narrative* (New York: Basic Books, 1981); and *The Art of Biblical Poetry* (New York: Basic Books, 1985).

[3]See John H. Stek, "When the Spirit Was Poetic," in *The NIV: The Making of a Contemporary Translation*, Kenneth L. Barker, ed. (Colorado Springs: International Bible Society, 1991), 79-80, and various references to Ridderbos therein.

[4]Calvin D. Linton, "The Importance of Literary Style in Bible Translation Today," in Barker, *The NIV*, 33.

[5]Richard Bauckham, *Bible and Mission: Christian Witness in a Postmodern World* (Grand Rapids: Baker Academic, 2003).

[6]Ibid., 13-15.

[7]Ibid., 16.

[8]For this and what follows, see ibid., 48-54.

[9]See N. T. Wright, *Jesus and the Victory of God* (Minneapolis: Fortress Press, 1996), 592-611.

[10]Bauckham, *Bible and Mission*, 52.

[11]Adam Lewis Greene, Bibliotheca Kickstarter video, www.kickstarter.com /projects/530877925/bibliotheca/description, 2014.

[12]Lisa Beth Anderson, "About This Book," *The Book of Psalms* (Colorado Springs: International Bible Society, 2006).

[13]Albert Borgmann, *Power Failure: Christianity in the Culture of Technology* (Grand Rapids: Brazos Press, 2003), 25.

[14]Ibid., 22.

[15]See Philip Goff, Arthur E. Farnsley II, and Peter J. Thuesen, "The Bible in American Life," a national study by the Center for the Study of Religion and American Culture, March 2014, p. 2.

CONCLUSION: RETURN

[1]William H. Armstrong, *Sounder* (New York: HarperCollins, 1969), 81. The overview of the story here is my retelling.

[2]Ibid., 50.

[3]Ibid., 77.

[4]Ibid., 82.

[5]Ibid., 9.